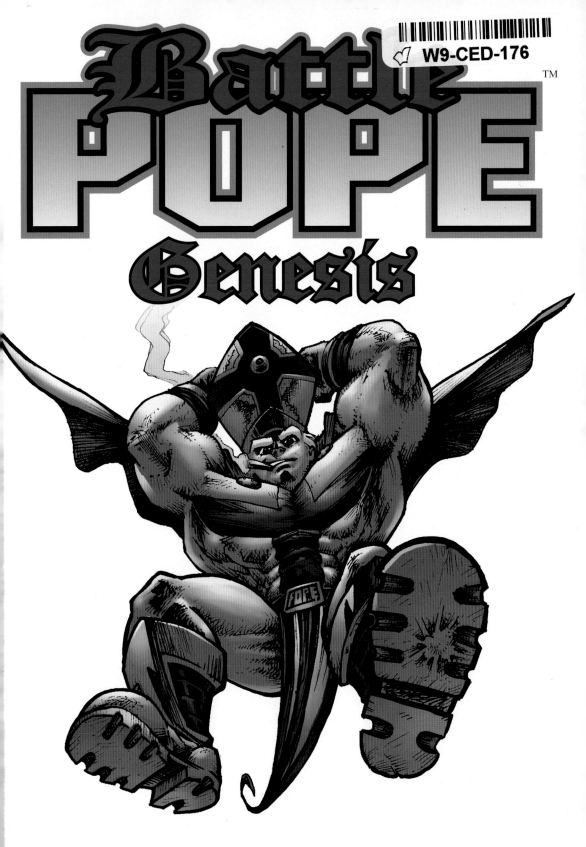

CREATED BY
**ROBERT KIRKMAN
& TONY MOORE**

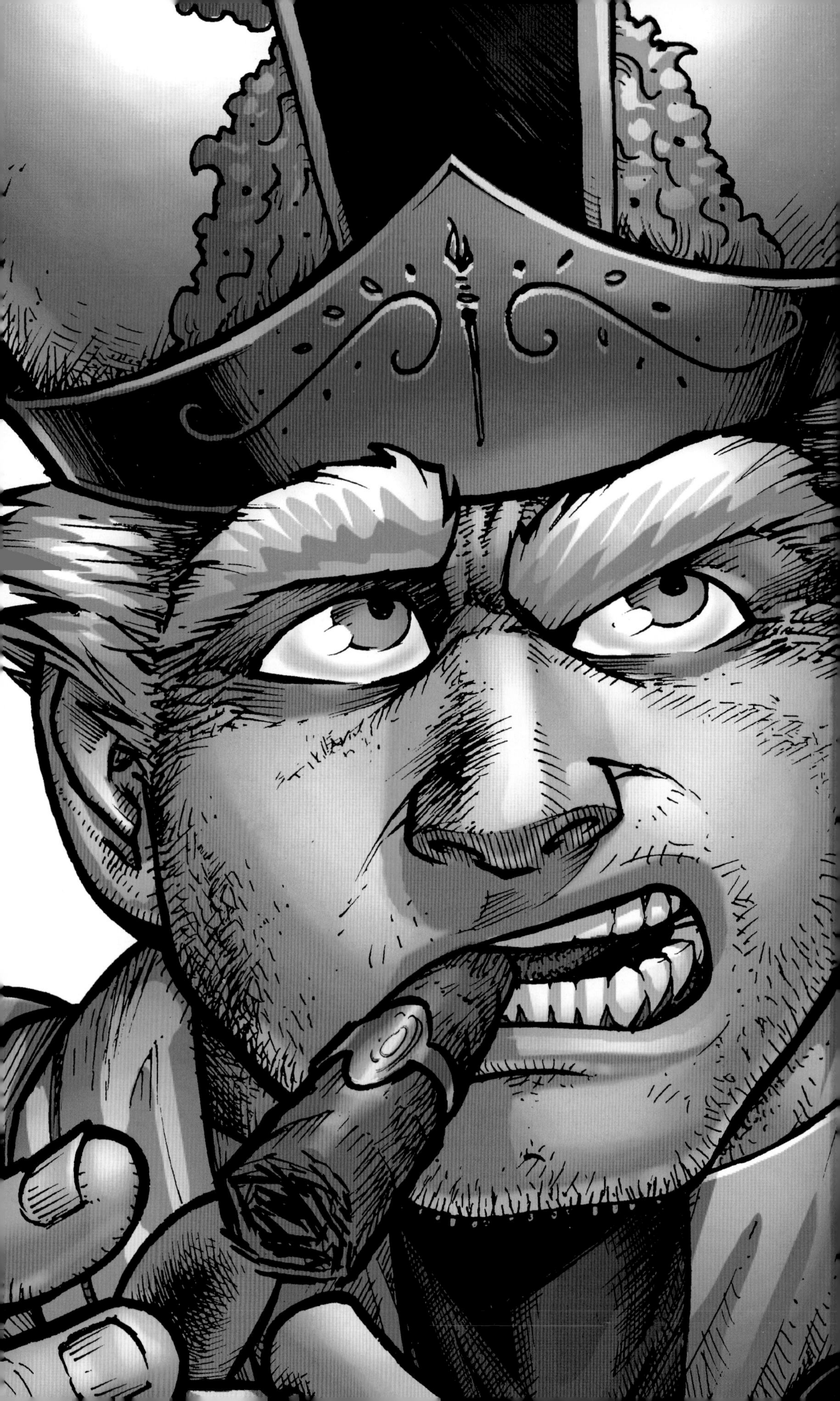

Robert Kirkman
writer, layout artist, letterer

Tony Moore
penciler, inker, story assist

Val Staples
colorist

FOR IMAGE COMICS

ROBERT KIRKMAN
chief operating officer
ERIK LARSEN
chief financial officer
TODD McFARLANE
president
MARC SILVESTRI
chief executive officer
JIM VALENTINO
vice-president

ericstephenson
publisher
JOE KEATINGE
pr & marketing coordinator
BRANWYN BIGGLESTONE
accounts manager
TYLER SHAINLINE
administrative assistant
TRACI HUI
traffic manager

ALLEN HUI
production manager
DREW GILL
production artist
JONATHAN CHAN
production artist
MONICA HOWARD
production artist

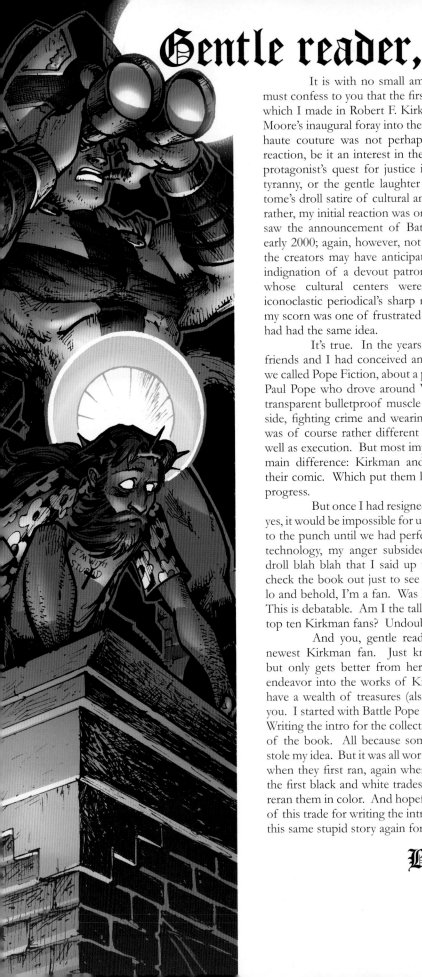

Gentle reader,

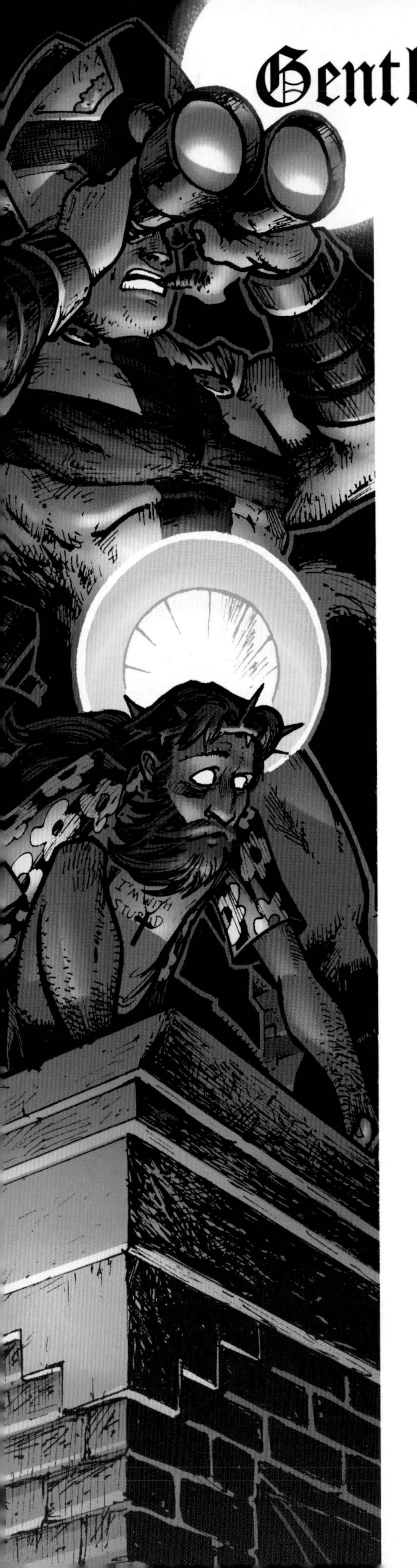
I'M WITH

It is with no small amount of chagrin that I must confess to you that the first emotional investment which I made in Robert F. Kirkman's and M. Anthony Moore's inaugural foray into the realm of the ninth art's haute couture was not perhaps the creators' desired reaction, be it an interest in the high adventure of the protagonist's quest for justice in a world of demonic tyranny, or the gentle laughter of appreciation at the tome's droll satire of cultural and religious mores. No, rather, my initial reaction was one of anger when I first saw the announcement of Battle Pope in late 1999/ early 2000; again, however, not anger in the sense that the creators may have anticipated: the lofty, righteous indignation of a devout patron of the denomination whose cultural centers were the quarry of this iconoclastic periodical's sharp nettle sting. No, again, my scorn was one of frustrated ambitions; I, dash it all, had had the same idea.

It's true. In the years around 1997-1999, my friends and I had conceived an idea for a book which we called Pope Fiction, about a protagonist named John Paul Pope who drove around Vatican City Beach in a transparent bulletproof muscle car, Desert Eagle at his side, fighting crime and wearing a mitre. Battle Pope was of course rather different in concept and tone as well as execution. But most importantly, there was one main difference: Kirkman and Moore actually made their comic. Which put them light years ahead of our progress.

But once I had resigned myself to the fact that, yes, it would be impossible for us to somehow beat them to the punch until we had perfected that flux capacitor technology, my anger subsided, and my interest and droll blah blah that I said up top grew. I decided to check the book out just to see how it would go. And, lo and behold, I'm a fan. Was I the first Kirkman fan? This is debatable. Am I the tallest of the chronological top ten Kirkman fans? Undoubtedly so.

And you, gentle reader, are conceivably the newest Kirkman fan. Just know that it starts here, but only gets better from here. If this is your first endeavor into the works of Kirkman and Moore, you have a wealth of treasures (also: Space Ace) ahead of you. I started with Battle Pope #1, and look at me now. Writing the intro for the collection of the color reprints of the book. All because some jerks from Kentucky stole my idea. But it was all worth it. I bought the books when they first ran, again when they were collected in the first black and white trades, and again when Image reran them in color. And hopefully I'll get a comp copy of this trade for writing the intro so I won't have to buy this same stupid story again for a fourth time.

Benito Cereno
February 2006

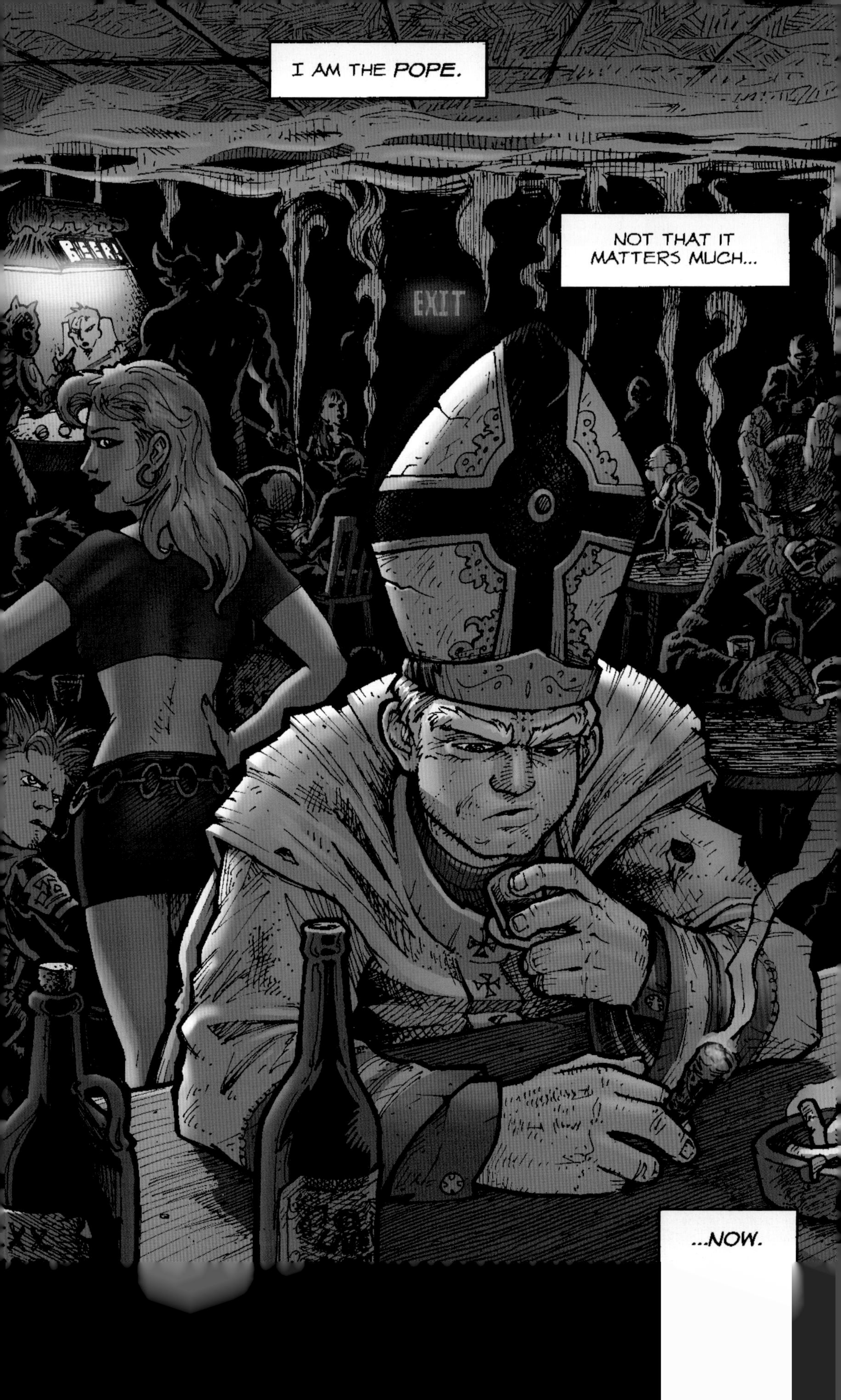
I AM THE POPE.
NOT THAT IT MATTERS MUCH...
BEER!
EXIT
...NOW.

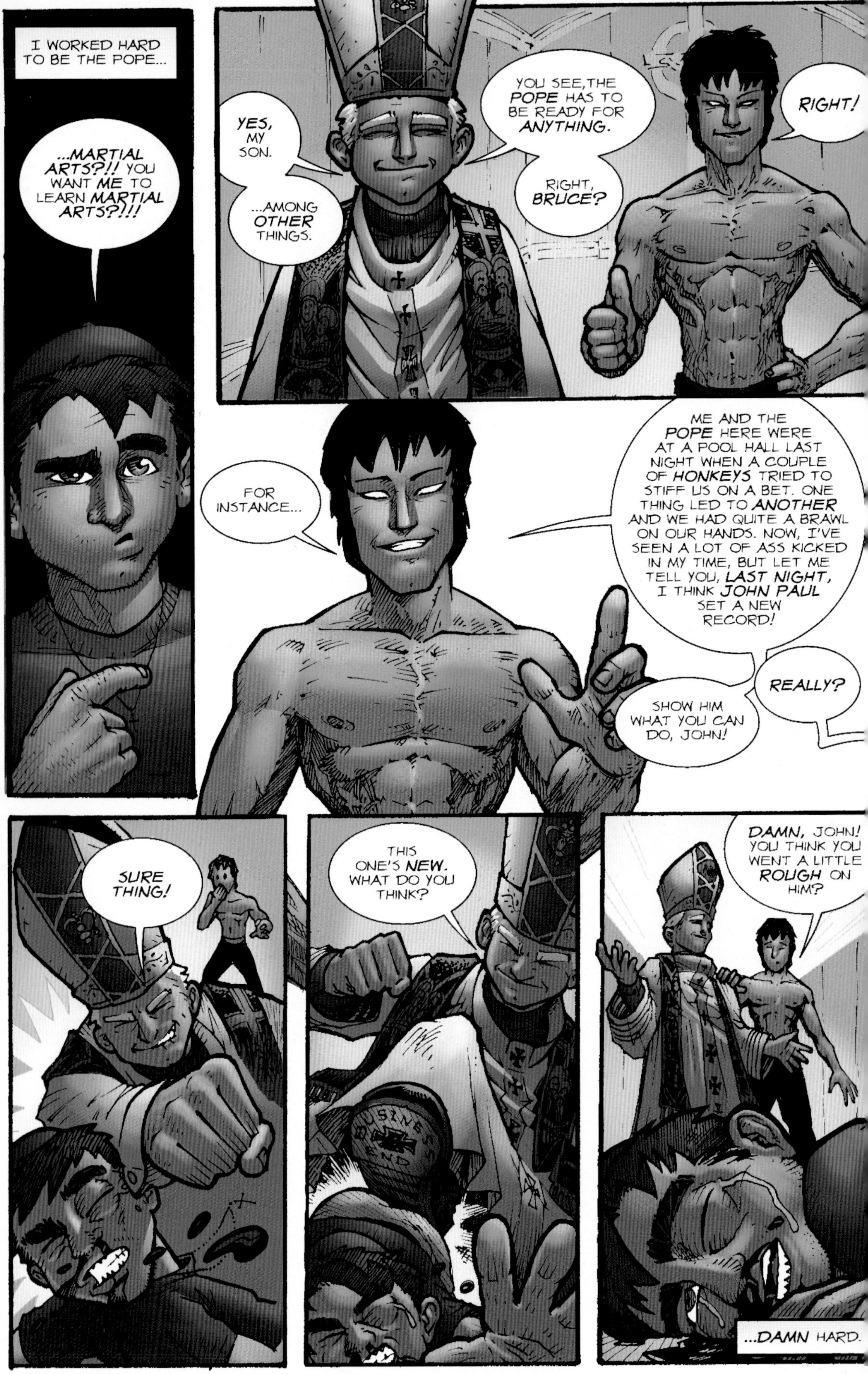

I WORKED HARD TO BE THE POPE...
...MARTIAL ARTS?!! YOU WANT ME TO LEARN MARTIAL ARTS?!!!
YES, MY SON.
...AMONG OTHER THINGS.
YOU SEE, THE POPE HAS TO BE READY FOR ANYTHING.
RIGHT, BRUCE?
RIGHT!
FOR INSTANCE...
ME AND THE POPE HERE WERE AT A POOL HALL LAST NIGHT WHEN A COUPLE OF HONKEYS TRIED TO STIFF US ON A BET. ONE THING LED TO ANOTHER AND WE HAD QUITE A BRAWL ON OUR HANDS. NOW, I'VE SEEN A LOT OF ASS KICKED IN MY TIME, BUT LET ME TELL YOU, LAST NIGHT, I THINK JOHN PAUL SET A NEW RECORD!
REALLY?
SHOW HIM WHAT YOU CAN DO, JOHN!
SURE THING!
THIS ONE'S NEW. WHAT DO YOU THINK?
DAMN, JOHN! YOU THINK YOU WENT A LITTLE ROUGH ON HIM?
...DAMN HARD.

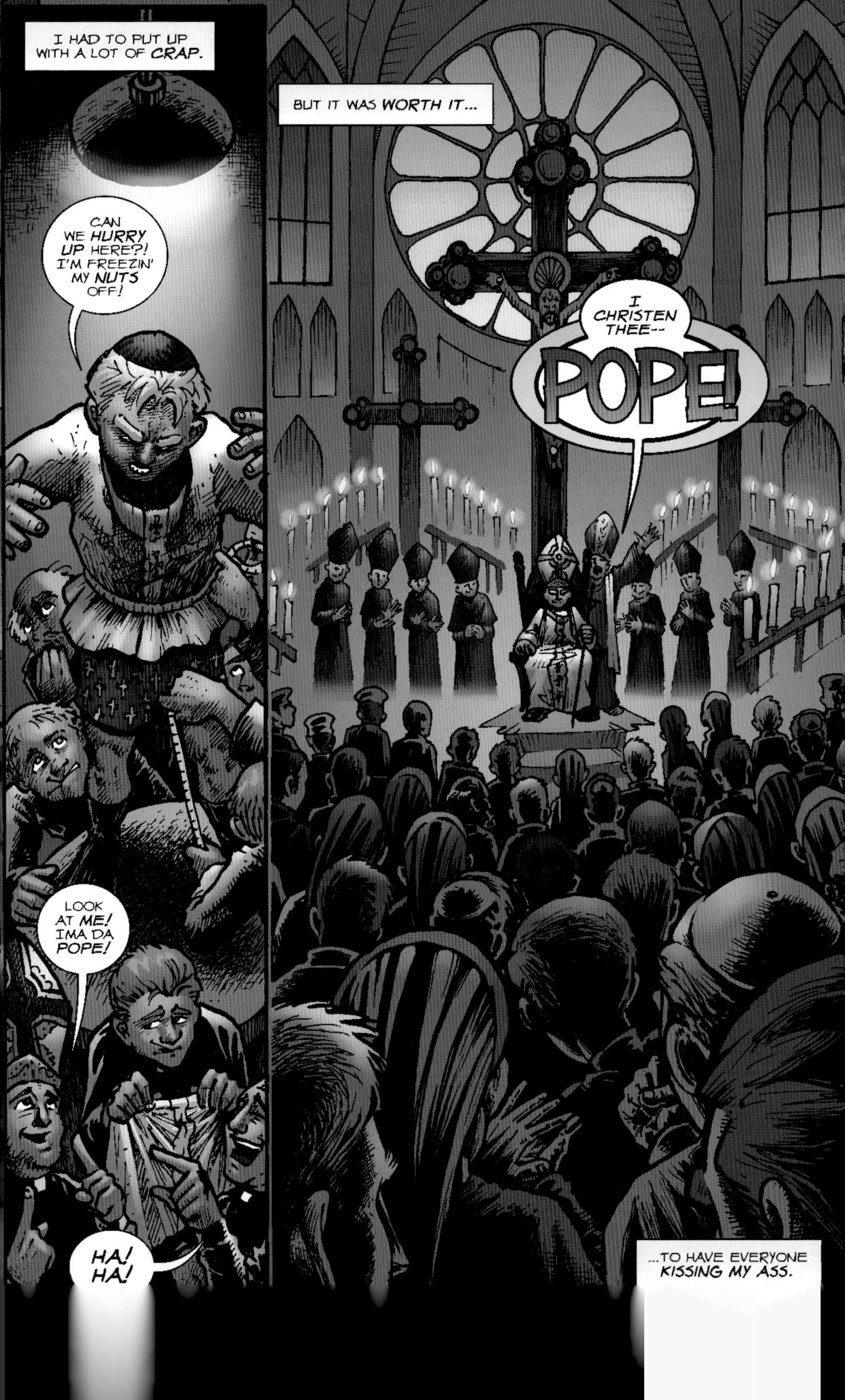
I HAD TO PUT UP WITH A LOT OF CRAP.
CAN WE HURRY UP HERE?! I'M FREEZIN' MY NUTS OFF!
LOOK AT ME! IMA DA POPE!
HA! HA!
BUT IT WAS WORTH IT...
I CHRISTEN THEE-- POPE!
...TO HAVE EVERYONE KISSING MY ASS.

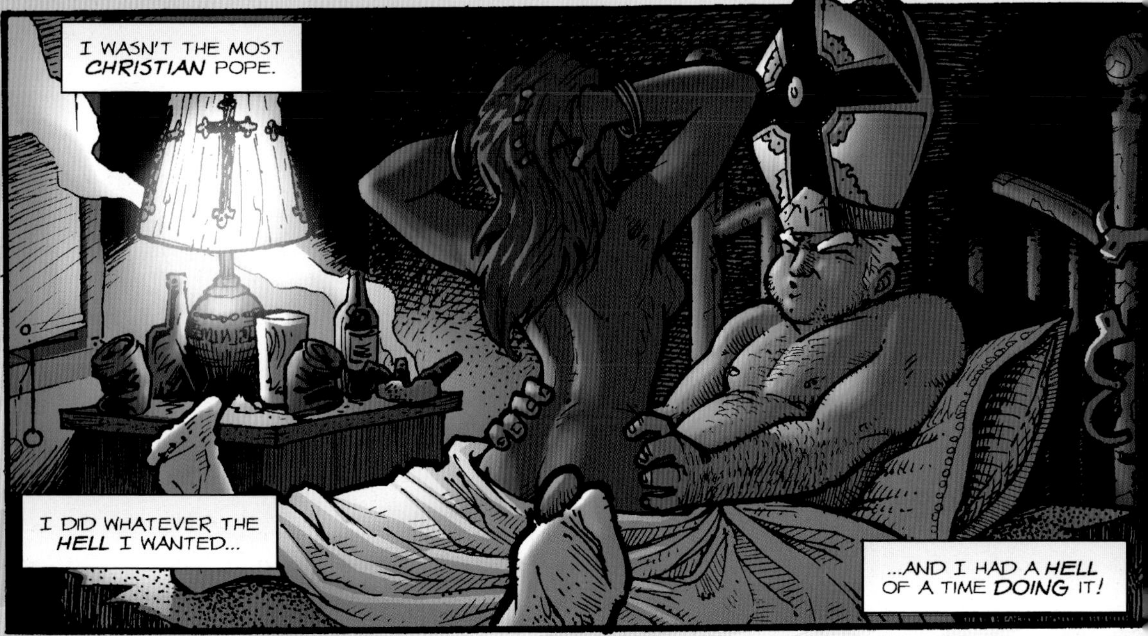
I WASN'T THE MOST CHRISTIAN POPE.
I DID WHATEVER THE HELL I WANTED...
...AND I HAD A HELL OF A TIME DOING IT!

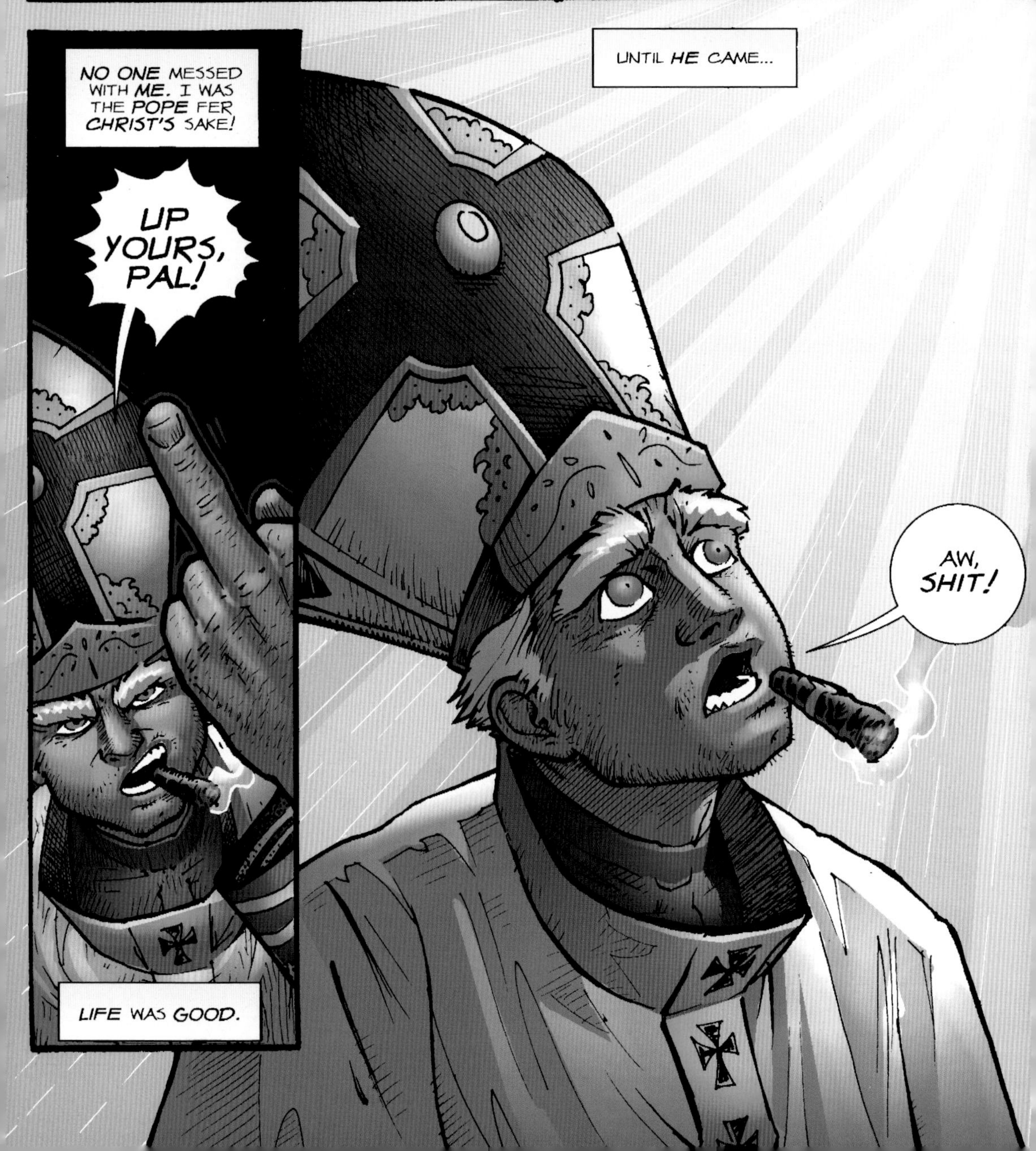
NO ONE MESSED WITH ME. I WAS THE POPE FER CHRIST'S SAKE!
UP YOURS, PAL!
LIFE WAS GOOD.
UNTIL HE CAME...
AW, SHIT!

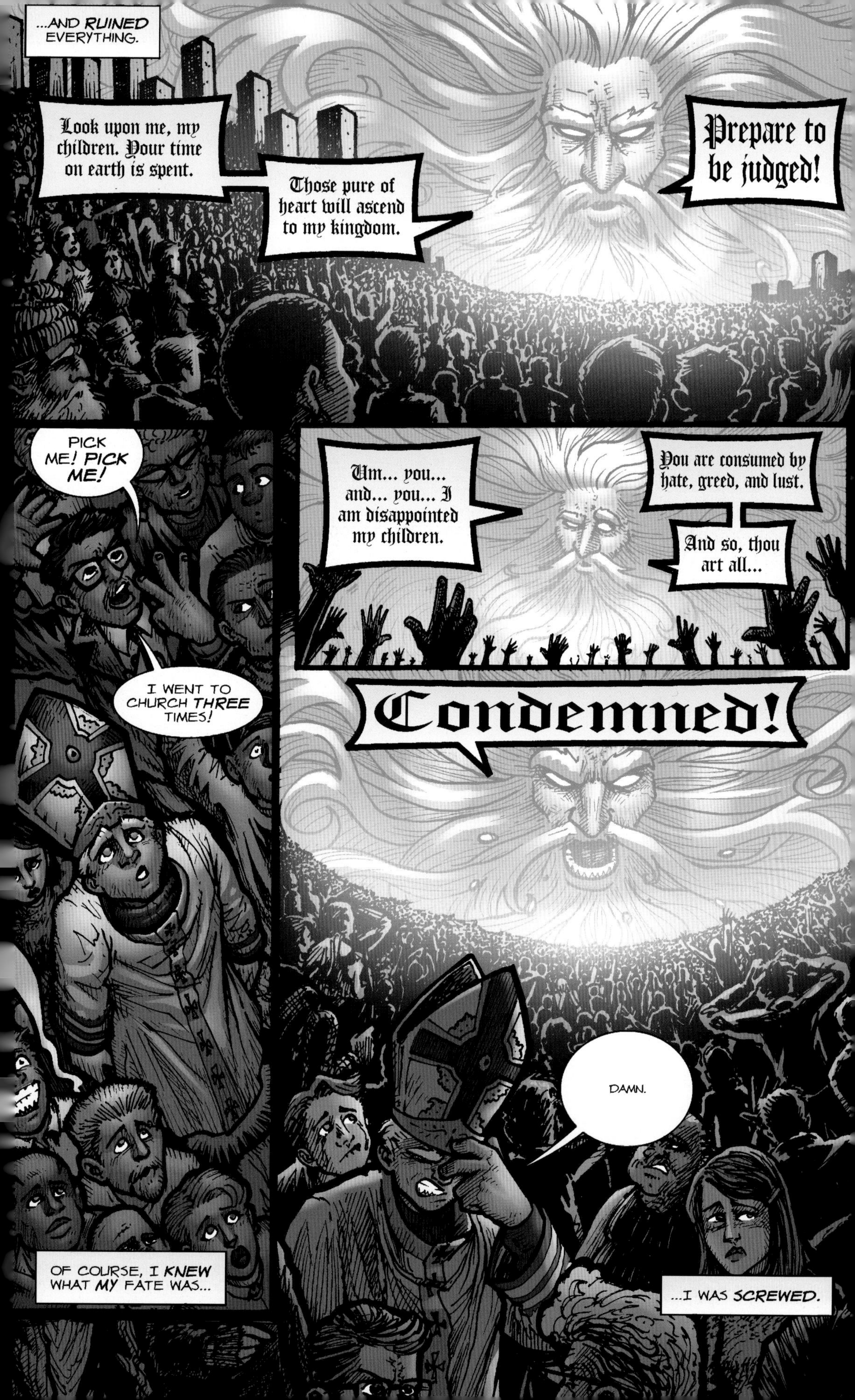

...AND RUINED EVERYTHING.
Look upon me, my children. Your time on earth is spent.
Those pure of heart will ascend to my kingdom.
Prepare to be judged!
PICK ME! PICK ME!
I WENT TO CHURCH THREE TIMES!
Um... you... and... you... I am disappointed my children.
You are consumed by hate, greed, and lust.
And so, thou art all...
Condemned!
OF COURSE, I KNEW WHAT MY FATE WAS...
DAMN.
...I WAS SCREWED.

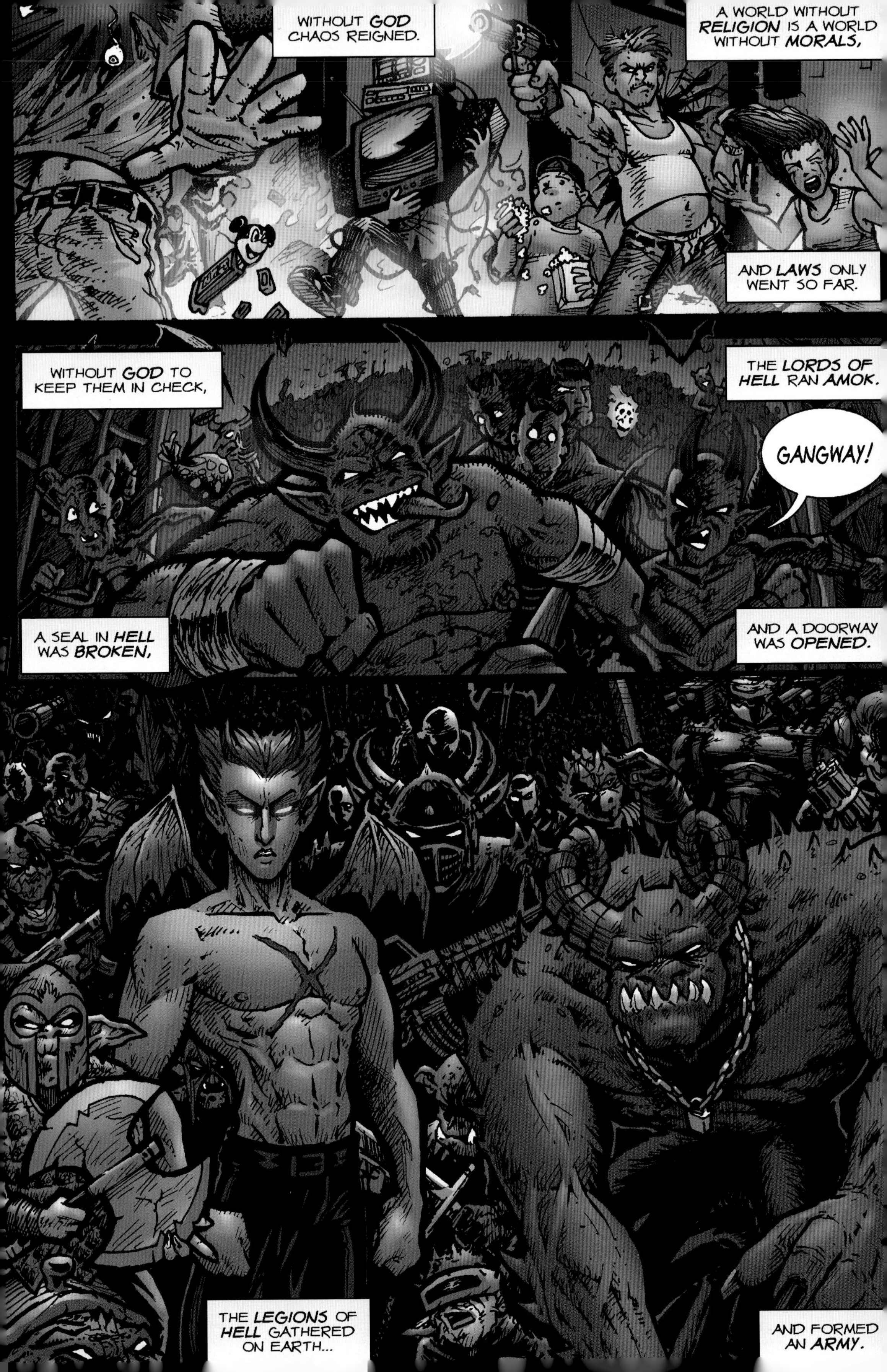
WITHOUT GOD CHAOS REIGNED.
A WORLD WITHOUT RELIGION IS A WORLD WITHOUT MORALS,
AND LAWS ONLY WENT SO FAR.
WITHOUT GOD TO KEEP THEM IN CHECK,
THE LORDS OF HELL RAN AMOK.
GANGWAY!
A SEAL IN HELL WAS BROKEN,
AND A DOORWAY WAS OPENED.
THE LEGIONS OF HELL GATHERED ON EARTH...
AND FORMED AN ARMY.

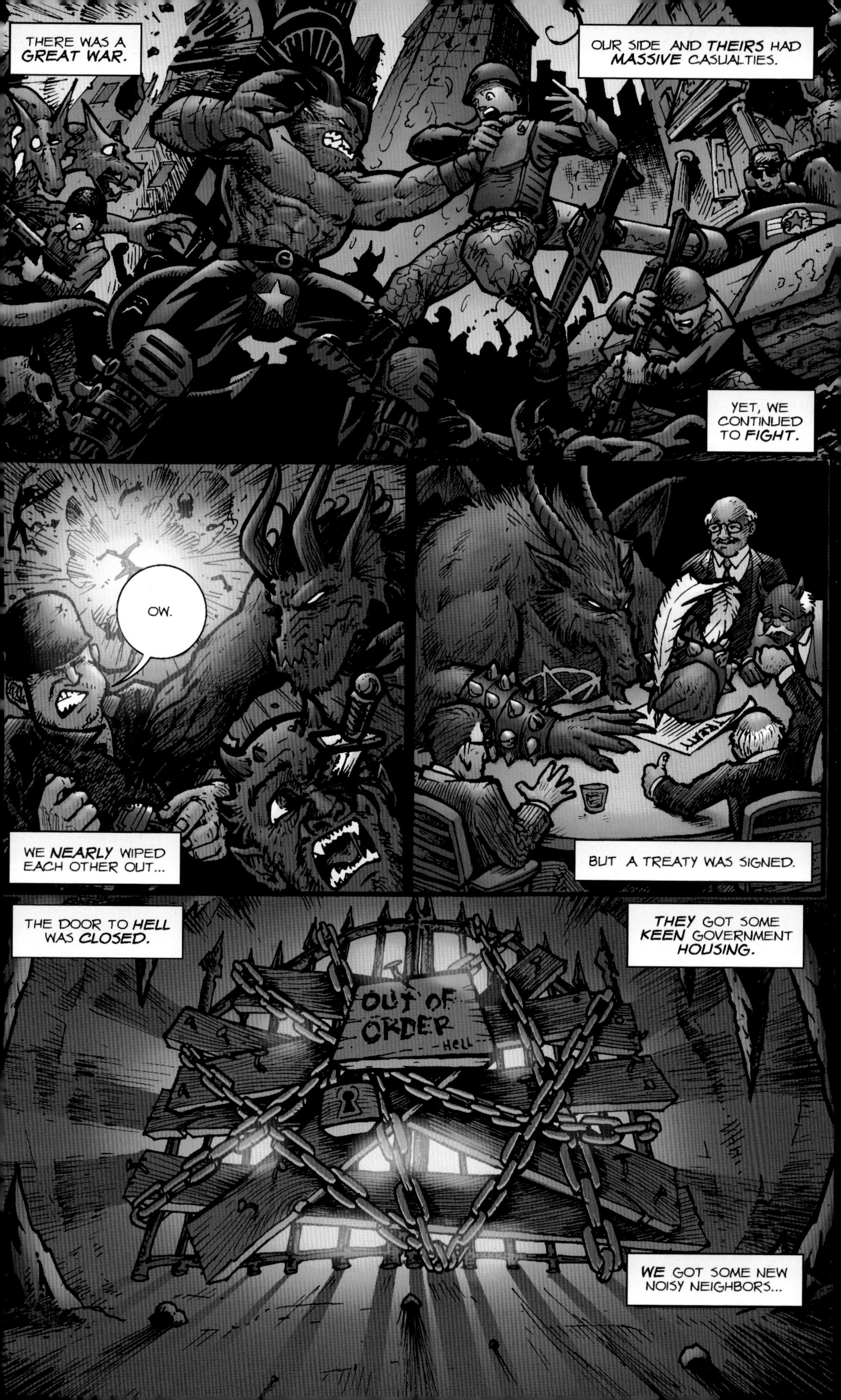
THERE WAS A GREAT WAR.
OUR SIDE AND THEIRS HAD MASSIVE CASUALTIES.
YET, WE CONTINUED TO FIGHT.
OW.
WE NEARLY WIPED EACH OTHER OUT...
BUT A TREATY WAS SIGNED.
THE DOOR TO HELL WAS CLOSED.
THEY GOT SOME KEEN GOVERNMENT HOUSING.
OUT OF ORDER
-HELL
WE GOT SOME NEW NOISY NEIGHBORS...

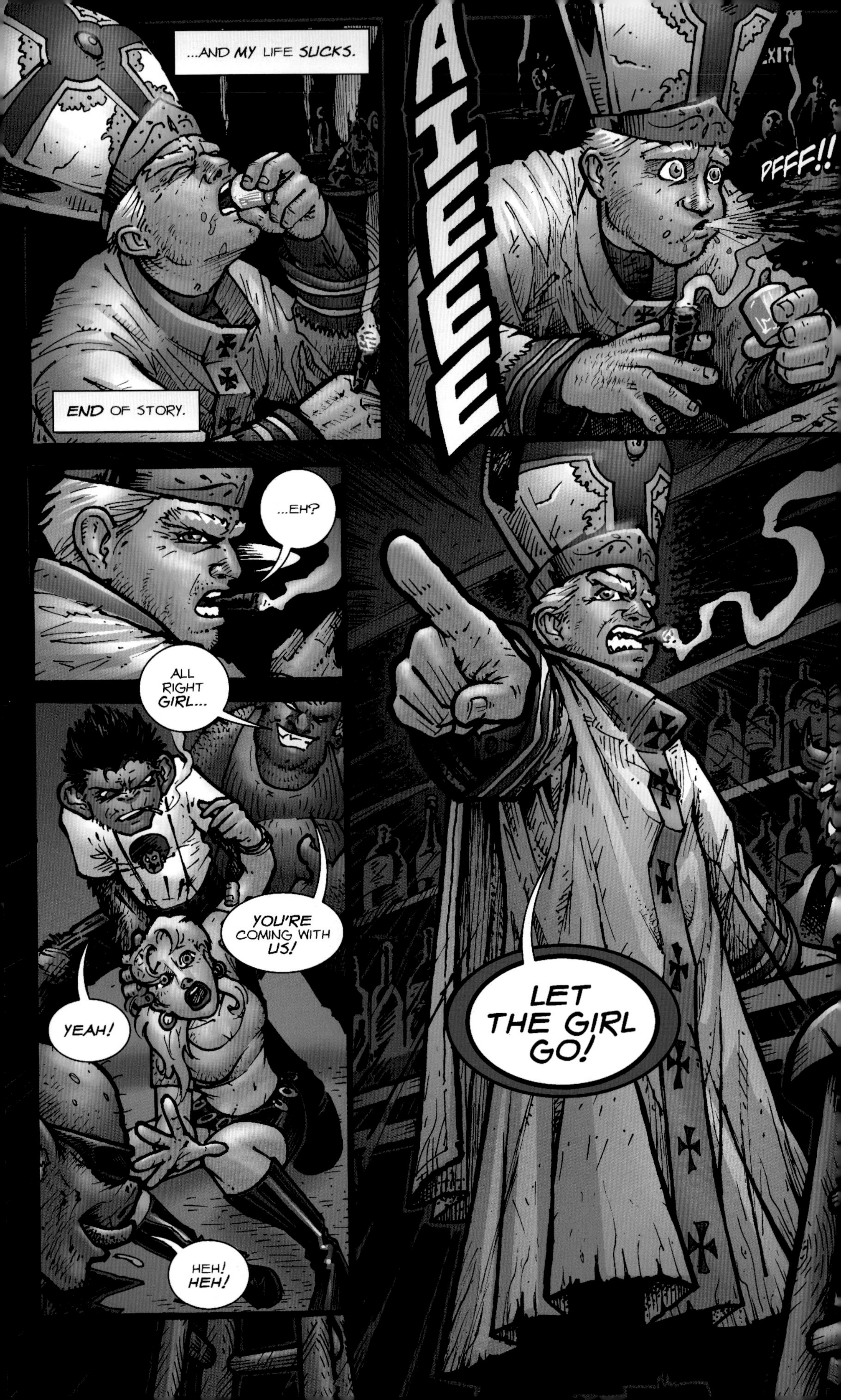

...AND MY LIFE SUCKS.
END OF STORY.
AIEEE
PFFF!!
...EH?
ALL RIGHT GIRL...
YOU'RE COMING WITH US!
YEAH!
HEH! HEH!
LET THE GIRL GO!

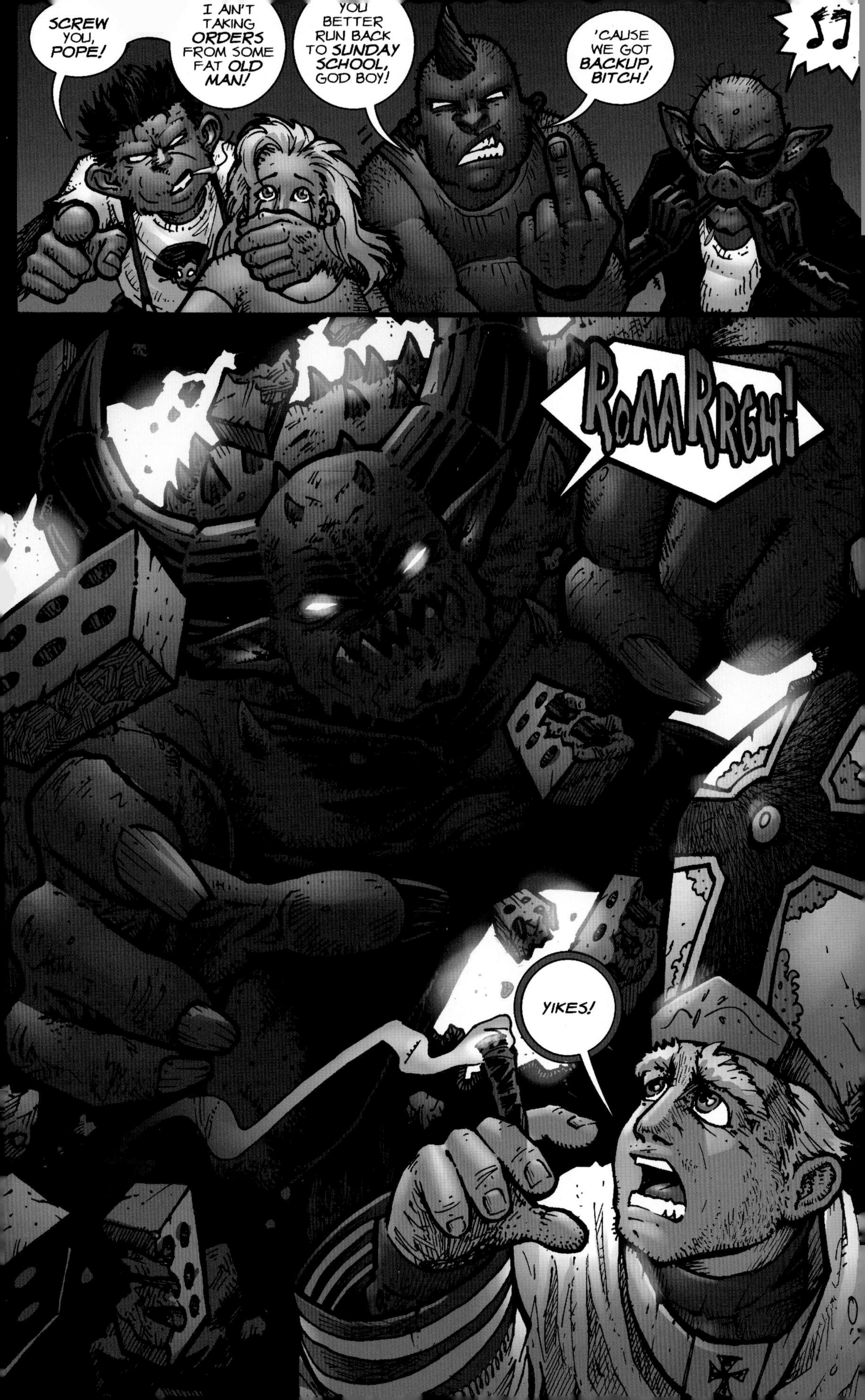
SCREW YOU, POPE!
I AIN'T TAKING ORDERS FROM SOME FAT OLD MAN!
YOU BETTER RUN BACK TO SUNDAY SCHOOL, GOD BOY!
'CAUSE WE GOT BACKUP, BITCH!
ROAARRGH!
YIKES!

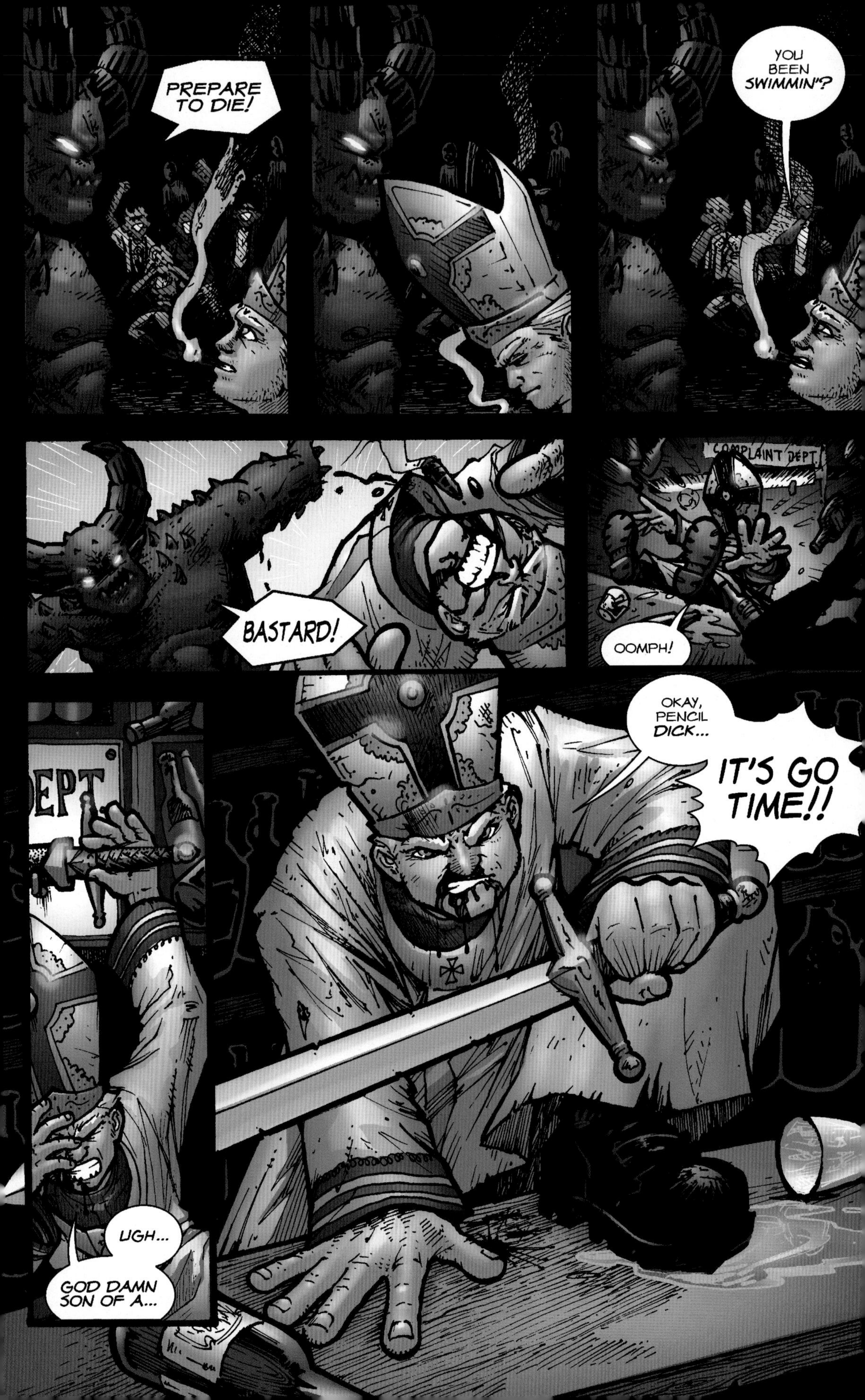
PREPARE TO DIE!
YOU BEEN SWIMMIN'?
BASTARD!
COMPLAINT DEPT
OOMPH!
OKAY, PENCIL DICK...
IT'S GO TIME!!
DEPT
UGH...
GOD DAMN SON OF A...

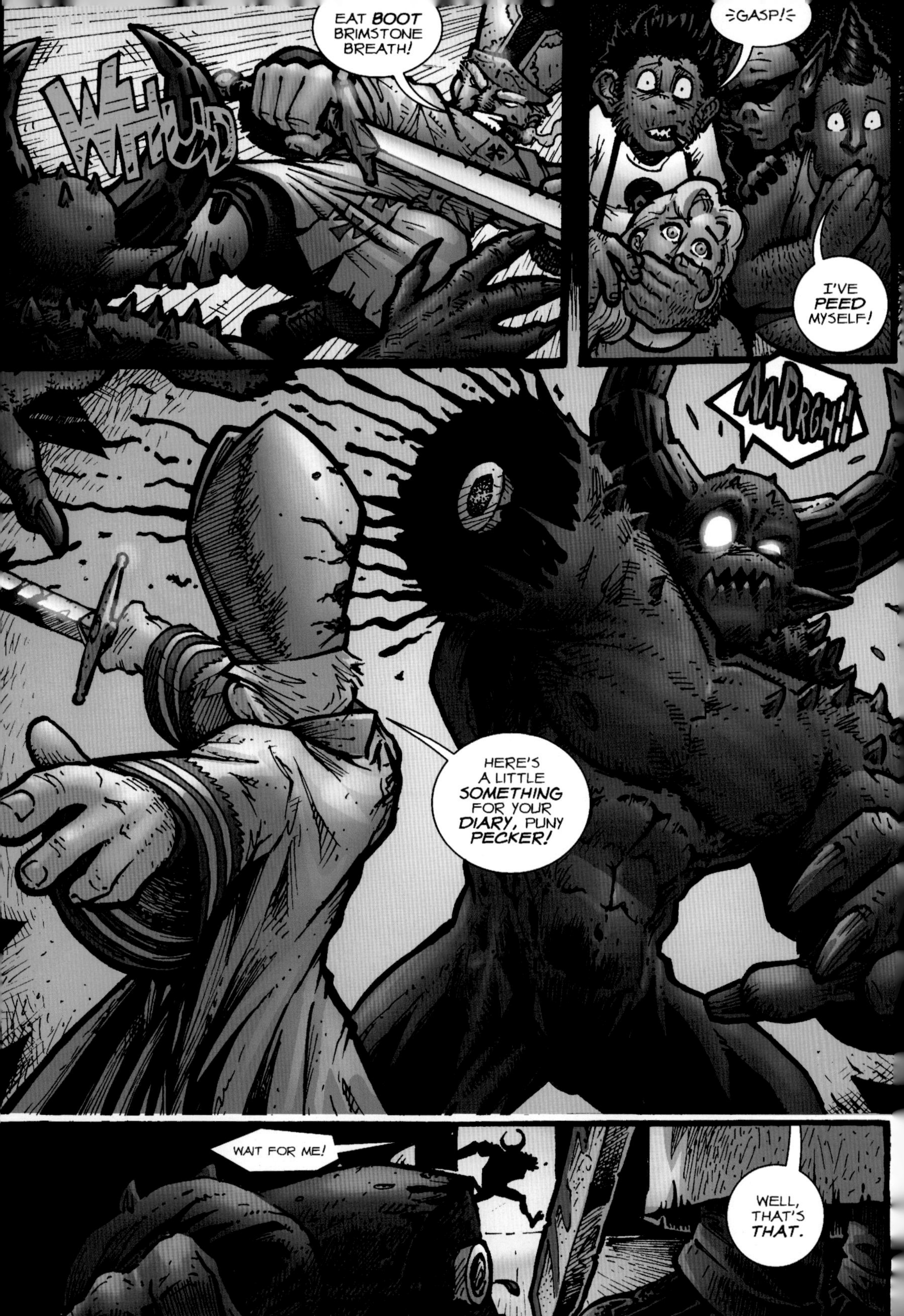
WHUD
EAT BOOT BRIMSTONE BREATH!
=GASP!=
I'VE PEED MYSELF!
AARRGHH!
HERE'S A LITTLE SOMETHING FOR YOUR DIARY, PUNY PECKER!
WAIT FOR ME!
WELL, THAT'S THAT.

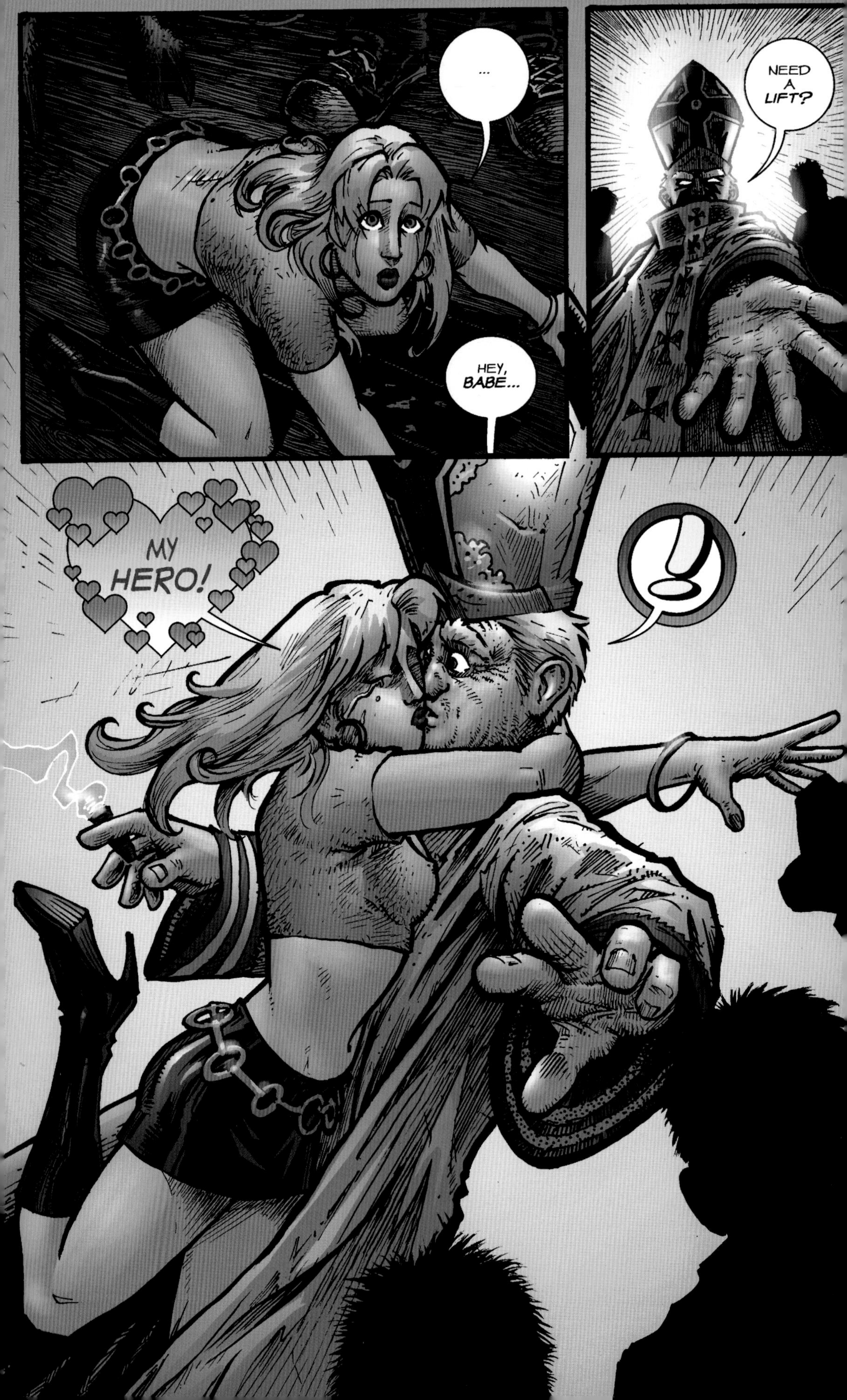
...
HEY, BABE...
NEED A LIFT?
MY HERO!
!

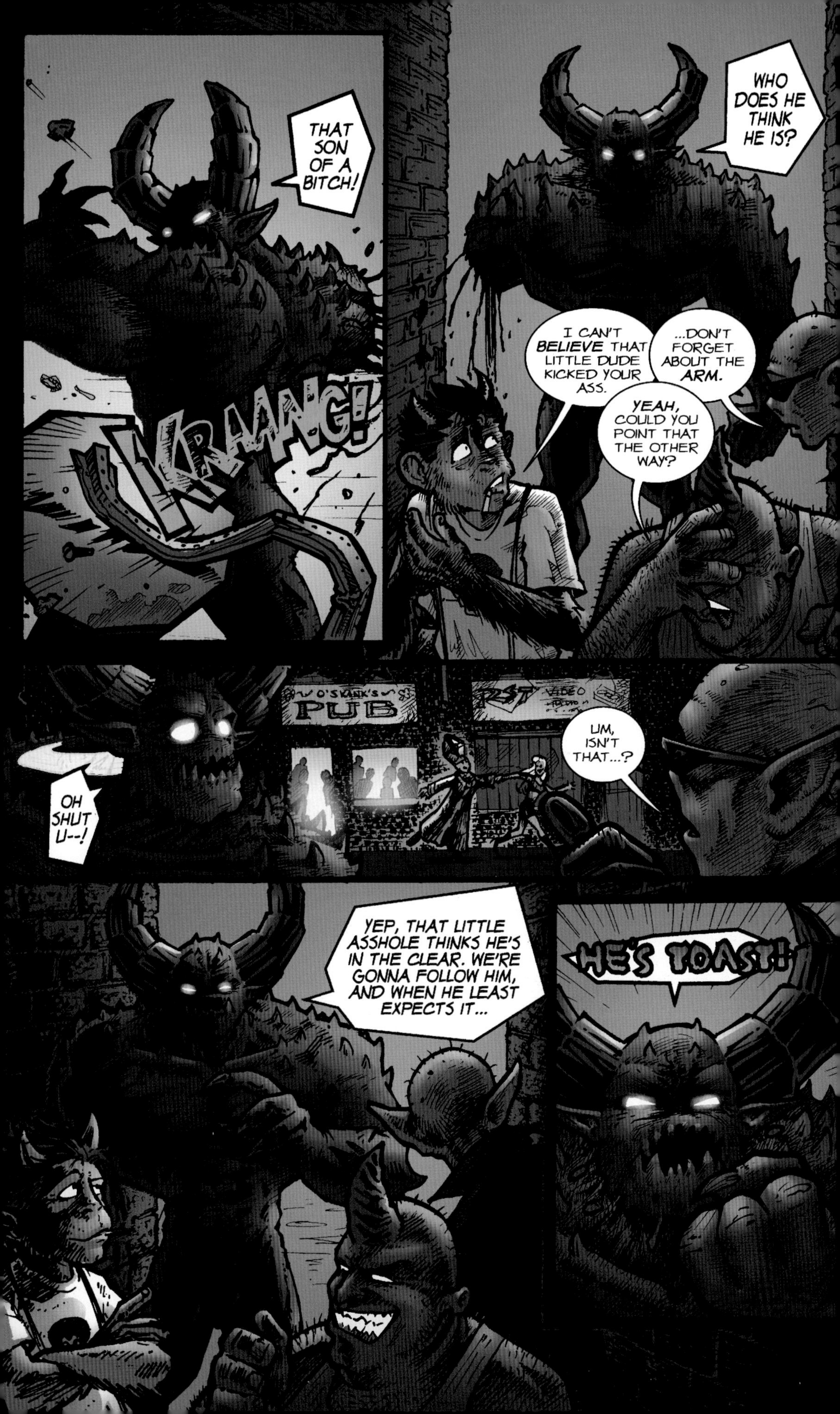
THAT SON OF A BITCH!
KRAANG!!
WHO DOES HE THINK HE IS?
I CAN'T BELIEVE THAT LITTLE DUDE KICKED YOUR ASS.
...DON'T FORGET ABOUT THE ARM.
YEAH, COULD YOU POINT THAT THE OTHER WAY?
O'SKANK'S PUB
VIDEO
OH SHUT U--!
UM, ISN'T THAT...?
YEP, THAT LITTLE ASSHOLE THINKS HE'S IN THE CLEAR. WE'RE GONNA FOLLOW HIM, AND WHEN HE LEAST EXPECTS IT...
HE'S TOAST!

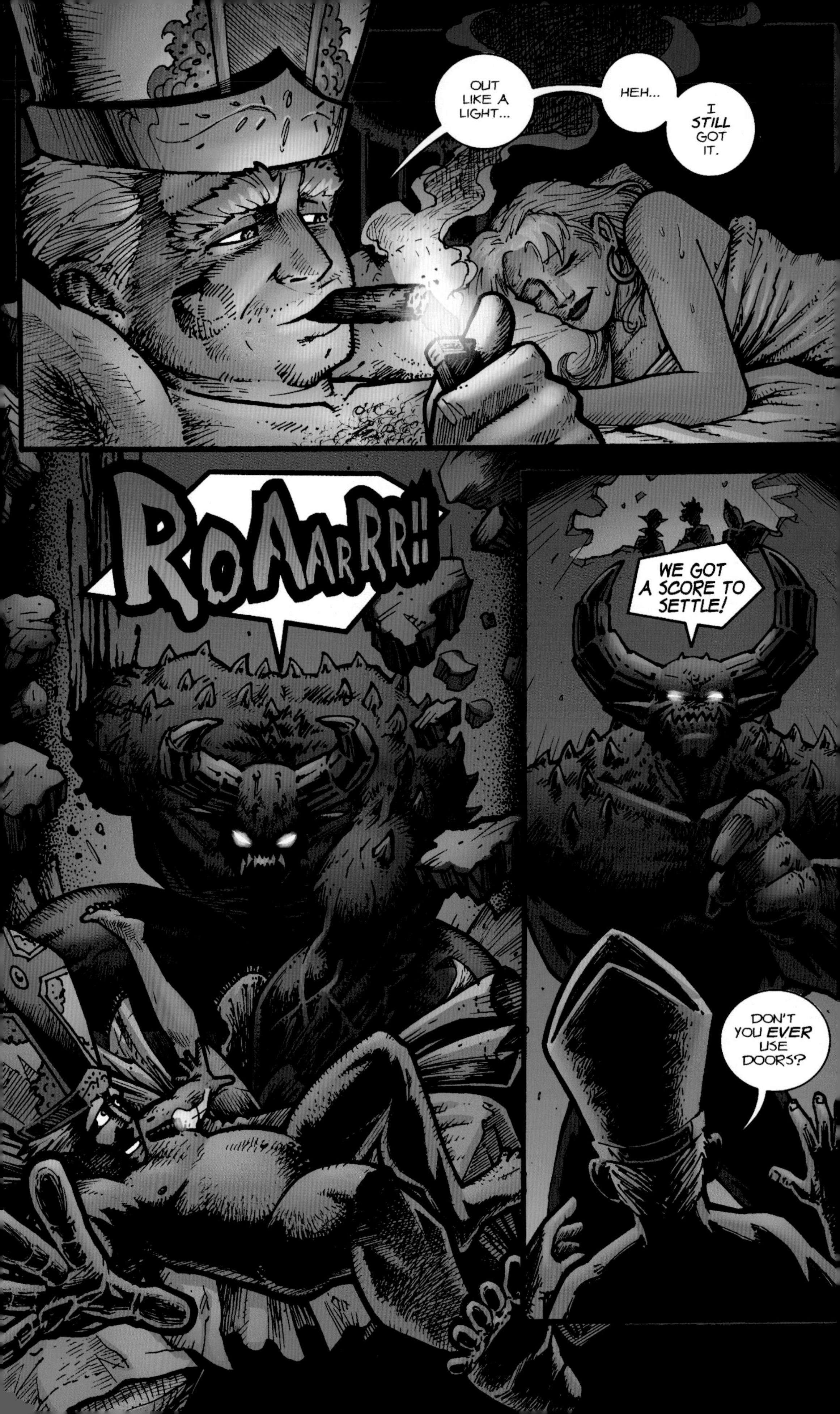
OUT LIKE A LIGHT...
HEH...
I *STILL* GOT IT.
ROAARRR!!
WE GOT A SCORE TO SETTLE!
DON'T YOU *EVER* USE DOORS?

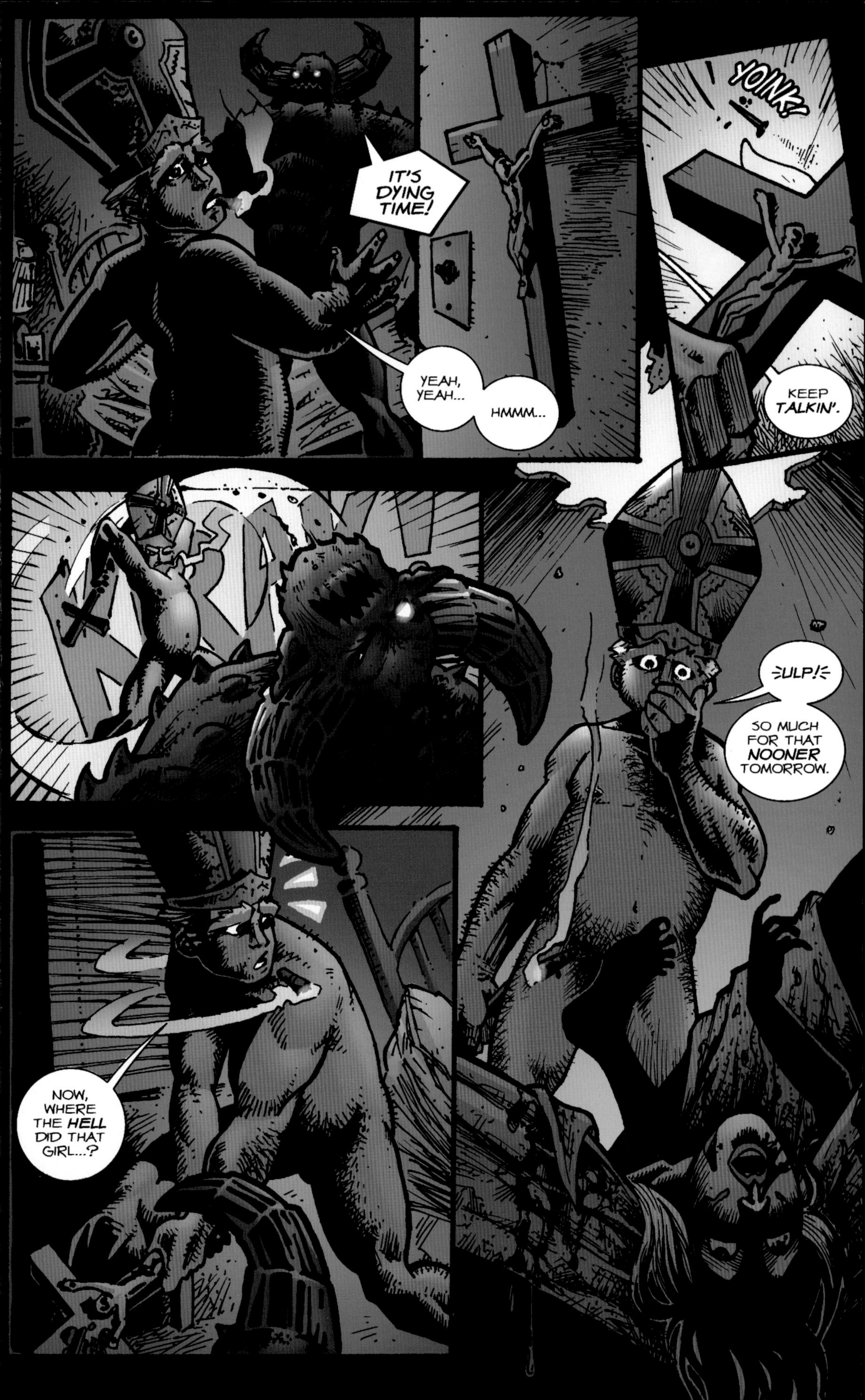
IT'S DYING TIME!
YEAH, YEAH...
HMMM...
YOINK!
KEEP TALKIN'.
ULP!
SO MUCH FOR THAT NOONER TOMORROW.
NOW, WHERE THE HELL DID THAT GIRL...?

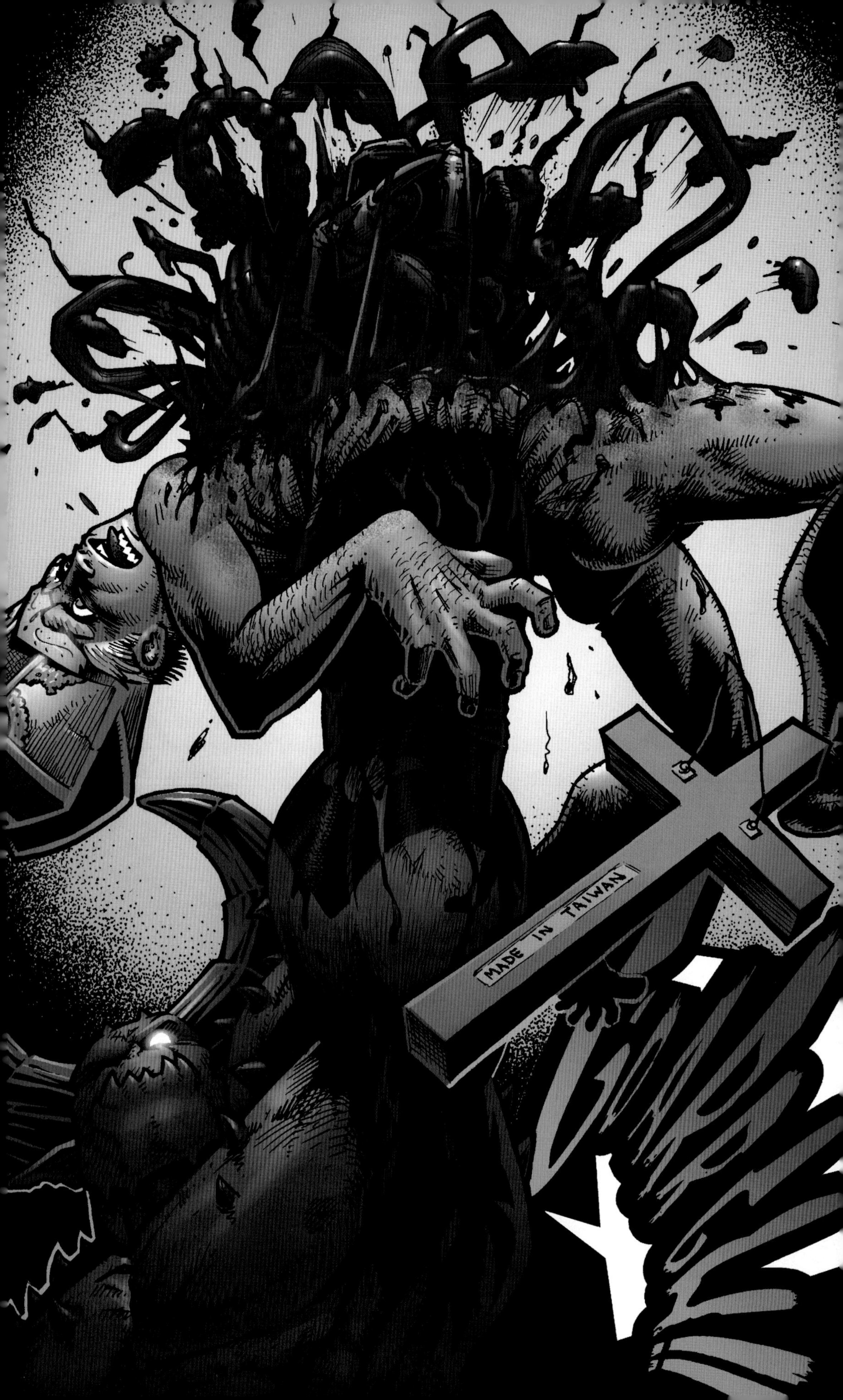
MADE IN TAIWAN

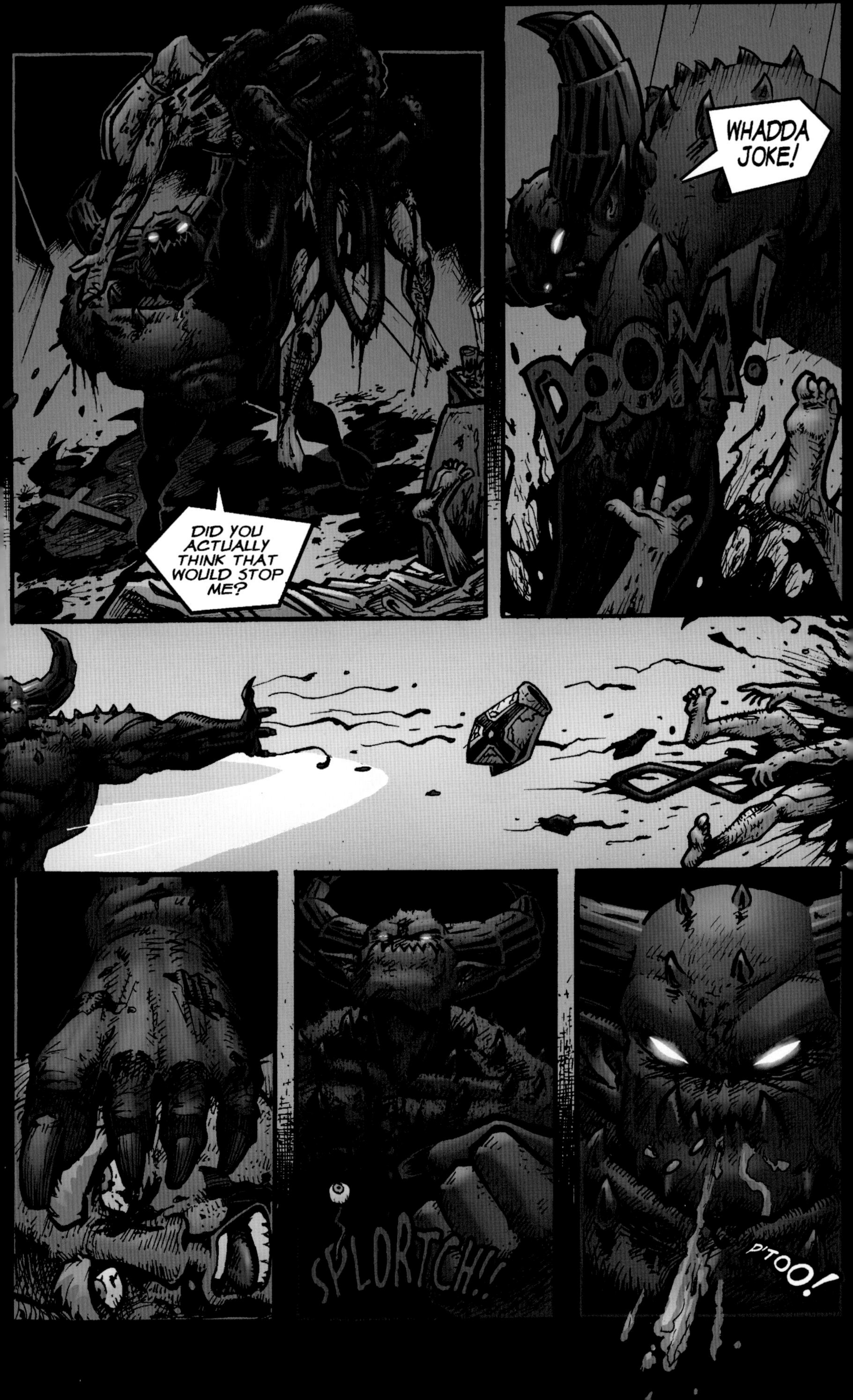
DID YOU ACTUALLY THINK THAT WOULD STOP ME?
WHADDA JOKE!
BOOM!
SPLORTCH!!
P'TOO!

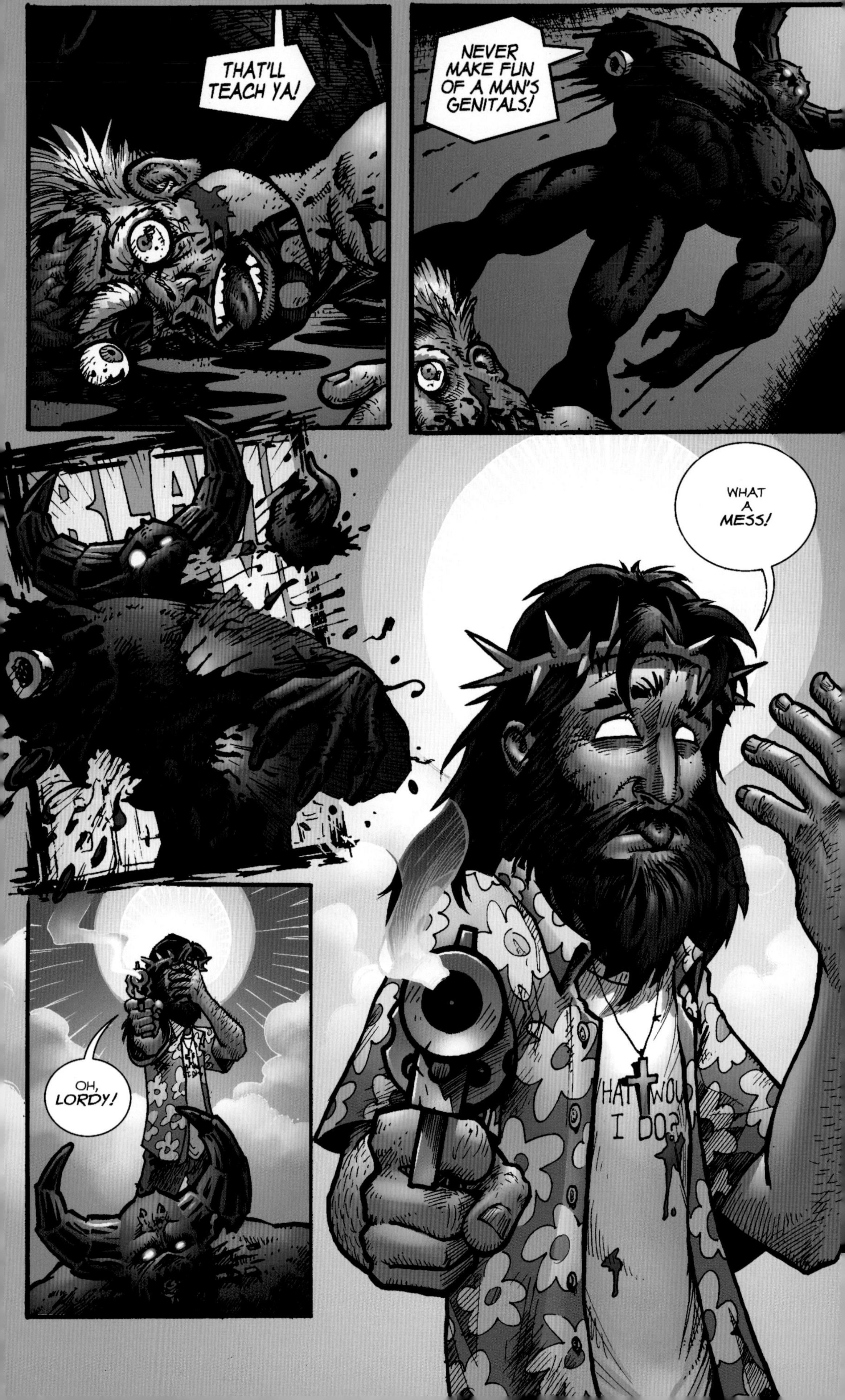
THAT'LL TEACH YA!
NEVER MAKE FUN OF A MAN'S GENITALS!
WHAT A MESS!
OH, LORDY!

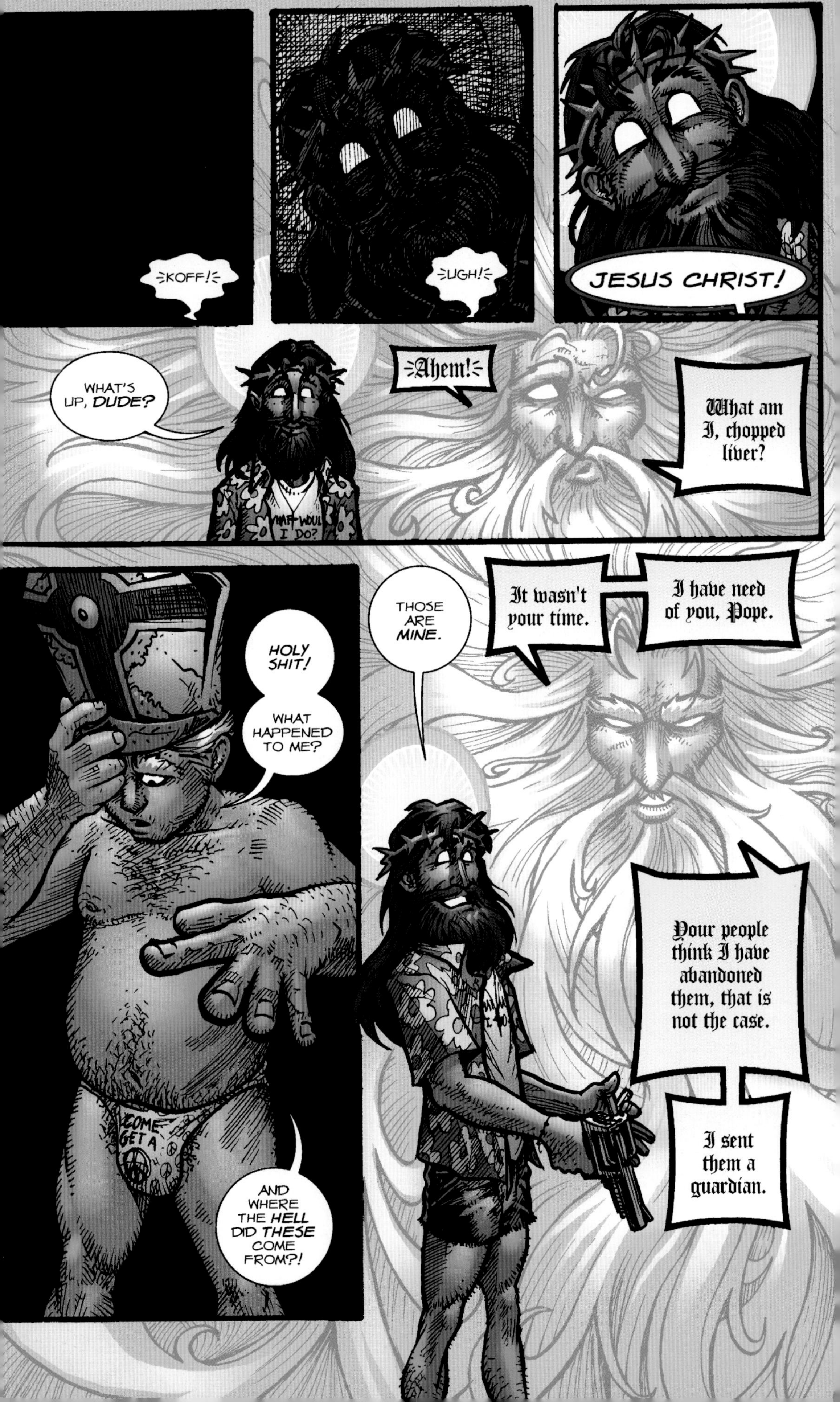
KOFF!
UGH!
JESUS CHRIST!
WHAT'S UP, DUDE?
Ahem!
What am I, chopped liver?
WHAT WOULD I DO?
HOLY SHIT!
WHAT HAPPENED TO ME?
THOSE ARE MINE.
It wasn't your time.
I have need of you, Pope.
AND WHERE THE HELL DID THESE COME FROM?!
COME GET A
Your people think I have abandoned them, that is not the case.
I sent them a guardian.

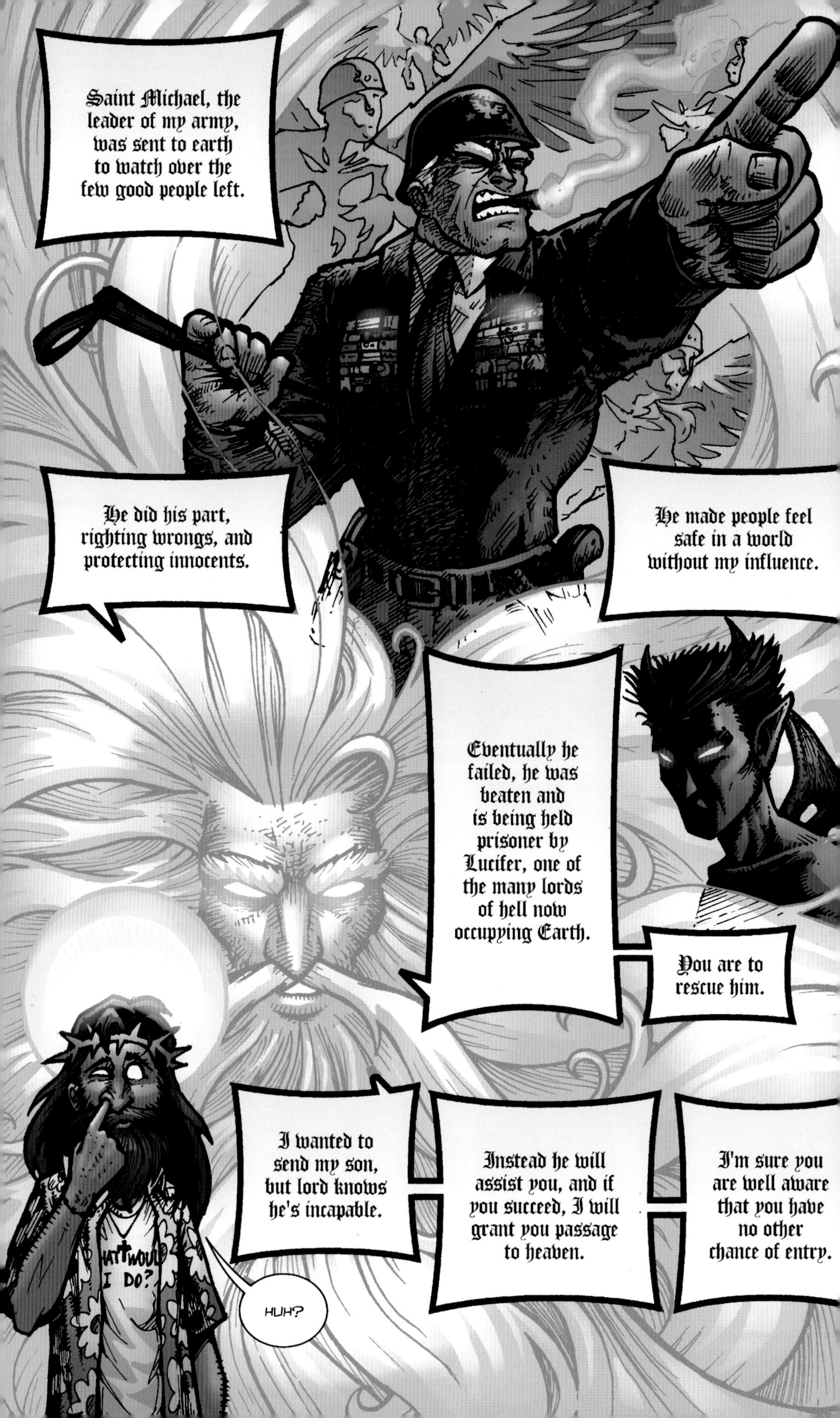
Saint Michael, the leader of my army, was sent to earth to watch over the few good people left.
He did his part, righting wrongs, and protecting innocents.
He made people feel safe in a world without my influence.
Eventually he failed, he was beaten and is being held prisoner by Lucifer, one of the many lords of hell now occupying Earth.
You are to rescue him.
I wanted to send my son, but lord knows he's incapable.
HUH?
Instead he will assist you, and if you succeed, I will grant you passage to heaven.
I'm sure you are well aware that you have no other chance of entry.

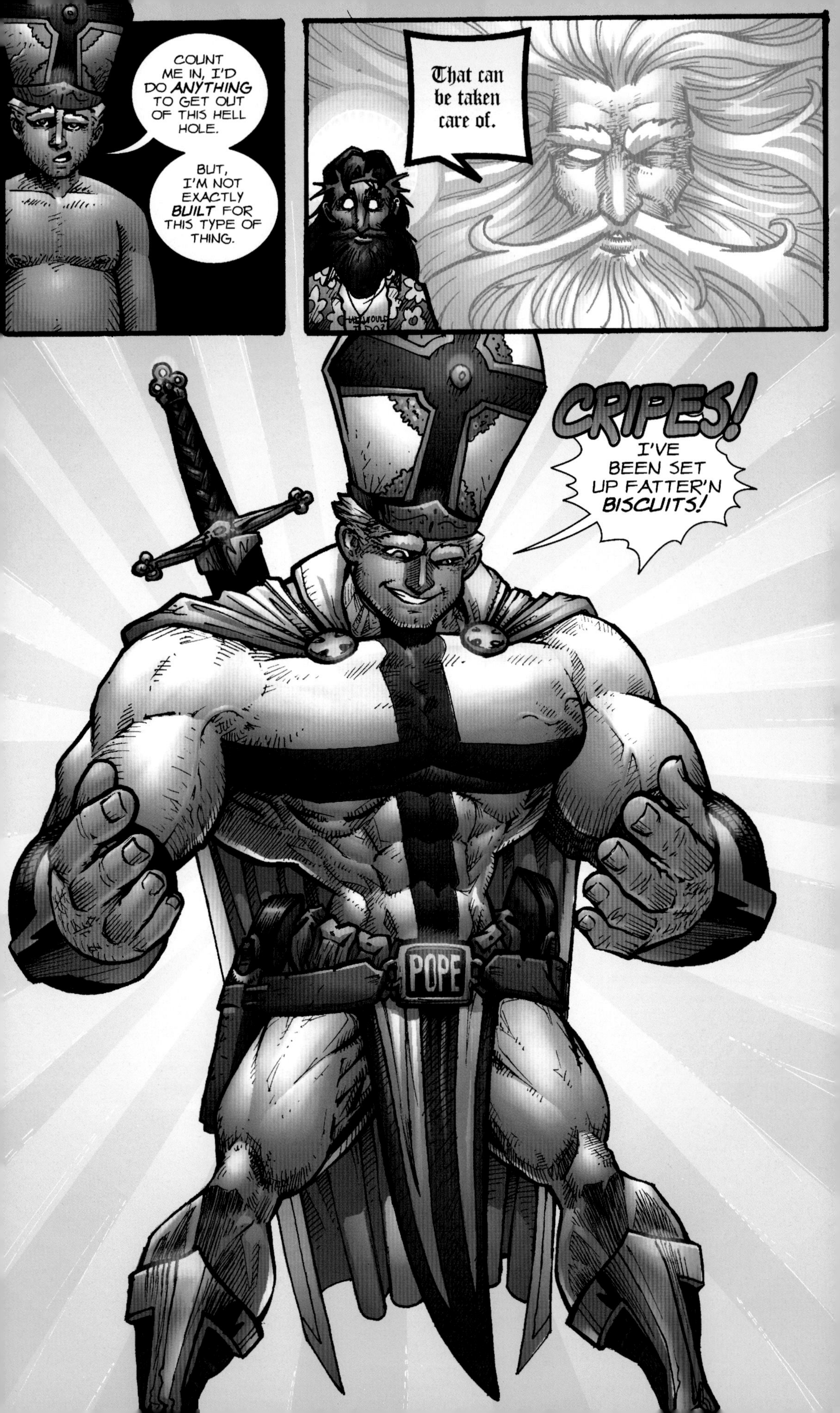
COUNT ME IN, I'D DO ANYTHING TO GET OUT OF THIS HELL HOLE.
BUT, I'M NOT EXACTLY BUILT FOR THIS TYPE OF THING.
That can be taken care of.
CRIPES!
I'VE BEEN SET UP FATTER'N BISCUITS!
POPE

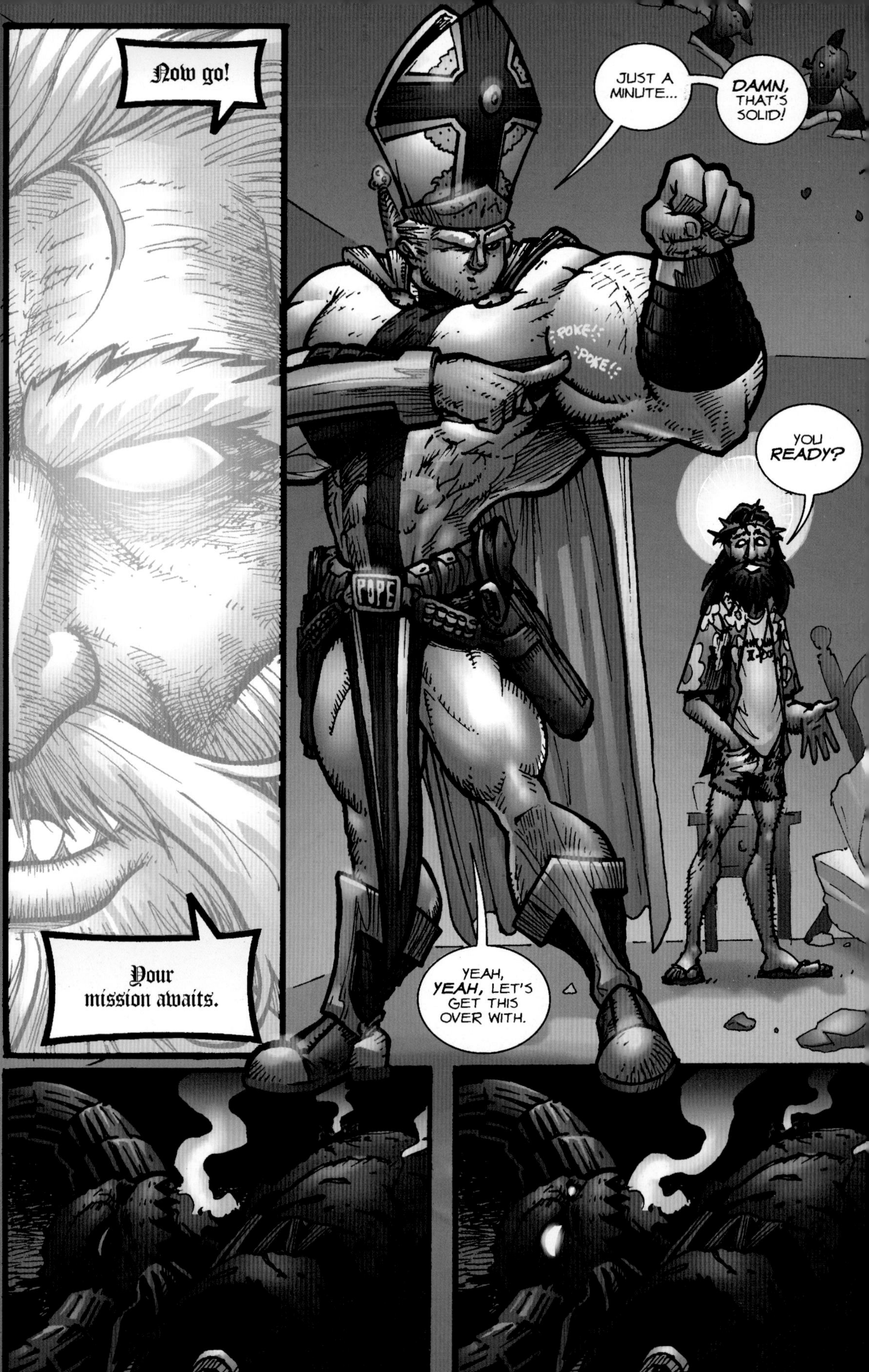
Now go!
Your mission awaits.
JUST A MINUTE...
DAMN, THAT'S SOLID!
POKE!!
POKE!!
YOU READY?
POPE
YEAH, YEAH, LET'S GET THIS OVER WITH.

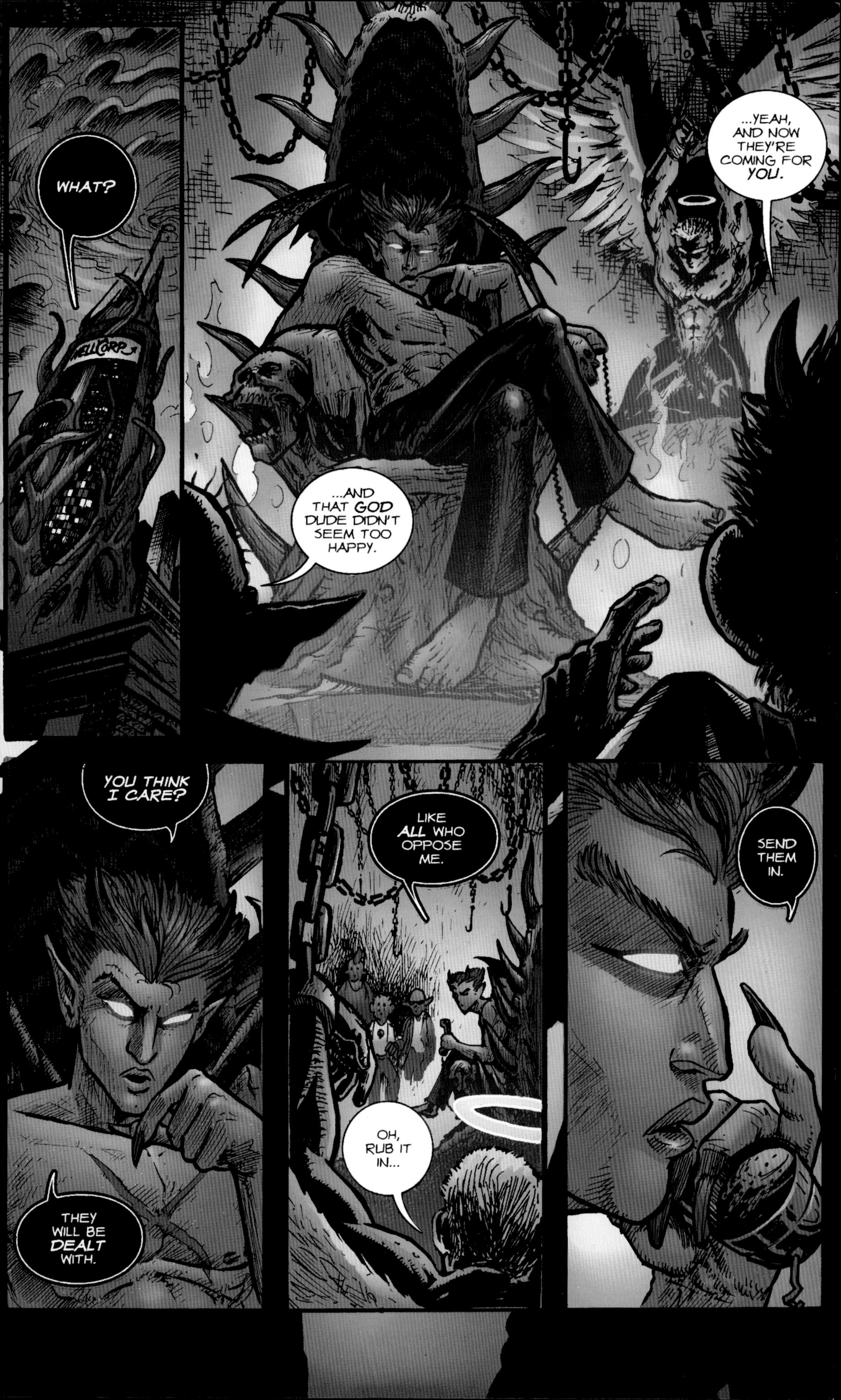
WHAT?
...AND THAT GOD DUDE DIDN'T SEEM TOO HAPPY.
...YEAH, AND NOW THEY'RE COMING FOR YOU.
YOU THINK I CARE?
THEY WILL BE DEALT WITH.
LIKE ALL WHO OPPOSE ME.
OH, RUB IT IN...
SEND THEM IN.

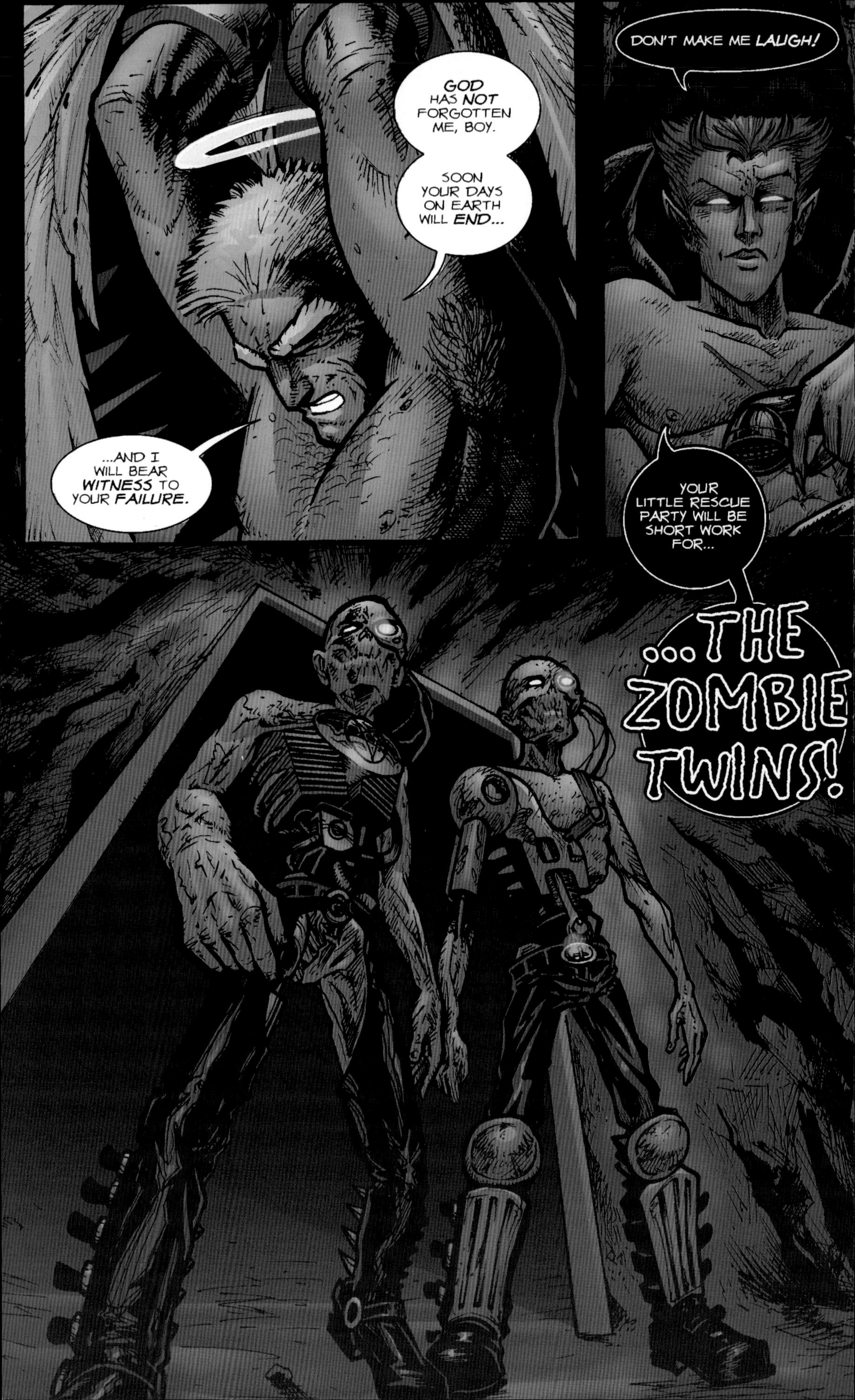
GOD HAS NOT FORGOTTEN ME, BOY.
SOON YOUR DAYS ON EARTH WILL END...
...AND I WILL BEAR WITNESS TO YOUR FAILURE.
DON'T MAKE ME LAUGH!
YOUR LITTLE RESCUE PARTY WILL BE SHORT WORK FOR...
...THE ZOMBIE TWINS!

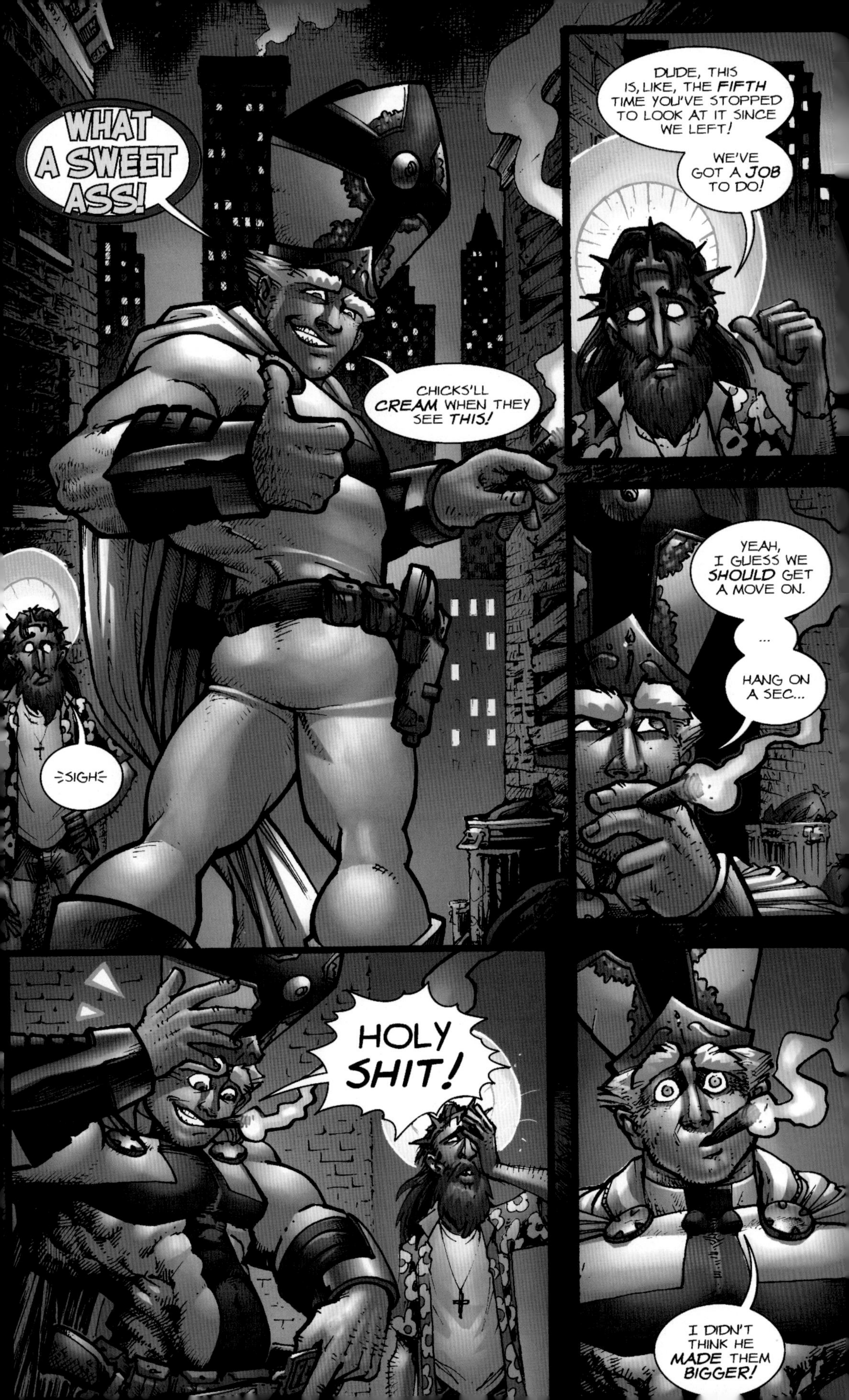
WHAT A SWEET ASS!
CHICKS'LL CREAM WHEN THEY SEE THIS!
=SIGH=
DUDE, THIS IS, LIKE, THE FIFTH TIME YOU'VE STOPPED TO LOOK AT IT SINCE WE LEFT!
WE'VE GOT A JOB TO DO!
YEAH, I GUESS WE SHOULD GET A MOVE ON.
...
HANG ON A SEC...
HOLY SHIT!
I DIDN'T THINK HE MADE THEM BIGGER!

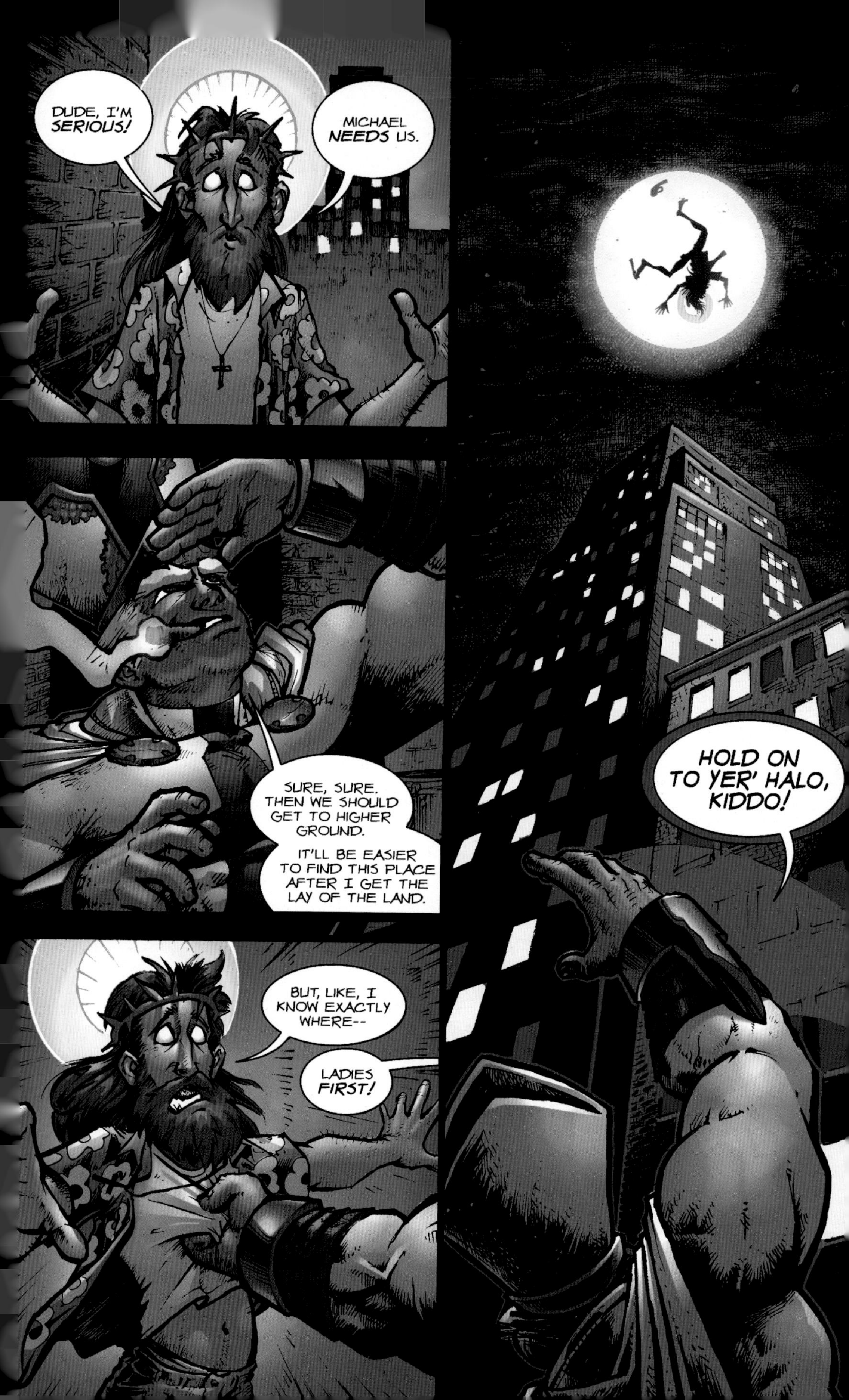
DUDE, I'M SERIOUS!
MICHAEL NEEDS US.
SURE, SURE. THEN WE SHOULD GET TO HIGHER GROUND.
IT'LL BE EASIER TO FIND THIS PLACE AFTER I GET THE LAY OF THE LAND.
BUT, LIKE, I KNOW EXACTLY WHERE--
LADIES FIRST!
HOLD ON TO YER' HALO, KIDDO!

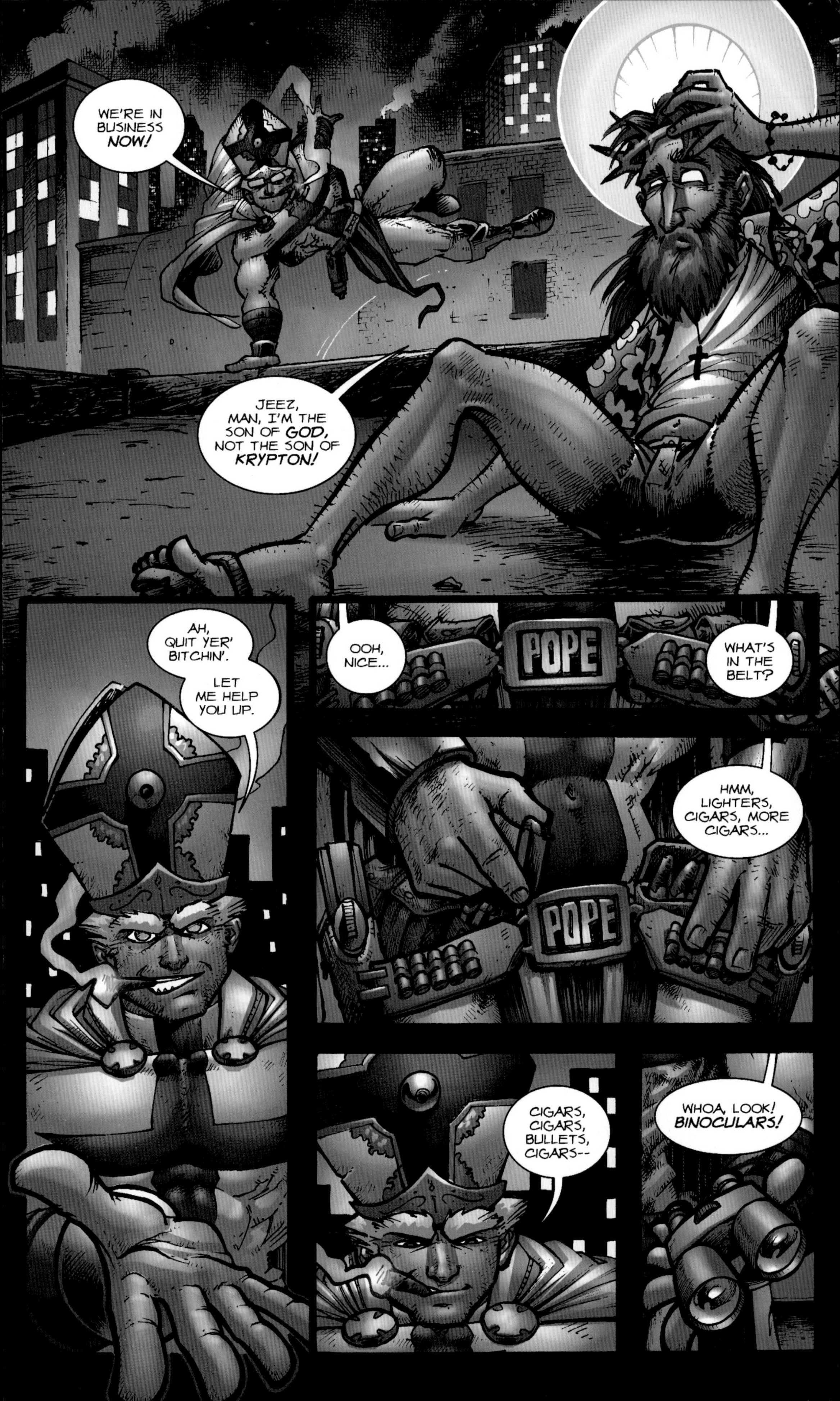
WE'RE IN BUSINESS NOW!
JEEZ, MAN, I'M THE SON OF GOD, NOT THE SON OF KRYPTON!
AH, QUIT YER' BITCHIN'.
LET ME HELP YOU UP.
OOH, NICE...
POPE
WHAT'S IN THE BELT?
HMM, LIGHTERS, CIGARS, MORE CIGARS...
POPE
CIGARS, CIGARS, BULLETS, CIGARS--
WHOA, LOOK! BINOCULARS!

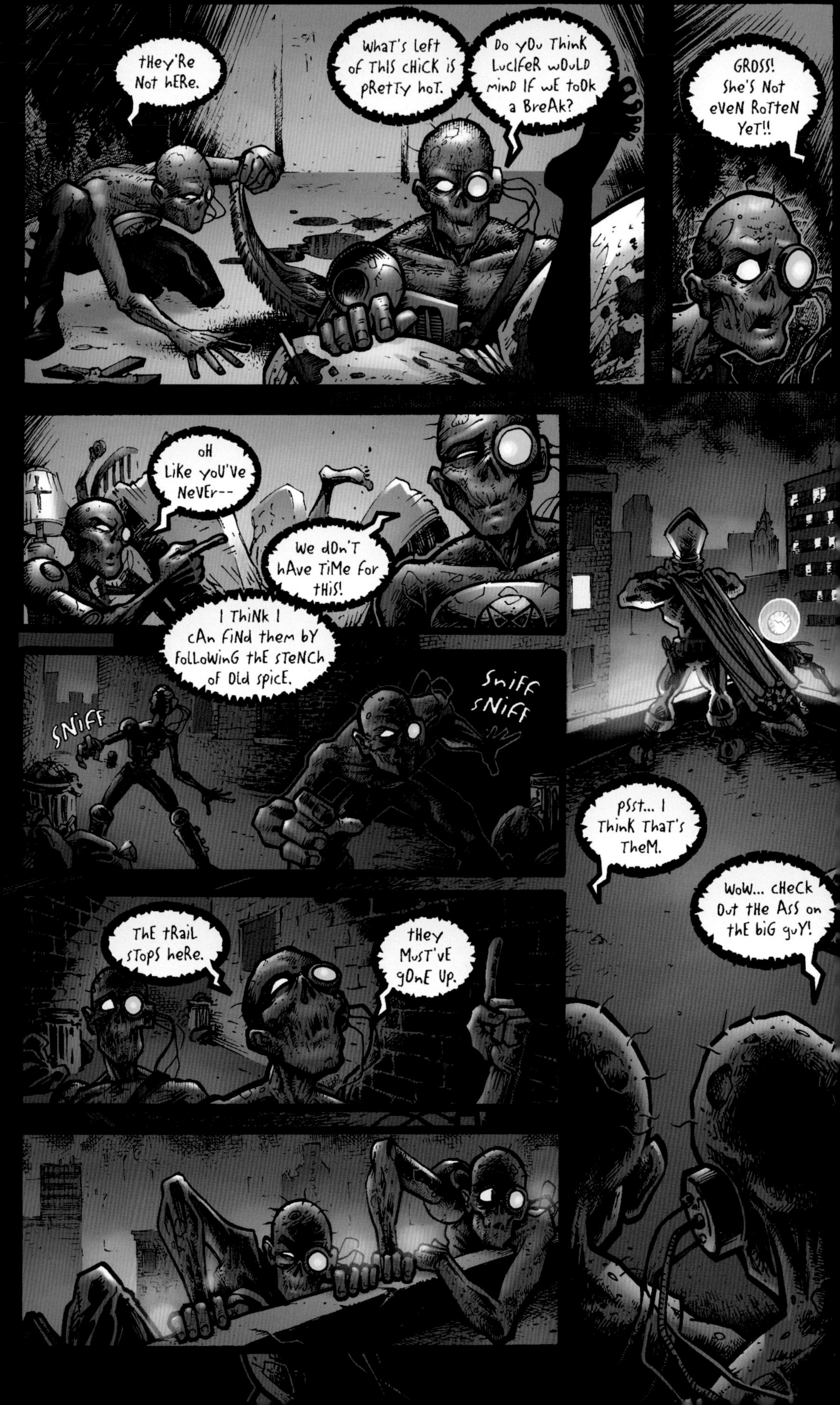
tHey'Re Not hERe.
WhaT's left of ThIS cHICK is pReTTy hoT.
Do yOu Think LucIfeR wOuLD minD If wE toOk a BreAk?
GROSS! She's Not eveN RoTTeN YeT!!
oH LiKe yoU'Ve NeVEr--
We dOn'T hAve TiMe for tHiS!
I ThiNk I cAn FiNd them bY FolLoWinG thE sTeNCh of Old spicE.
SNiFF
SNiFF SNiFF
ThE tRaiL sTops heRe.
tHey MusT'vE gOnE Up.
pSst... I Think ThaT's TheM.
WoW... cHeCk Out tHe Ass on thE biG guY!

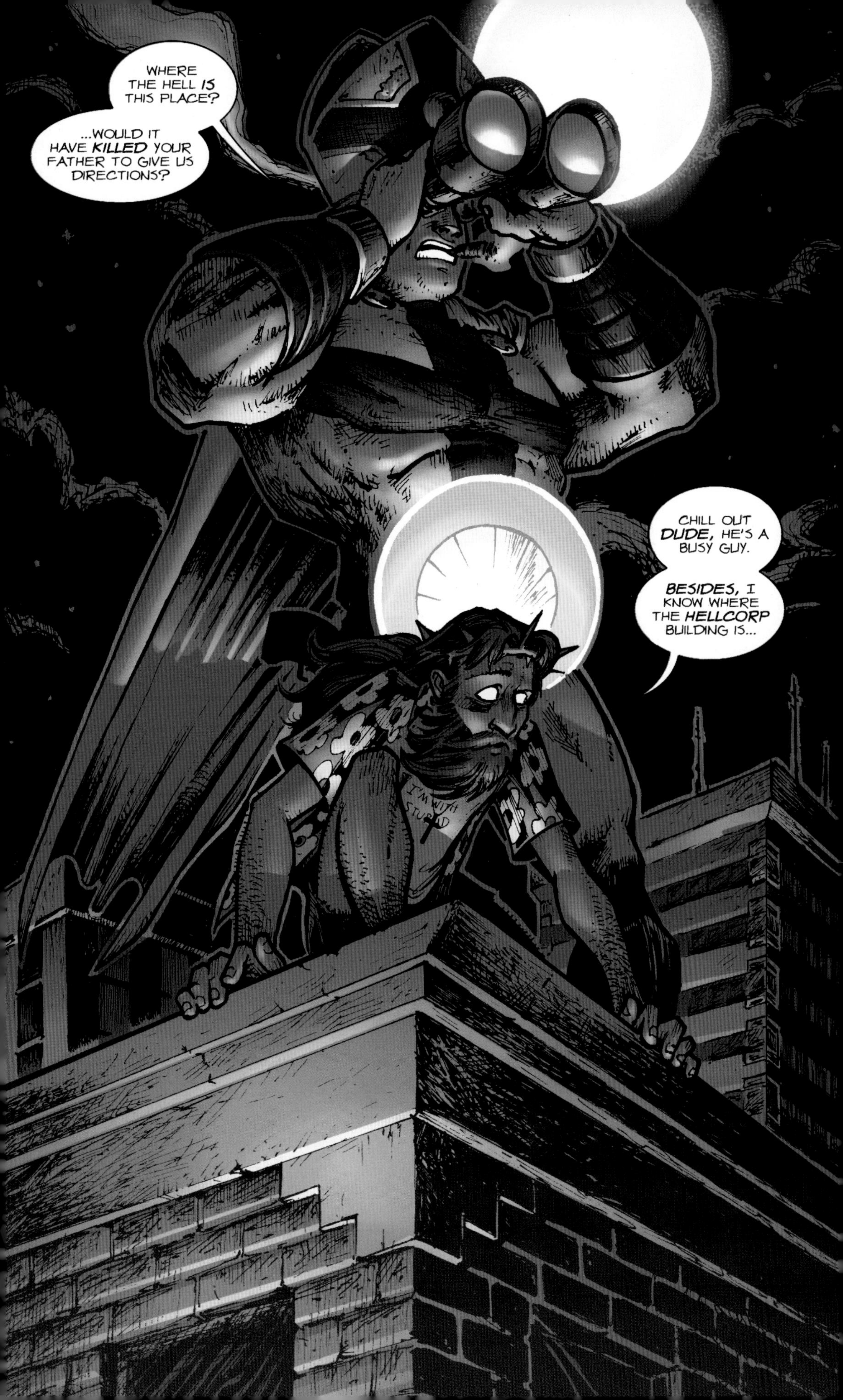
WHERE THE HELL IS THIS PLACE?
...WOULD IT HAVE KILLED YOUR FATHER TO GIVE US DIRECTIONS?
CHILL OUT DUDE, HE'S A BUSY GUY.
BESIDES, I KNOW WHERE THE HELLCORP BUILDING IS...

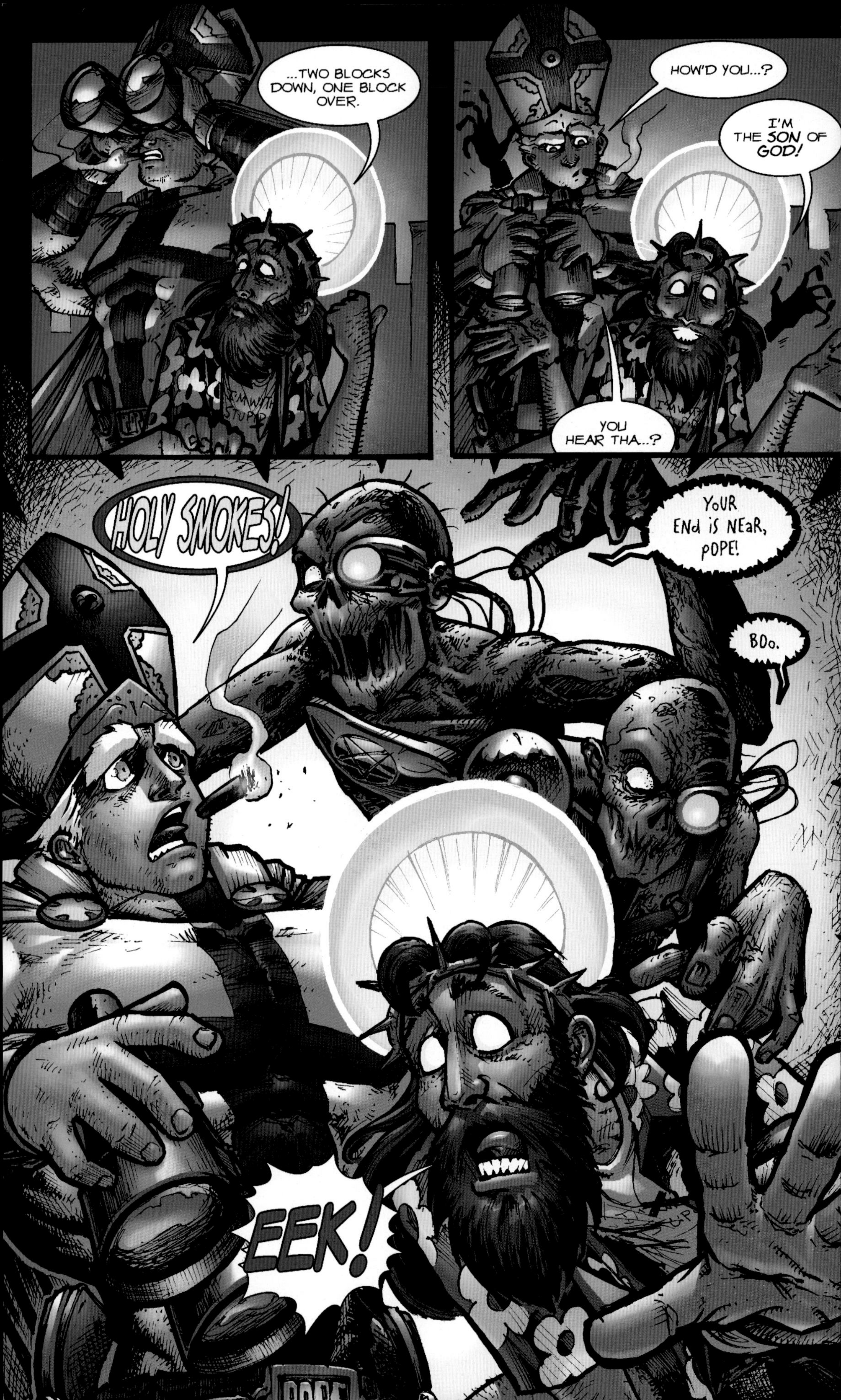
...TWO BLOCKS DOWN, ONE BLOCK OVER.
HOW'D YOU...?
I'M THE SON OF GOD!
YOU HEAR THA...?
HOLY SMOKES!
YoUR ENd is NEaR, POPE!
BOo.
EEK!

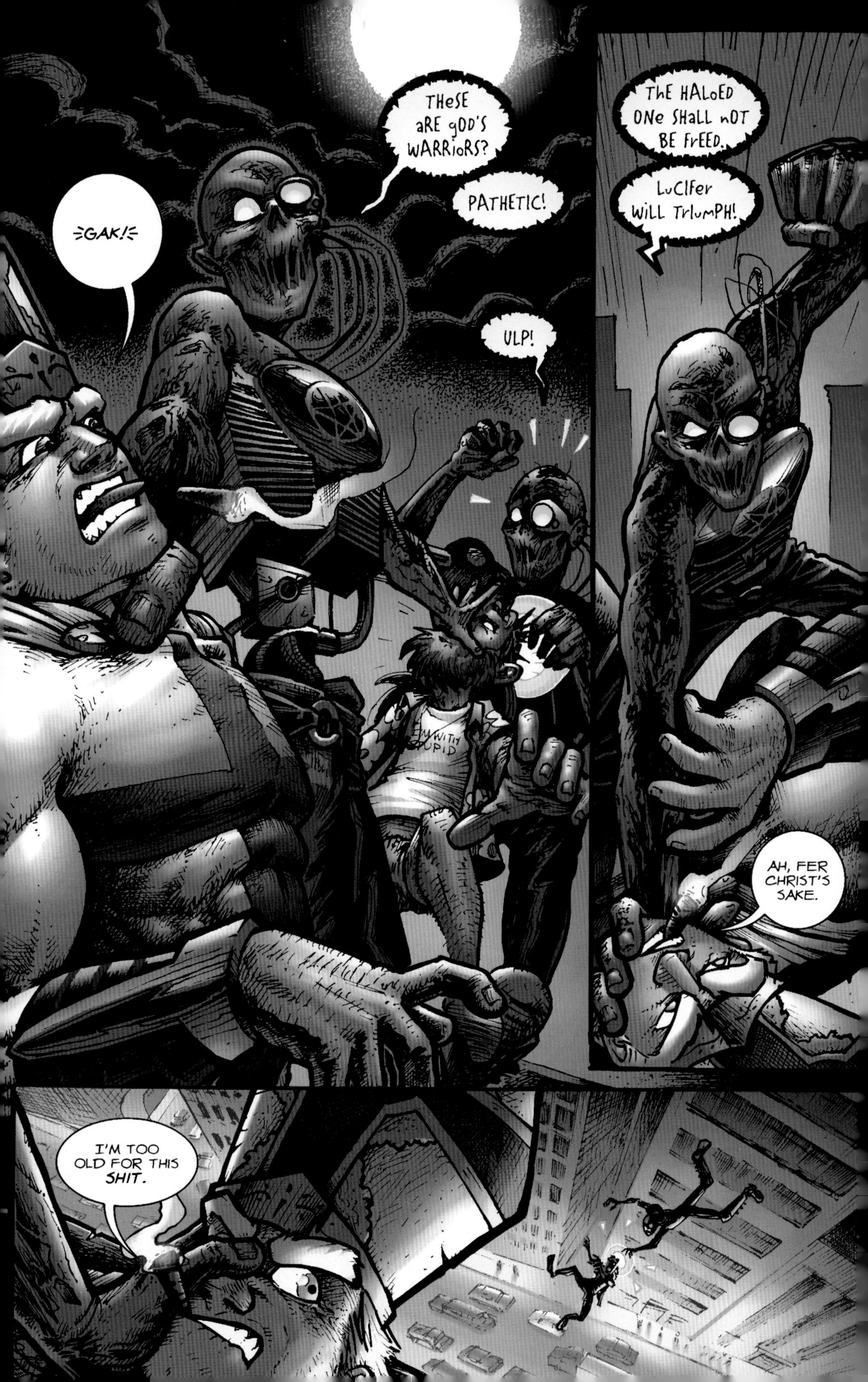

≡GAK!≡
THESE ARE GOD'S WARRIORS?
PATHETIC!
ULP!
THE HALOED ONE SHALL NOT BE FREED.
LUCIFER WILL TRIUMPH!
AH, FER CHRIST'S SAKE.
I'M TOO OLD FOR THIS SHIT.

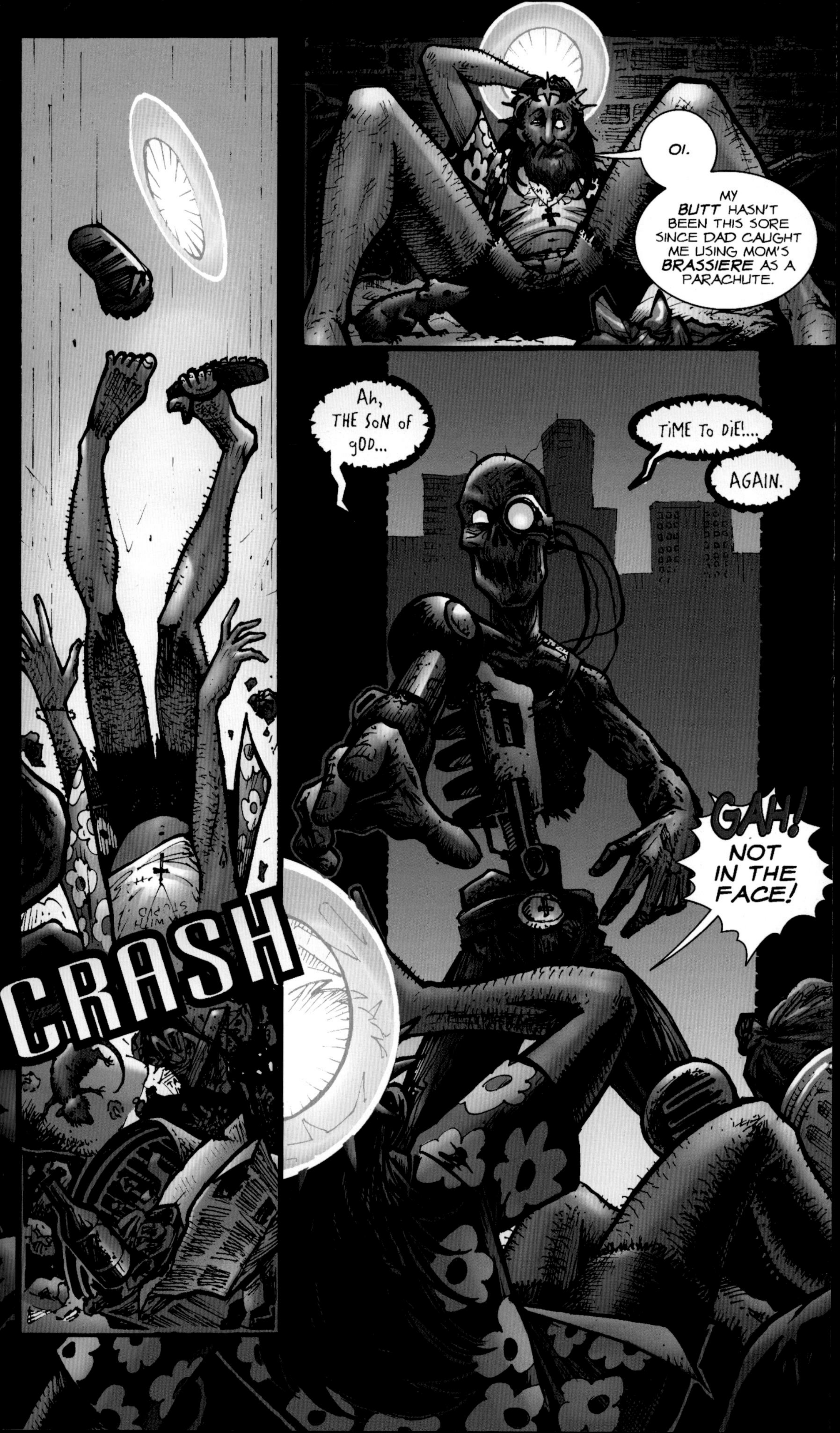
CRASH
OI.
MY BUTT HASN'T BEEN THIS SORE SINCE DAD CAUGHT ME USING MOM'S BRASSIERE AS A PARACHUTE.
Ah, THE SoN of goD...
TiME To DiE!...
AGAIN.
GAH! NOT IN THE FACE!

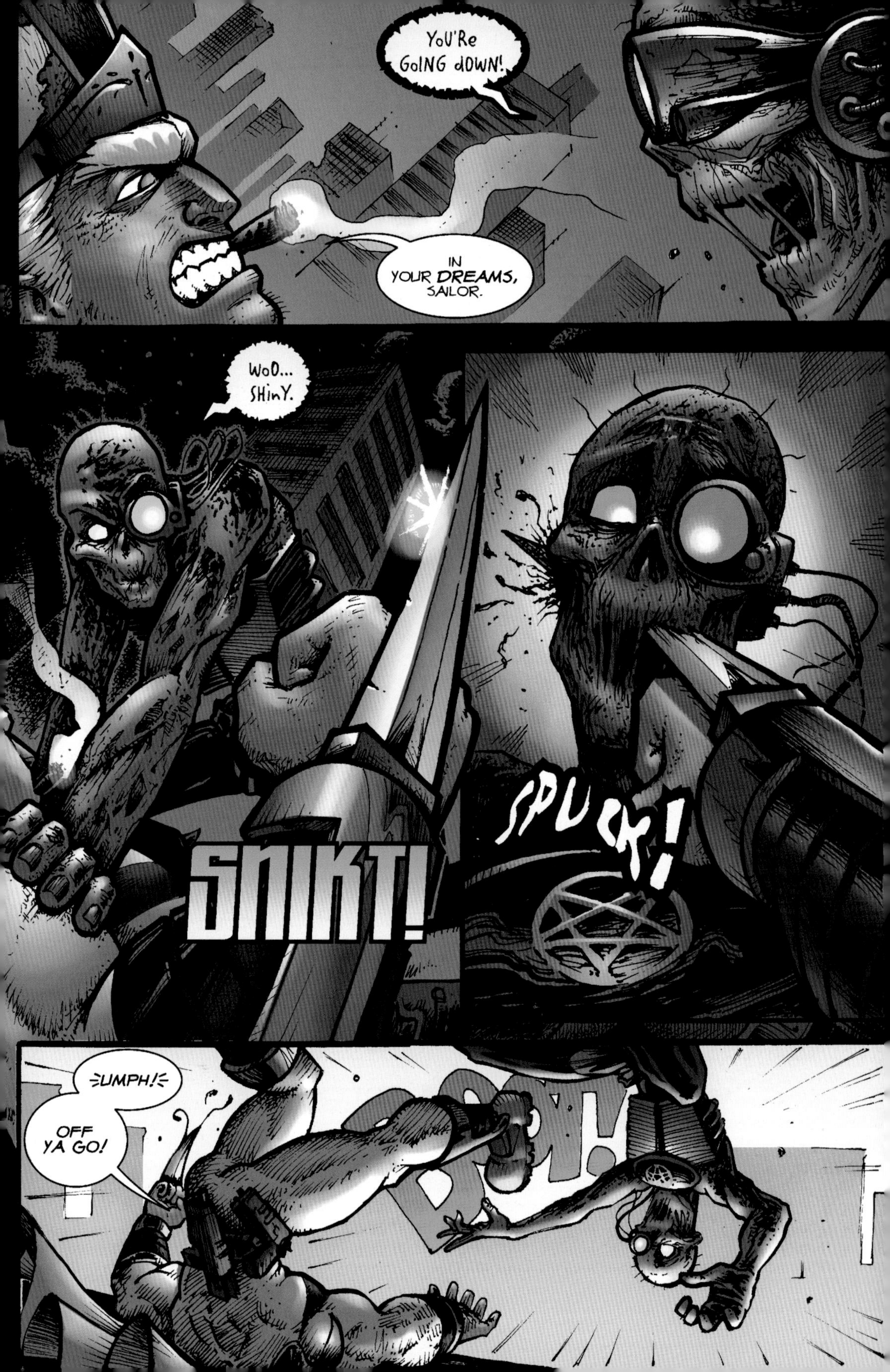
YOU'RE GOING DOWN!
IN YOUR DREAMS, SAILOR.
WOO... SHINY.
SNIKT!
SPLUCK!
UMPH!
OFF YA GO!

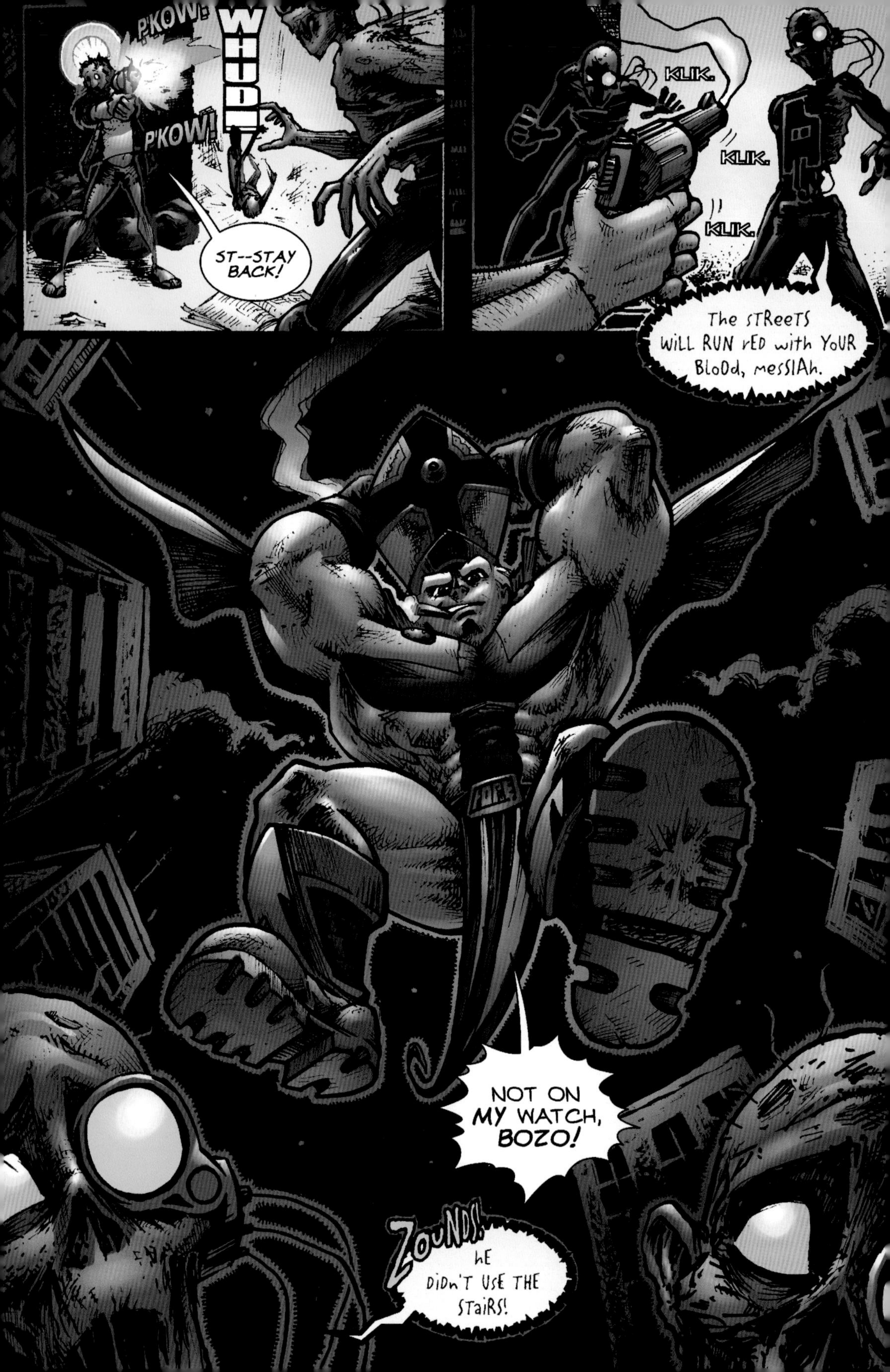
P'KOW!
WHUD!
P'KOW!
ST--STAY BACK!
KLIK.
KLIK.
KLIK.
The STReeTS WiLL RUN rED with YoUR BloOd, mesSIAh.
NOT ON MY WATCH, BOZO!
ZOUNDS!
hE DiDn'T USE THE STaiRS!

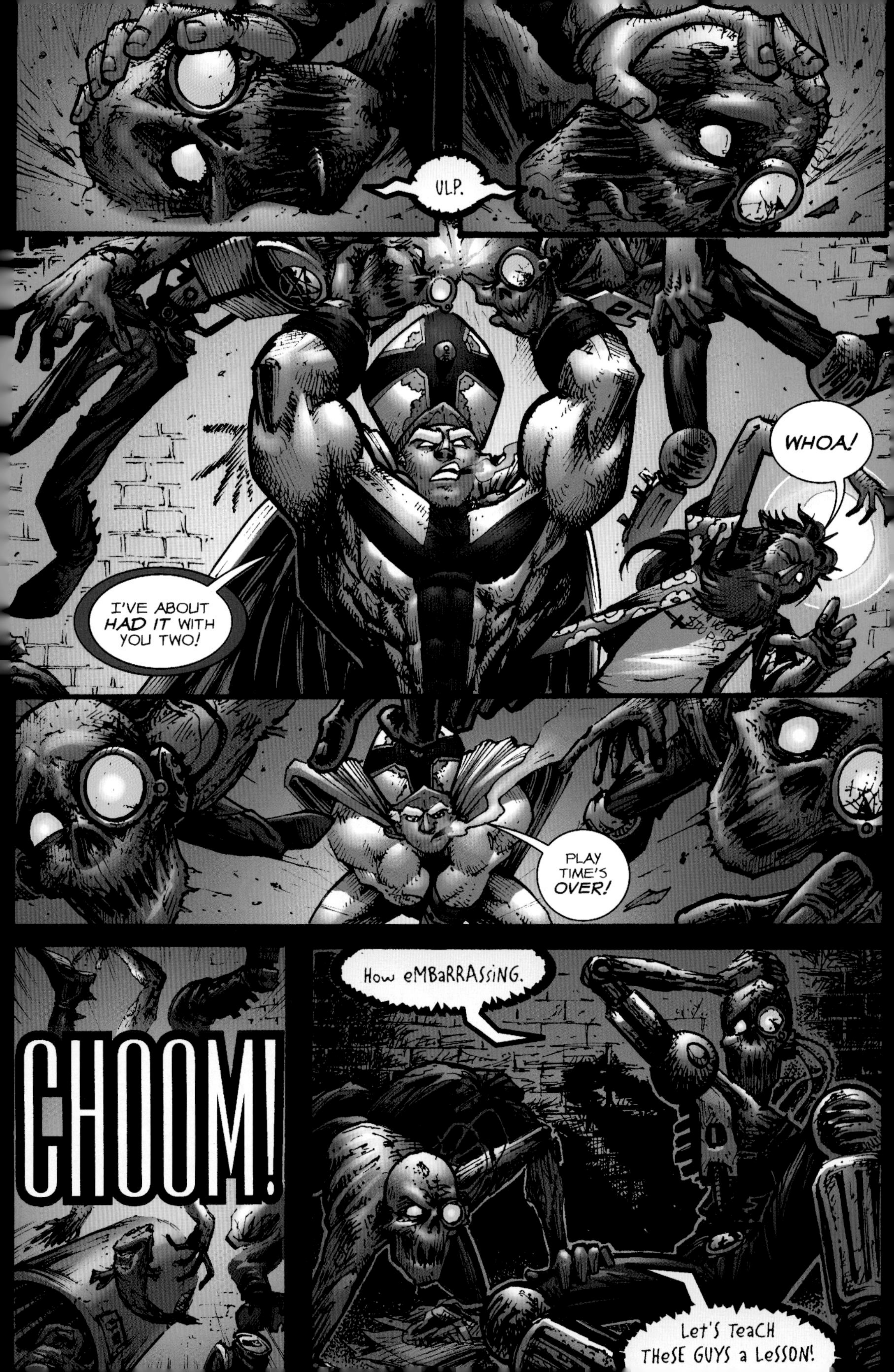

ULP.
WHOA!
I'VE ABOUT HAD IT WITH YOU TWO!
PLAY TIME'S OVER!
CHOOM!
How eMBaRRASSiNG.
Let'S TeaCH THeSE GUYS a LeSSON!

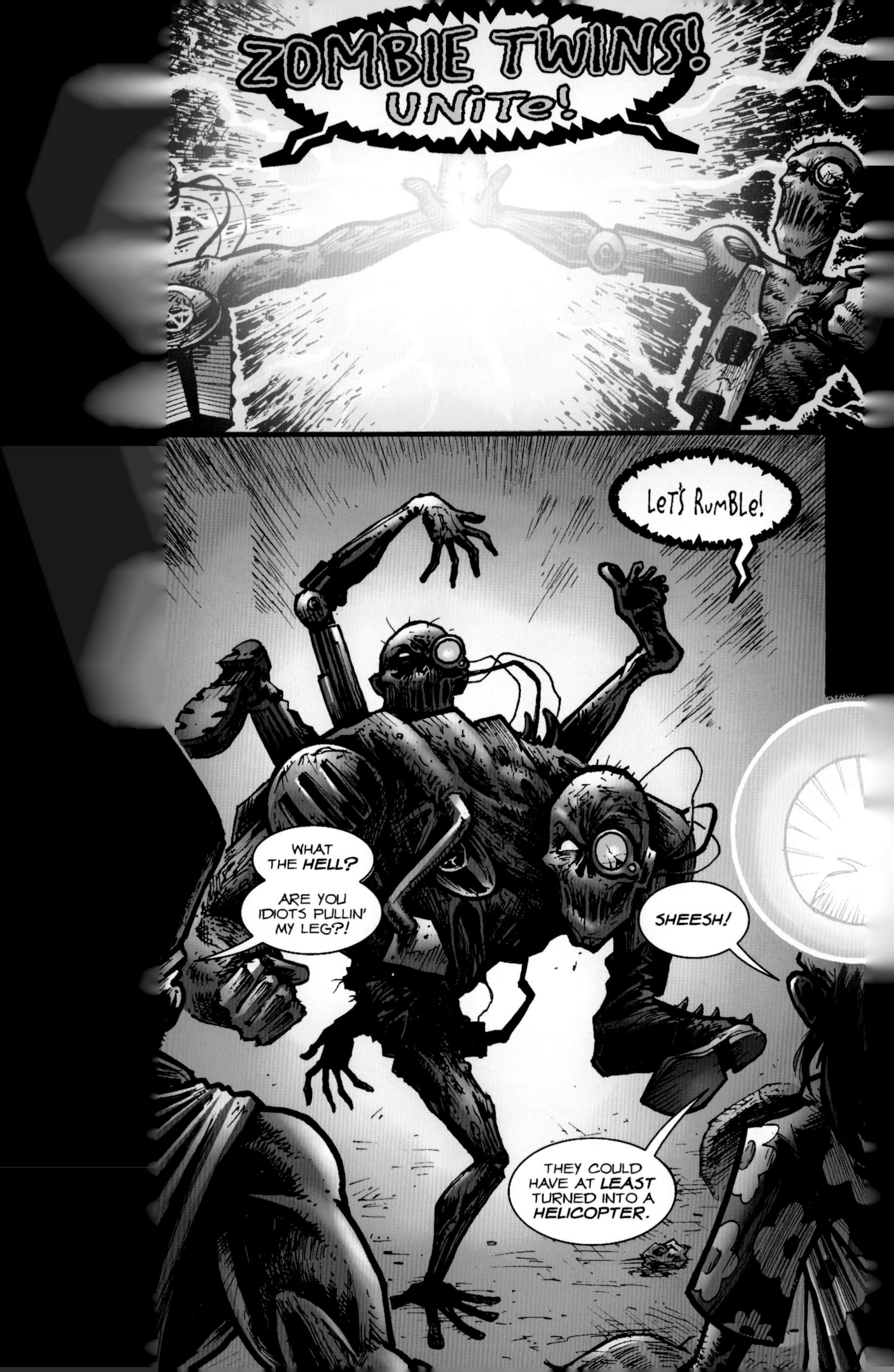
ZOMBIE TWINS! UNITE!
LET'S RUMBLE!
WHAT THE HELL?
ARE YOU IDIOTS PULLIN' MY LEG?!
SHEESH!
THEY COULD HAVE AT LEAST TURNED INTO A HELICOPTER.

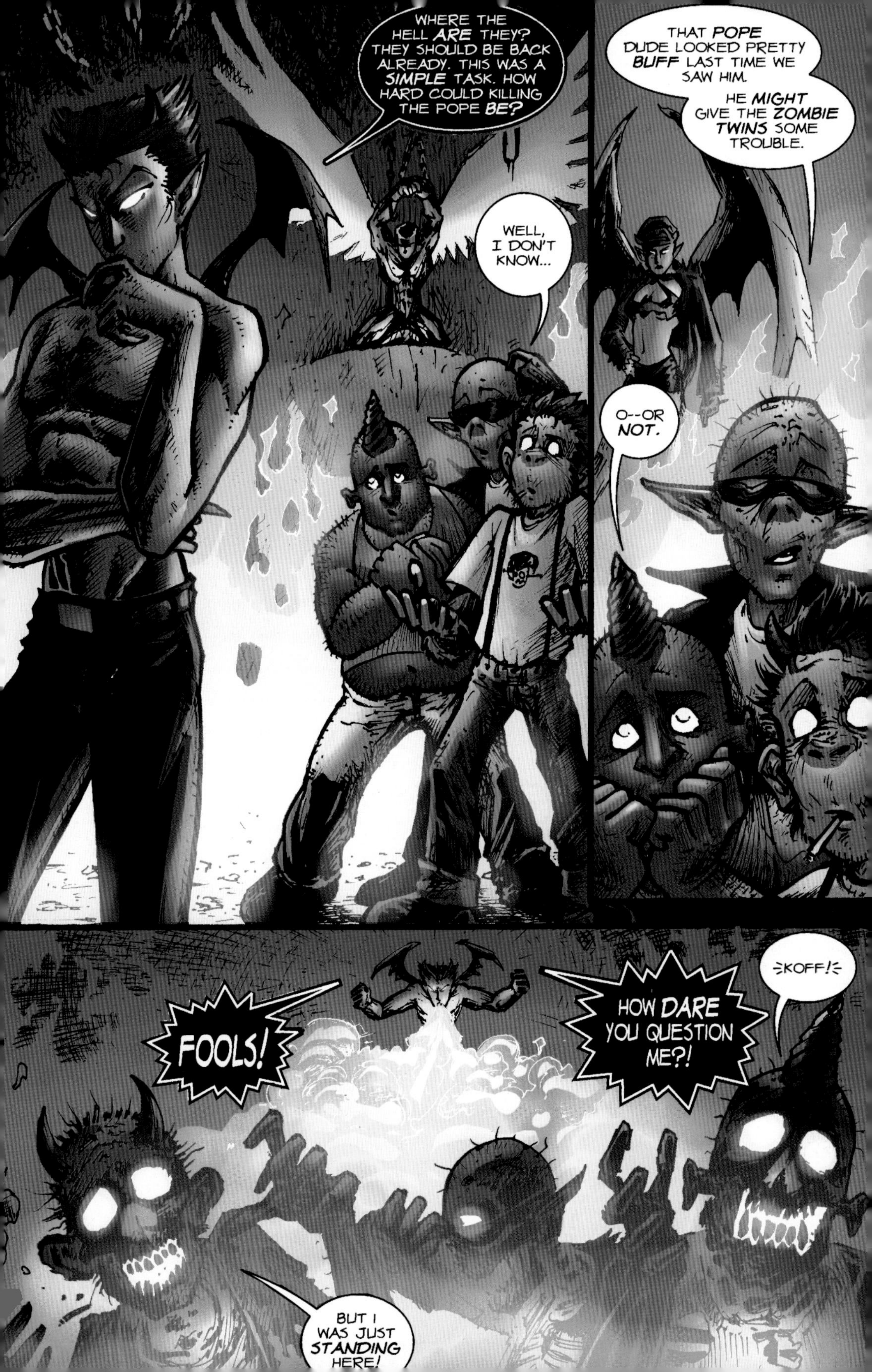
WHERE THE HELL ARE THEY? THEY SHOULD BE BACK ALREADY. THIS WAS A SIMPLE TASK. HOW HARD COULD KILLING THE POPE BE?
WELL, I DON'T KNOW...
THAT POPE DUDE LOOKED PRETTY BUFF LAST TIME WE SAW HIM.
HE MIGHT GIVE THE ZOMBIE TWINS SOME TROUBLE.
O--OR NOT.
FOOLS!
HOW DARE YOU QUESTION ME?!
KOFF!
BUT I WAS JUST STANDING HERE!

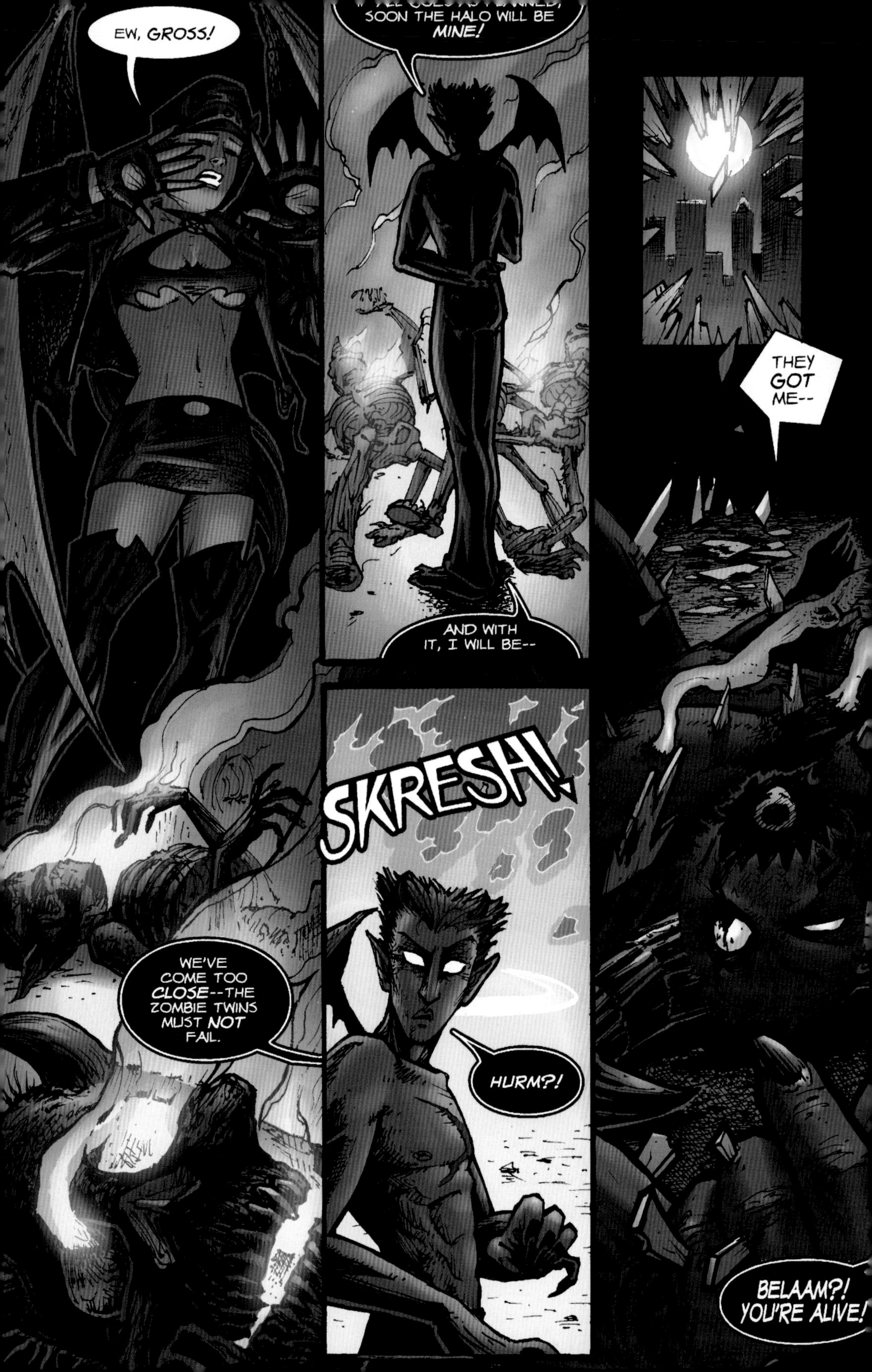
EW, GROSS!
SOON THE HALO WILL BE MINE!
AND WITH IT, I WILL BE--
WE'VE COME TOO CLOSE--THE ZOMBIE TWINS MUST NOT FAIL.
SKRESH!
HURM?!
THEY GOT ME--
BELAAM?! YOU'RE ALIVE!

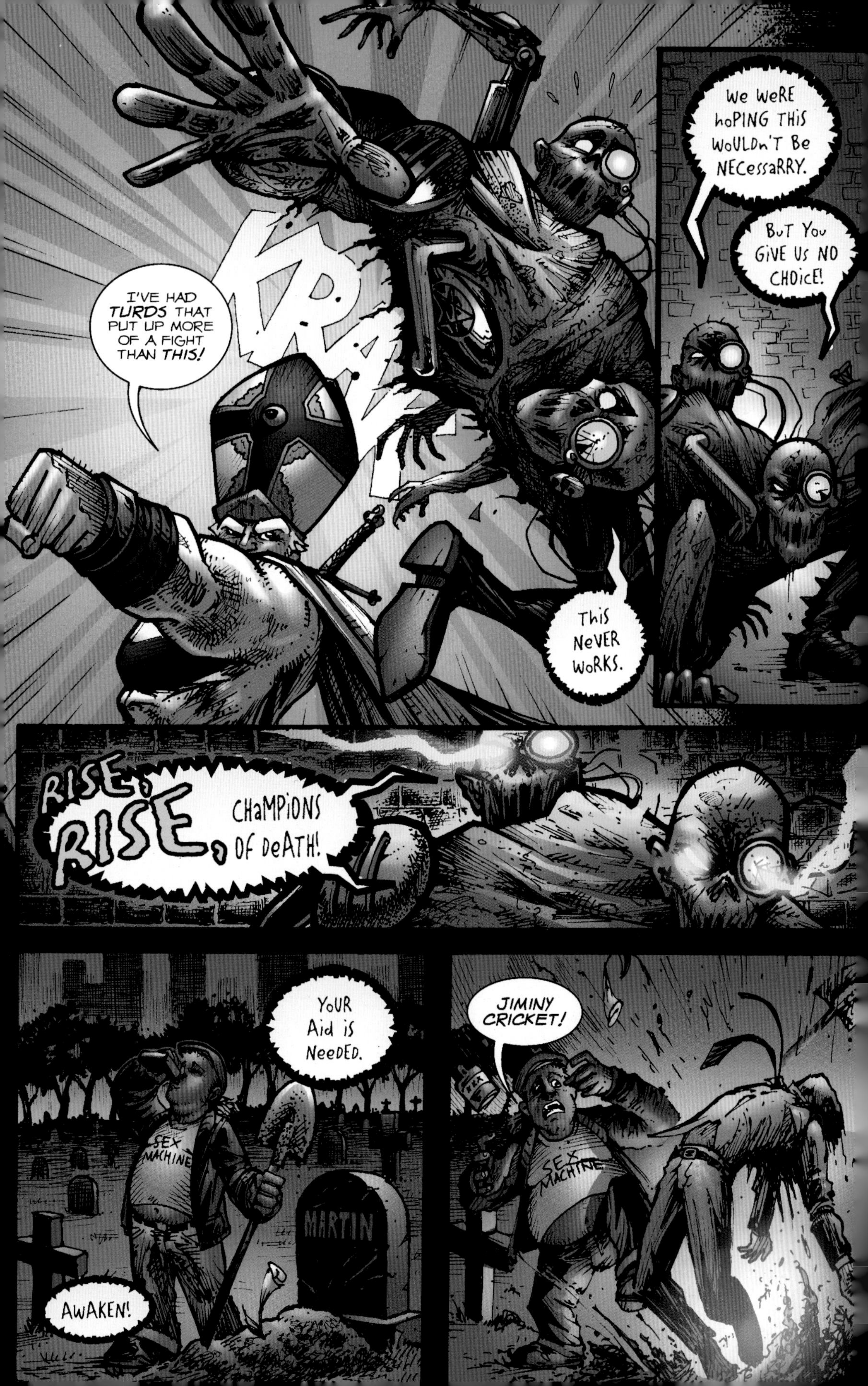
KRAK
I'VE HAD TURDS THAT PUT UP MORE OF A FIGHT THAN THIS!
We WeRE hoPING THIS WoULDn'T Be NECessaRRY.
BuT You GiVE Us NO CHOicE!
This NeVER WoRKS.
RISE, RISE, CHaMPioNS OF DeATH!
YoUR Aid is NeeDED.
AWAKEN!
SEX MACHINE
MARTIN
JIMINY CRICKET!
SEX MACHINE

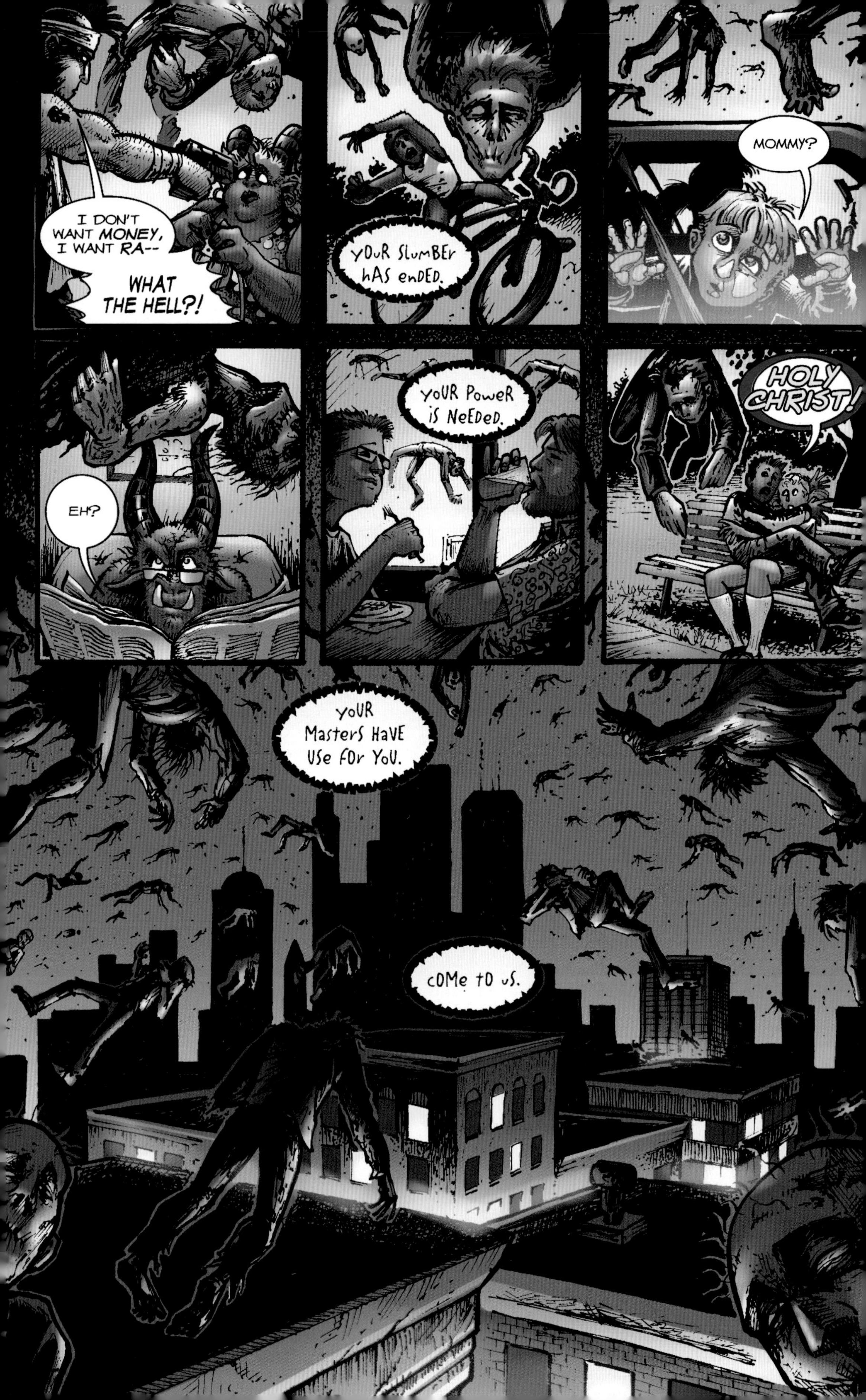
I DON'T WANT MONEY, I WANT RA--
WHAT THE HELL?!
YOUR SLUMBER HAS ENDED.
MOMMY?
EH?
YOUR POWER IS NEEDED.
HOLY CHRIST!
YOUR MASTERS HAVE USE FOR YOU.
COME TO US.

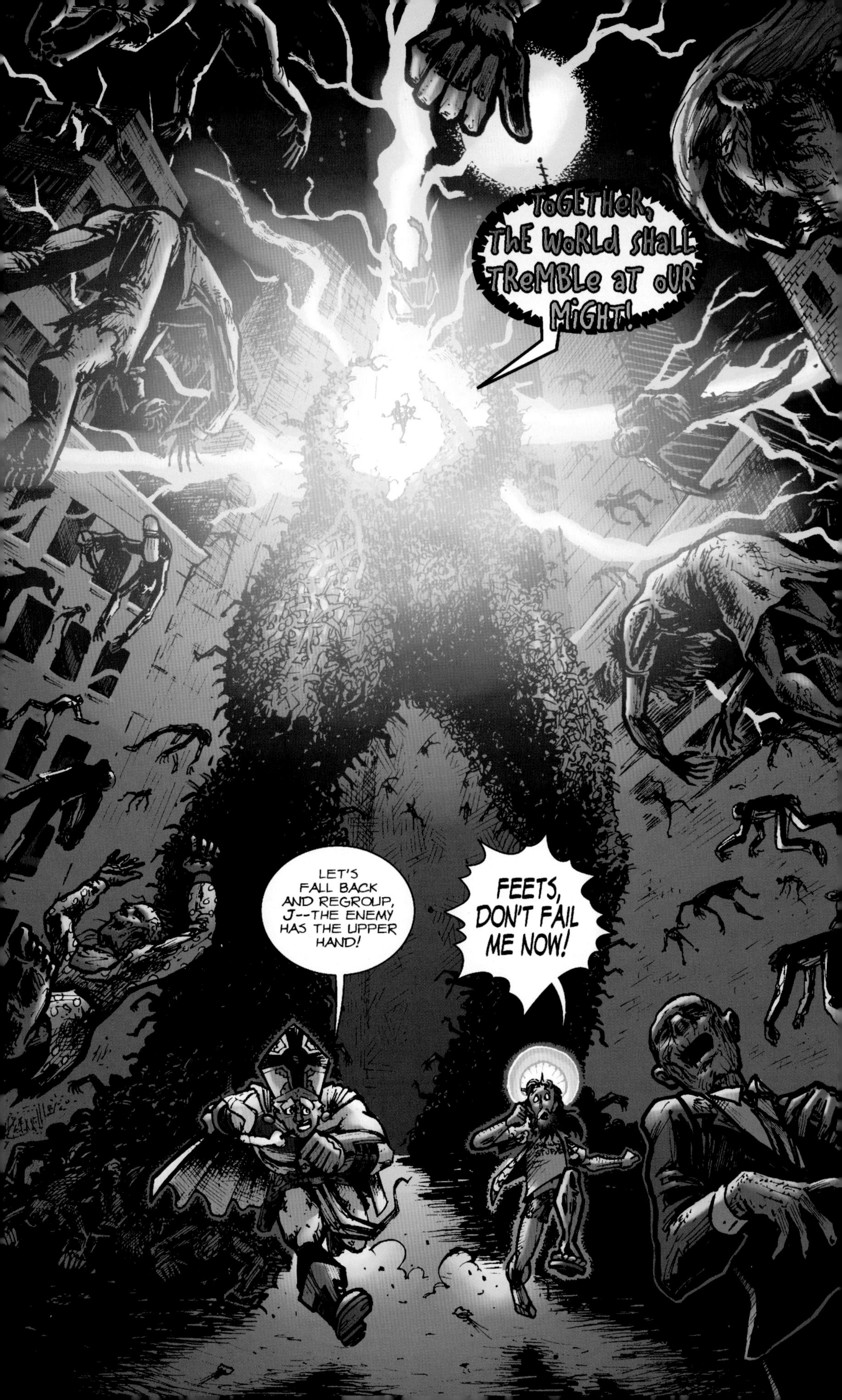
TOGETHER, THE WORLD SHALL TREMBLE AT OUR MIGHT!
LET'S FALL BACK AND REGROUP, J--THE ENEMY HAS THE UPPER HAND!
FEETS, DON'T FAIL ME NOW!

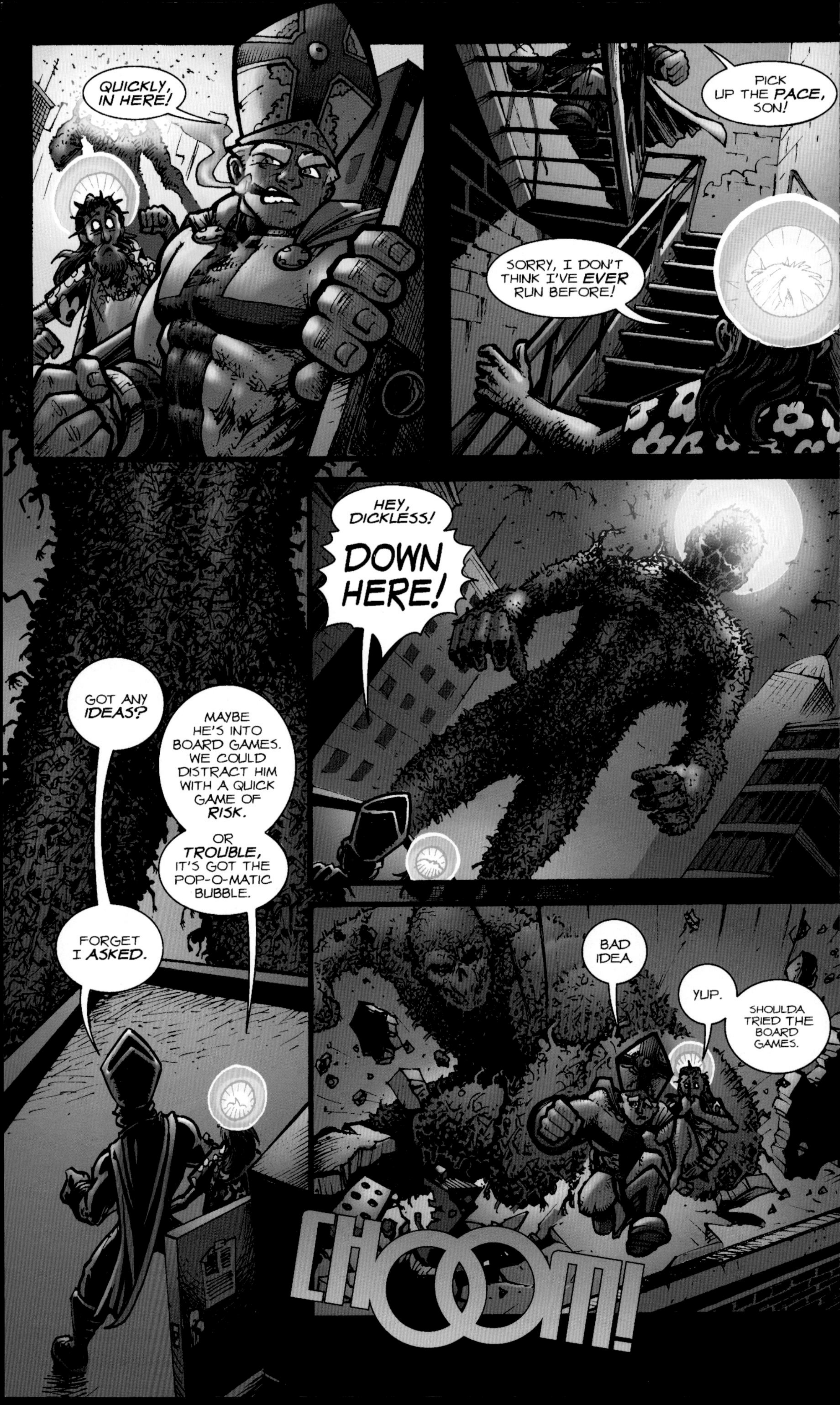

QUICKLY, IN HERE!
PICK UP THE PACE, SON!
SORRY, I DON'T THINK I'VE EVER RUN BEFORE!
HEY, DICKLESS!
DOWN HERE!
GOT ANY IDEAS?
MAYBE HE'S INTO BOARD GAMES. WE COULD DISTRACT HIM WITH A QUICK GAME OF RISK.
OR TROUBLE, IT'S GOT THE POP-O-MATIC BUBBLE.
FORGET I ASKED.
BAD IDEA.
YUP.
SHOULDA TRIED THE BOARD GAMES.
CHOOM!

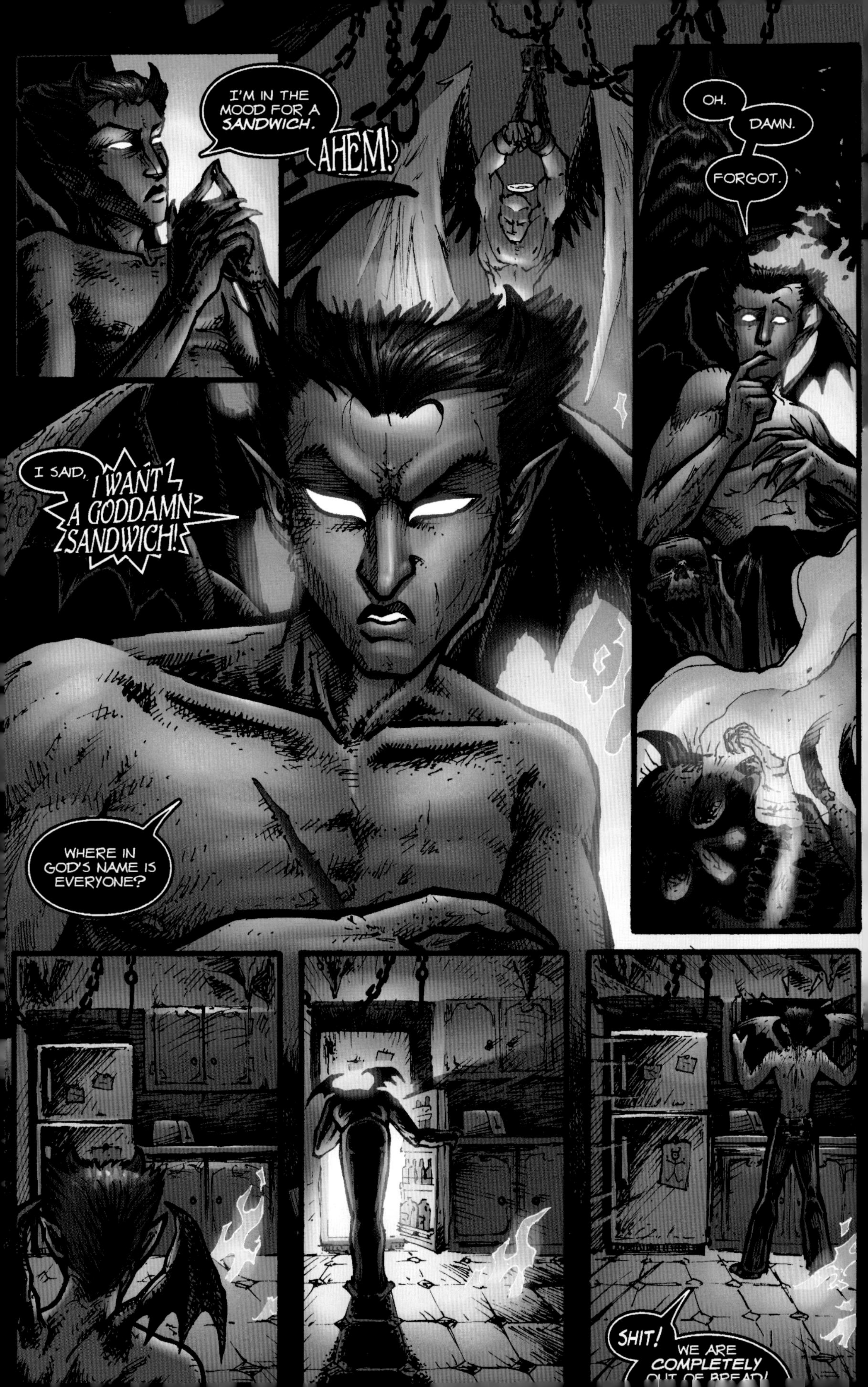
I'M IN THE MOOD FOR A SANDWICH.
AHEM!
OH.
DAMN.
FORGOT.
I SAID, I WANT A GODDAMN SANDWICH!
WHERE IN GOD'S NAME IS EVERYONE?
SHIT!
WE ARE COMPLETELY OUT OF BREAD!

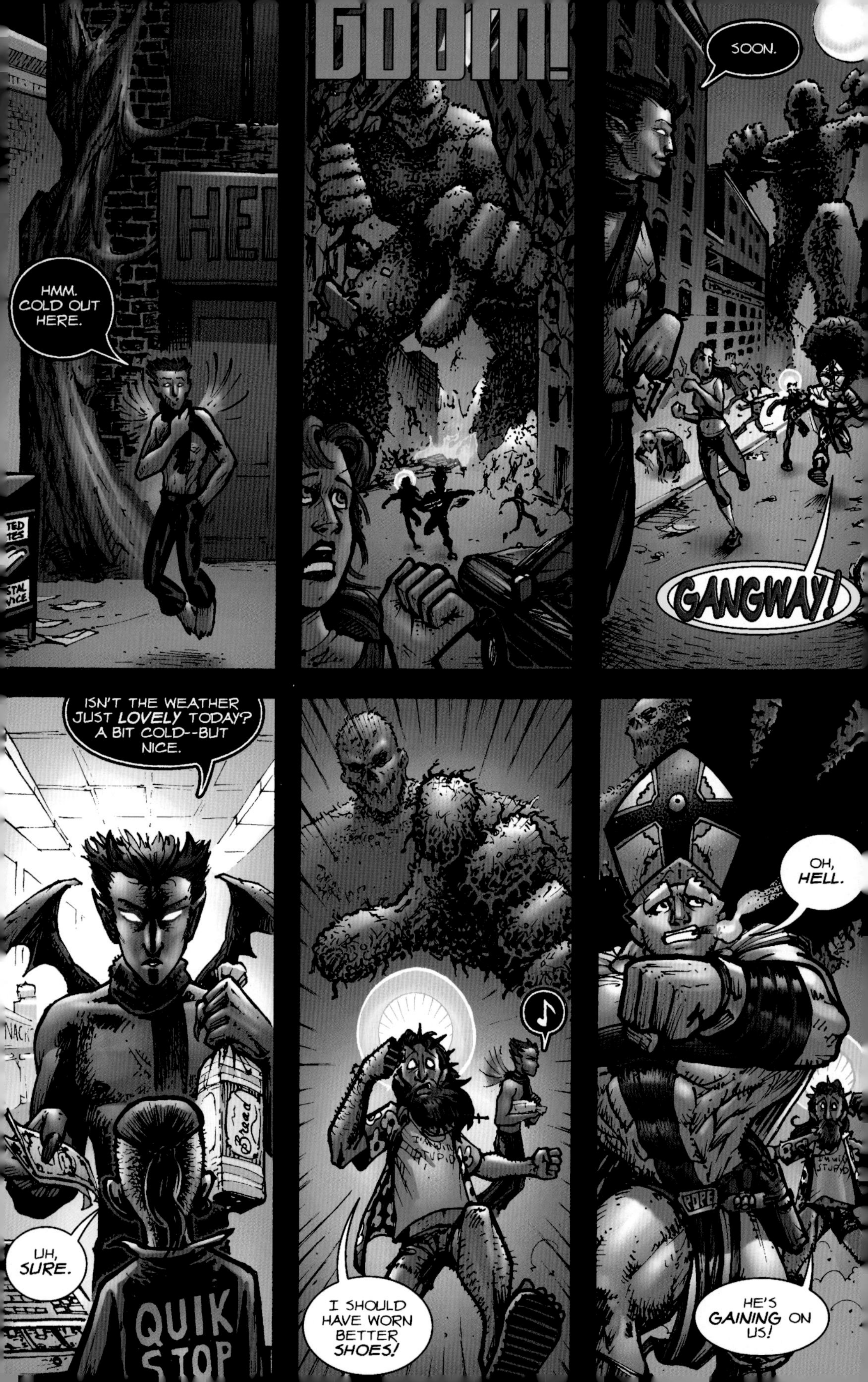

HMM. COLD OUT HERE.
BOOM!
SOON.
GANGWAY!
ISN'T THE WEATHER JUST LOVELY TODAY? A BIT COLD--BUT NICE.
UH, SURE.
QUIK STOP
I SHOULD HAVE WORN BETTER SHOES!
OH, HELL.
HE'S GAINING ON US!

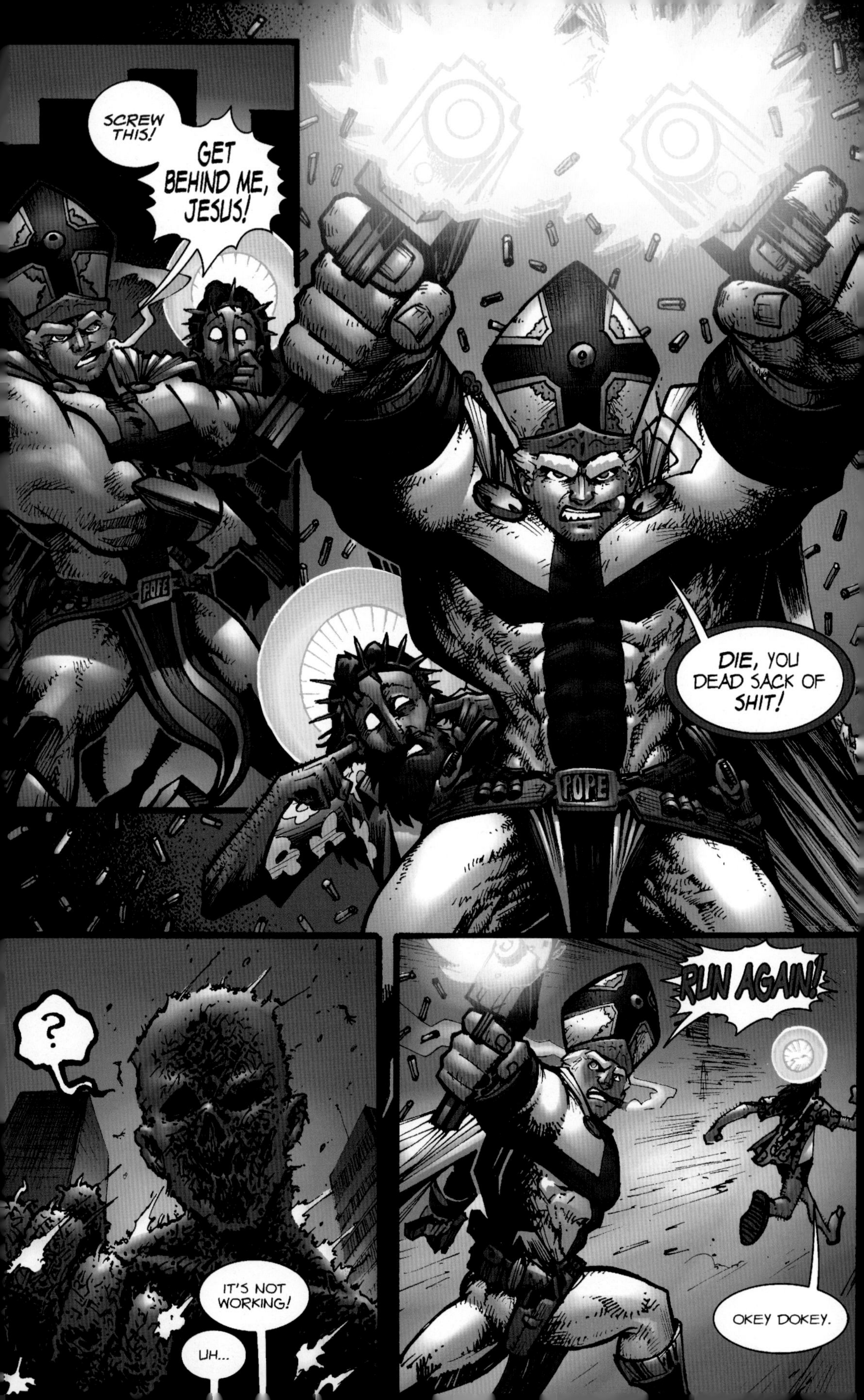
SCREW THIS!
GET BEHIND ME, JESUS!
DIE, YOU DEAD SACK OF SHIT!
POPE
POPE
?
IT'S NOT WORKING!
UH...
RUN AGAIN!
OKEY DOKEY.

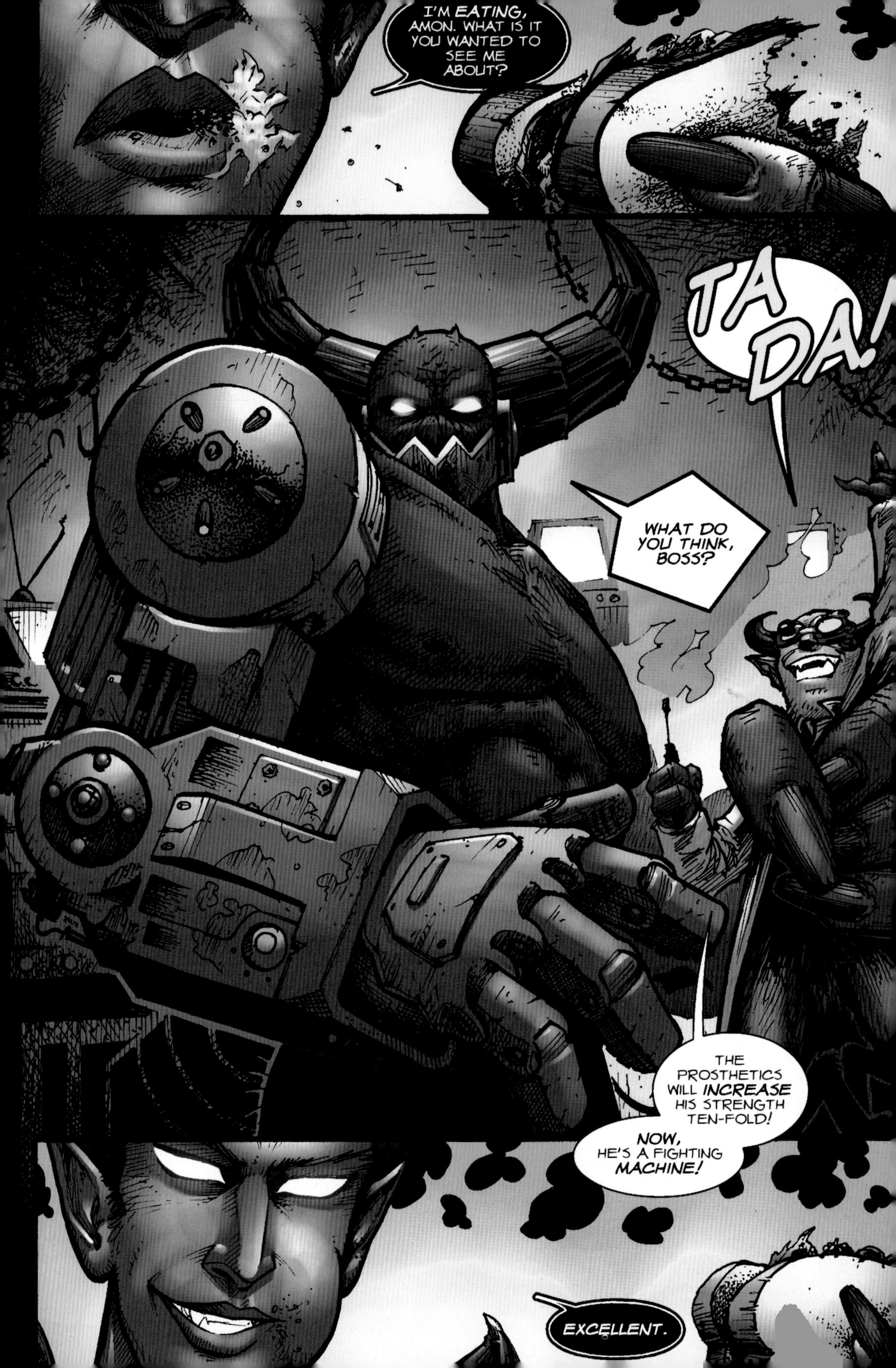
I'M EATING, AMON. WHAT IS IT YOU WANTED TO SEE ME ABOUT?
TA DA!
WHAT DO YOU THINK, BOSS?
THE PROSTHETICS WILL INCREASE HIS STRENGTH TEN-FOLD!
NOW, HE'S A FIGHTING MACHINE!
EXCELLENT.

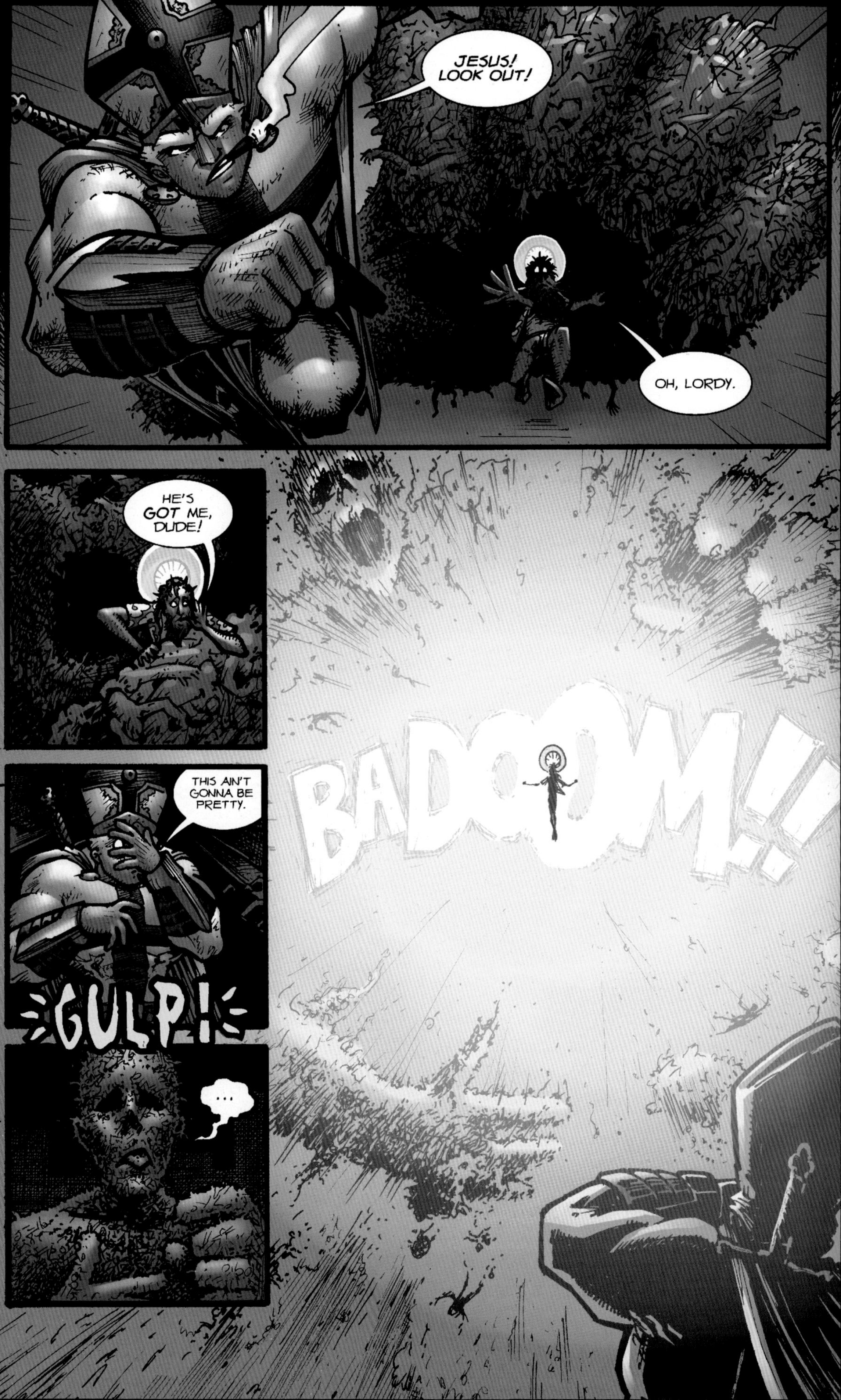
JESUS! LOOK OUT!
OH, LORDY.
HE'S GOT ME, DUDE!
THIS AIN'T GONNA BE PRETTY.
GULP!
...
BADOOM!!

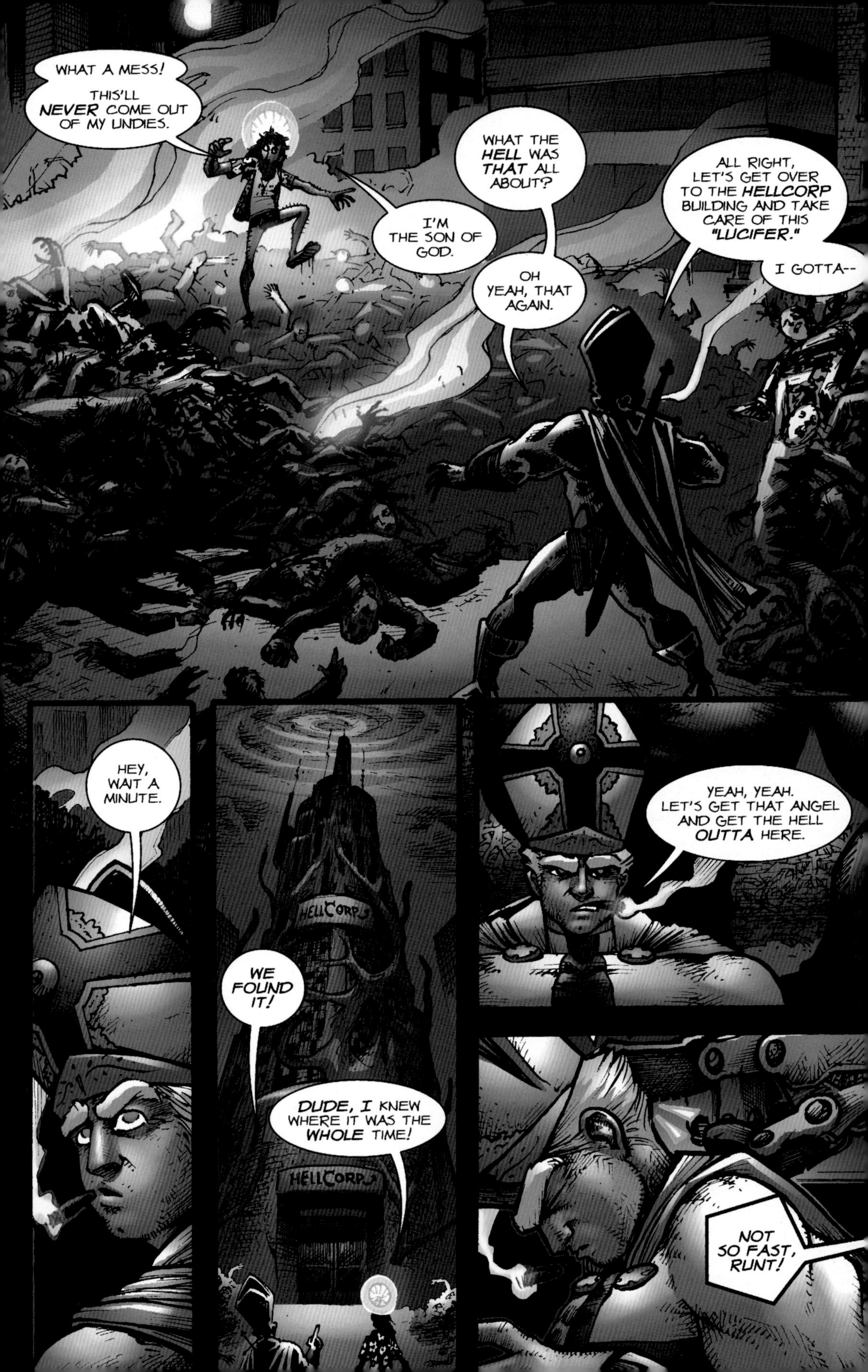
WHAT A MESS!
THIS'LL NEVER COME OUT OF MY UNDIES.
I'M THE SON OF GOD.
WHAT THE HELL WAS THAT ALL ABOUT?
OH YEAH, THAT AGAIN.
ALL RIGHT, LET'S GET OVER TO THE HELLCORP BUILDING AND TAKE CARE OF THIS "LUCIFER."
I GOTTA--
HEY, WAIT A MINUTE.
WE FOUND IT!
HELLCORP
DUDE, I KNEW WHERE IT WAS THE WHOLE TIME!
HELLCORP
YEAH, YEAH. LET'S GET THAT ANGEL AND GET THE HELL OUTTA HERE.
NOT SO FAST, RUNT!

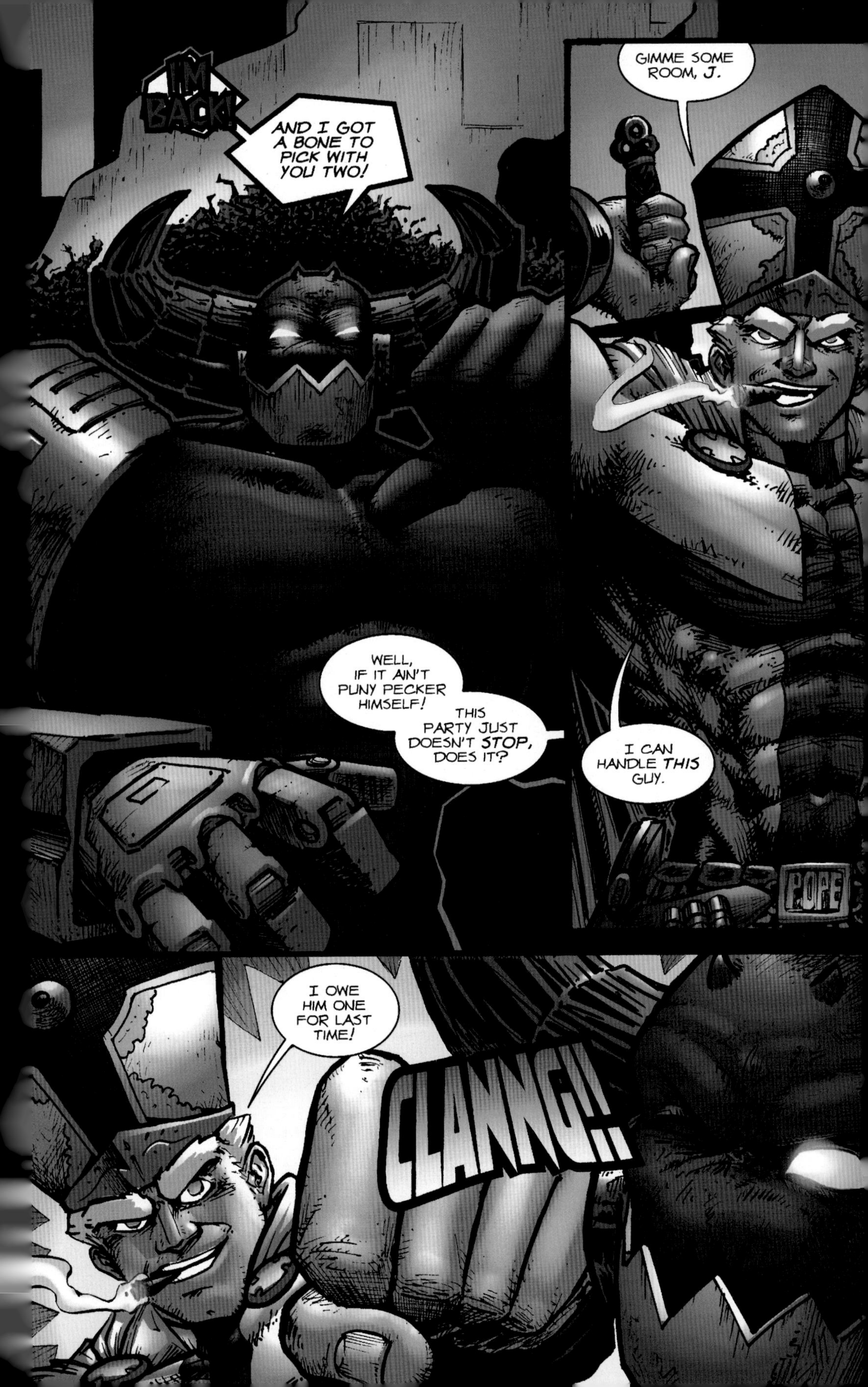
I'M BACK!
AND I GOT A BONE TO PICK WITH YOU TWO!
GIMME SOME ROOM, J.
WELL, IF IT AIN'T PUNY PECKER HIMSELF!
THIS PARTY JUST DOESN'T STOP, DOES IT?
I CAN HANDLE THIS GUY.
POPE
I OWE HIM ONE FOR LAST TIME!
CLANNG!!

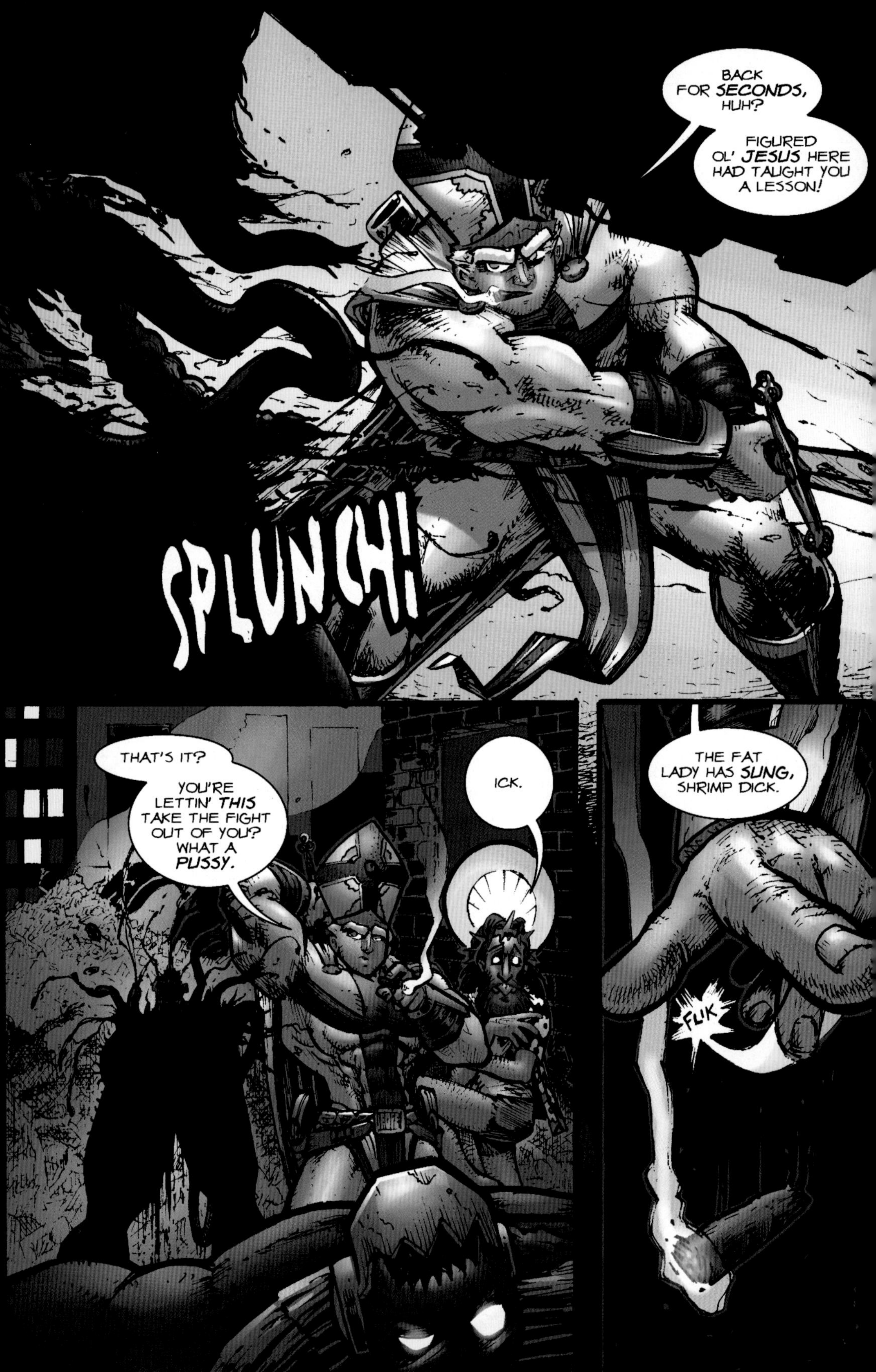
BACK FOR SECONDS, HUH?
FIGURED OL' JESUS HERE HAD TAUGHT YOU A LESSON!
SPLUNCH!
THAT'S IT?
YOU'RE LETTIN' THIS TAKE THE FIGHT OUT OF YOU? WHAT A PUSSY.
ICK.
THE FAT LADY HAS SUNG, SHRIMP DICK.
FLIK

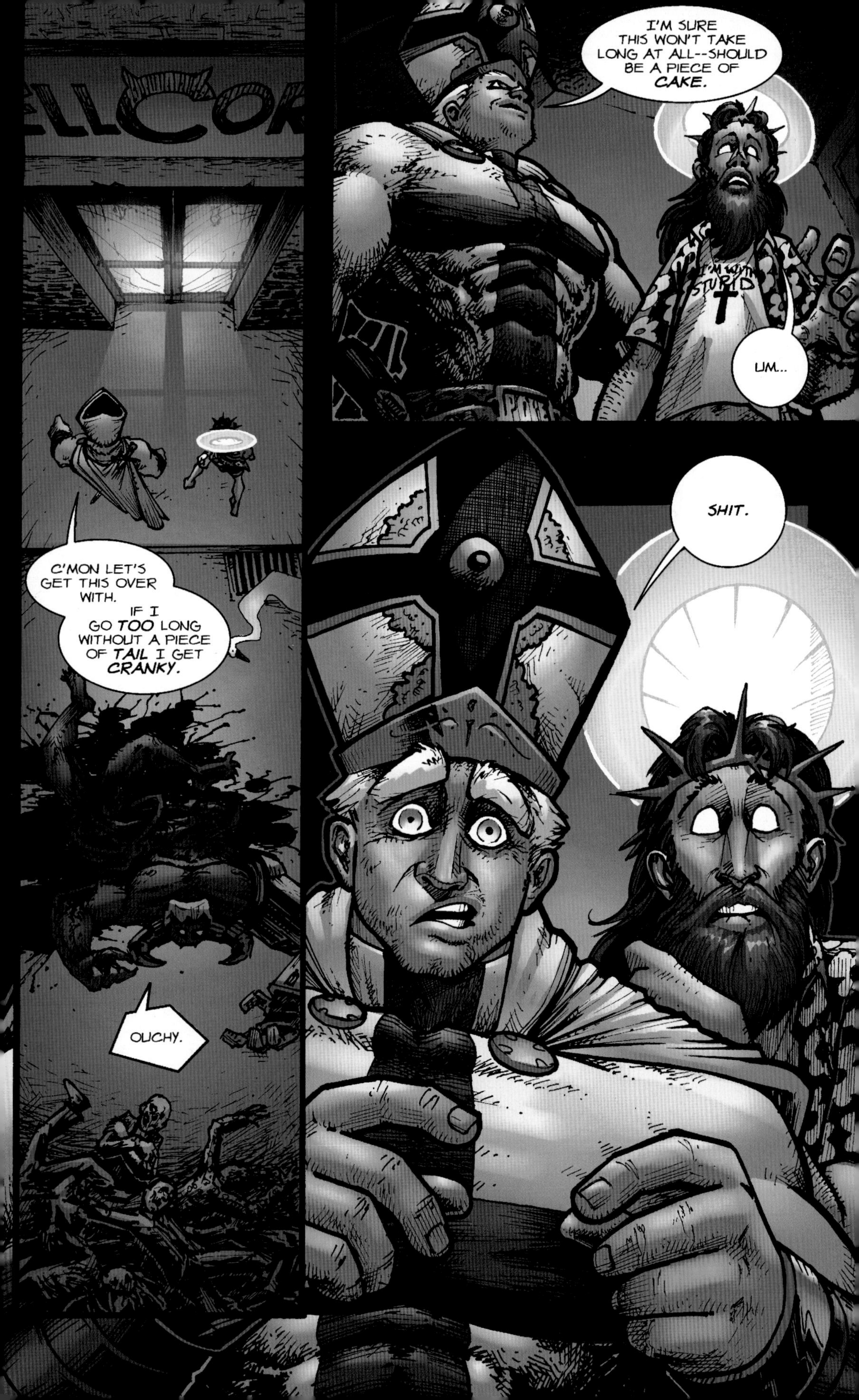

I'M SURE THIS WON'T TAKE LONG AT ALL--SHOULD BE A PIECE OF **CAKE.**
UM..
C'MON LET'S GET THIS OVER WITH.
IF I GO **TOO** LONG WITHOUT A PIECE OF **TAIL** I GET **CRANKY.**
OUCHY.
SHIT.

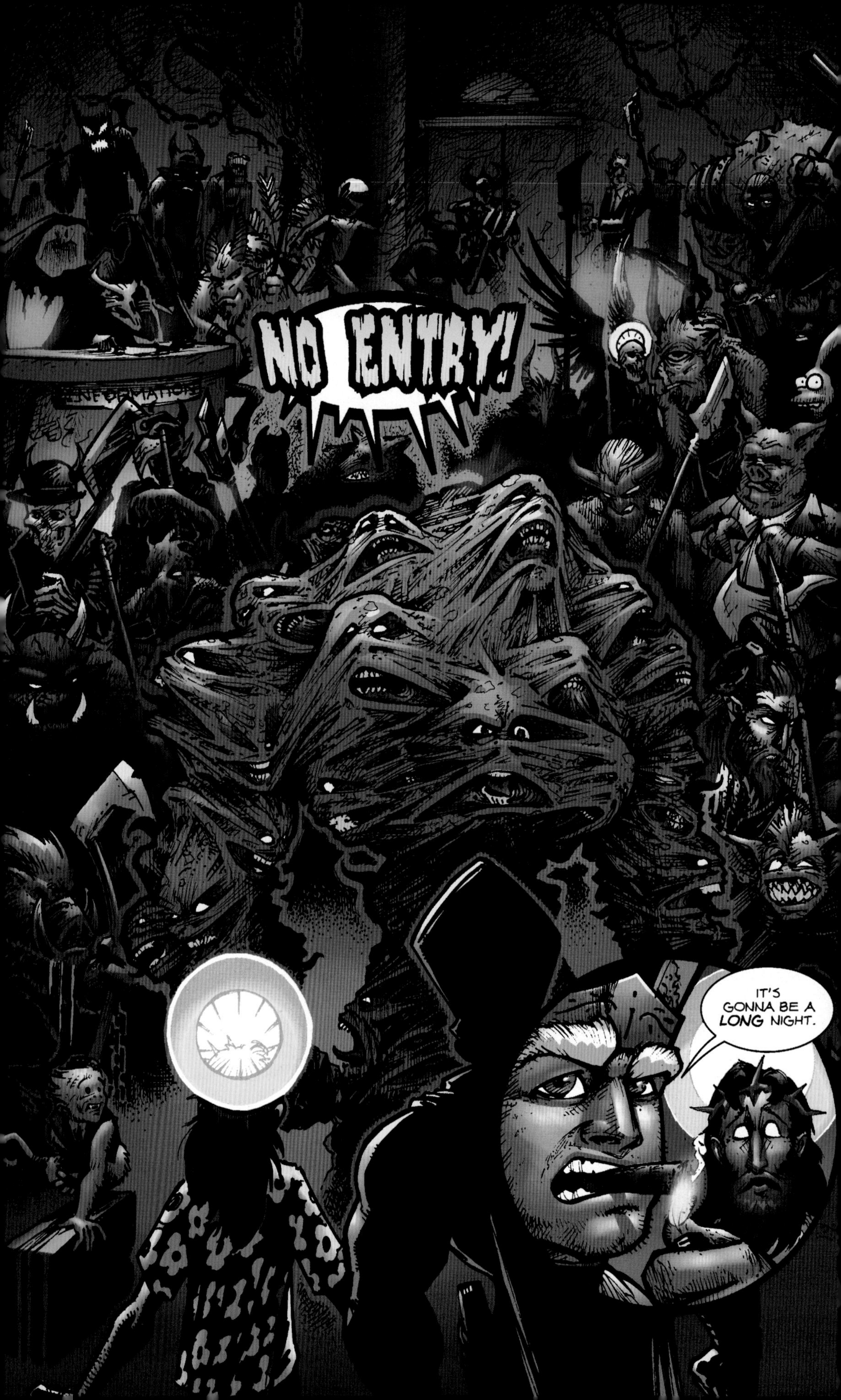
NO ENTRY!
IT'S GONNA BE A LONG NIGHT.

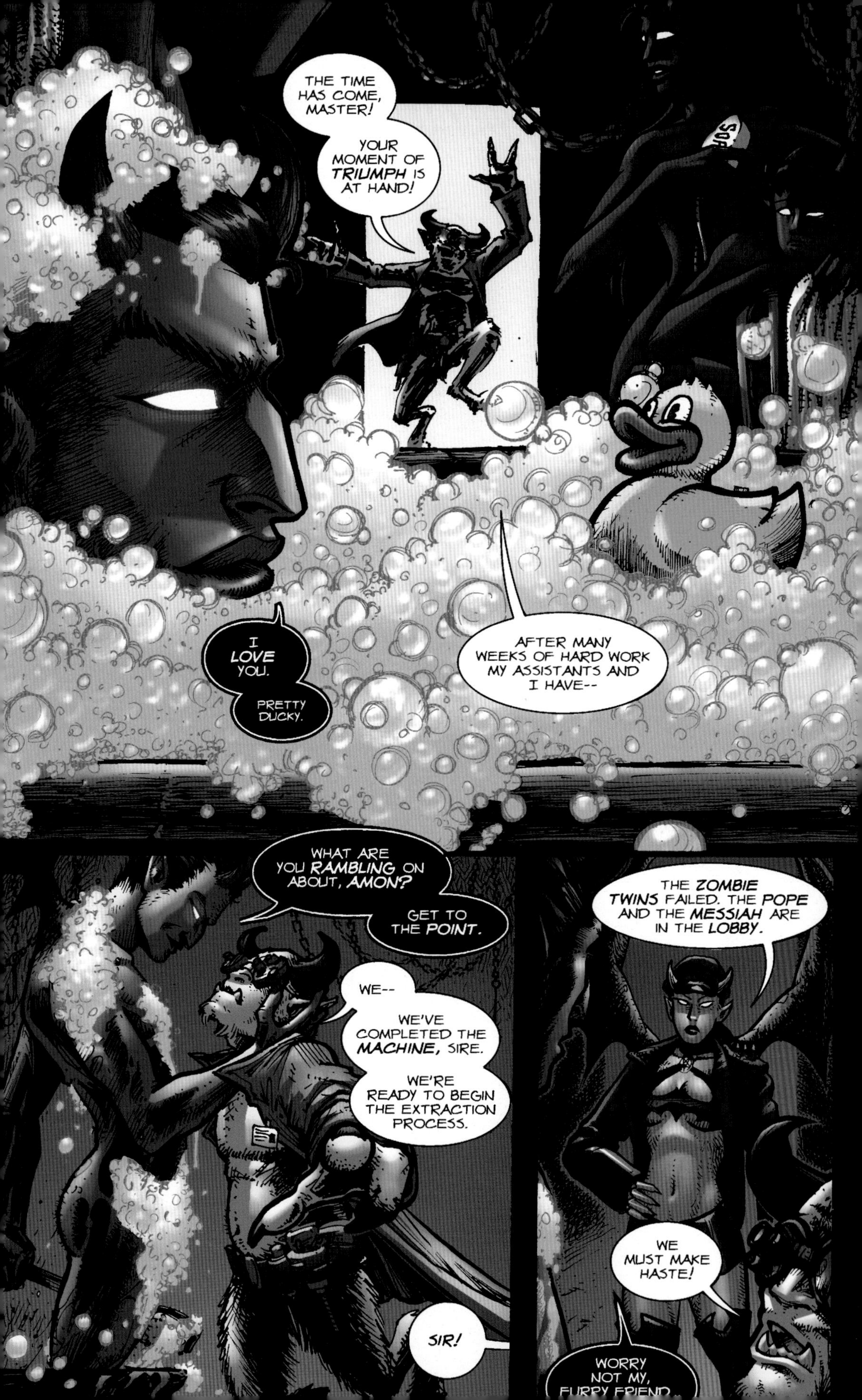
THE TIME HAS COME, MASTER!
YOUR MOMENT OF TRIUMPH IS AT HAND!
I LOVE YOU.
PRETTY DUCKY.
AFTER MANY WEEKS OF HARD WORK MY ASSISTANTS AND I HAVE--
WHAT ARE YOU RAMBLING ON ABOUT, AMON?
GET TO THE POINT.
WE--
WE'VE COMPLETED THE MACHINE, SIRE.
WE'RE READY TO BEGIN THE EXTRACTION PROCESS.
SIR!
THE ZOMBIE TWINS FAILED. THE POPE AND THE MESSIAH ARE IN THE LOBBY.
WE MUST MAKE HASTE!
WORRY NOT MY, FURRY FRIEND.

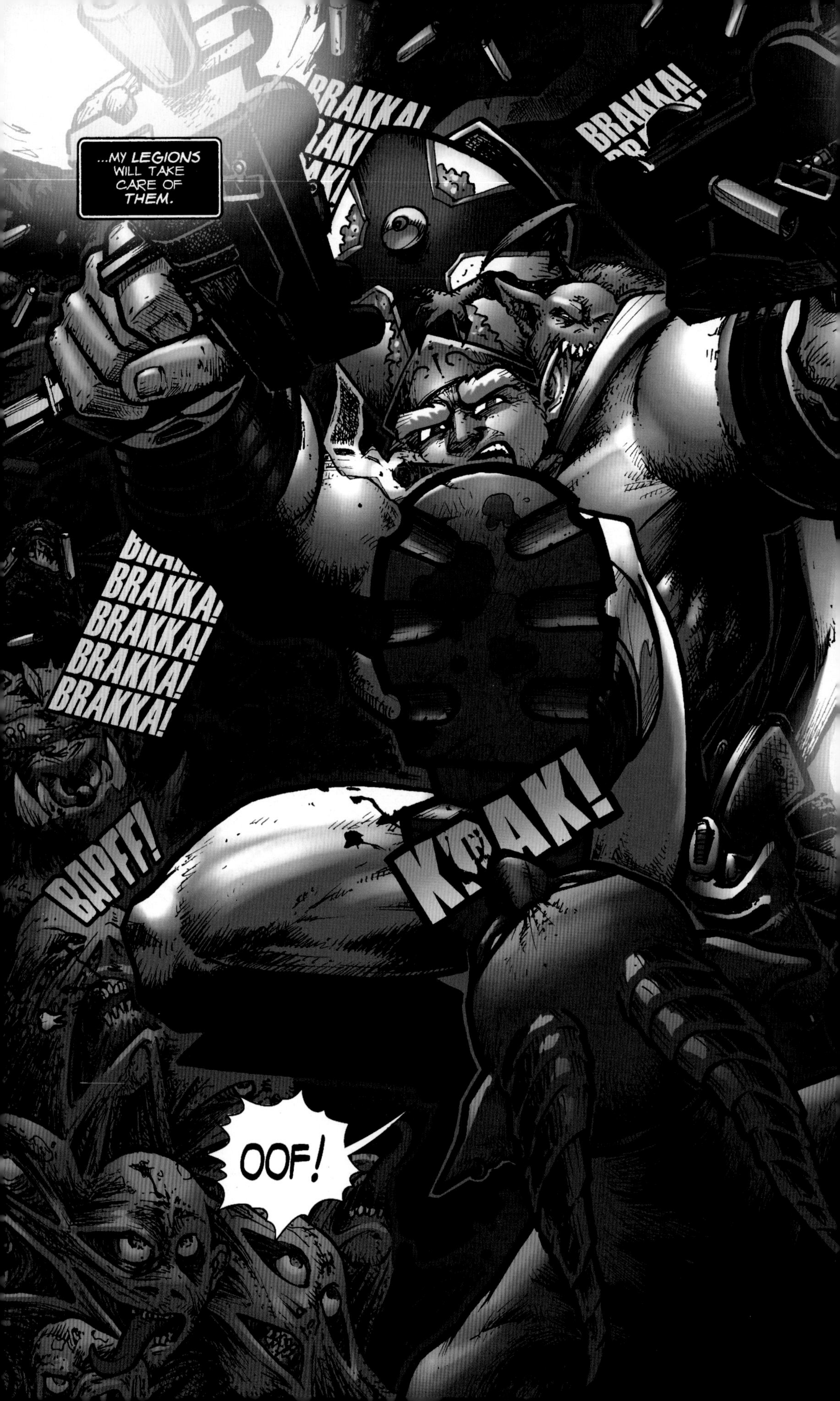
...MY LEGIONS WILL TAKE CARE OF THEM.
BRAKKA!
BRAKKA!
BRAKKA!
BRAKKA!
BRAKKA!
BRAKKA!
BAPFF!
OOF!

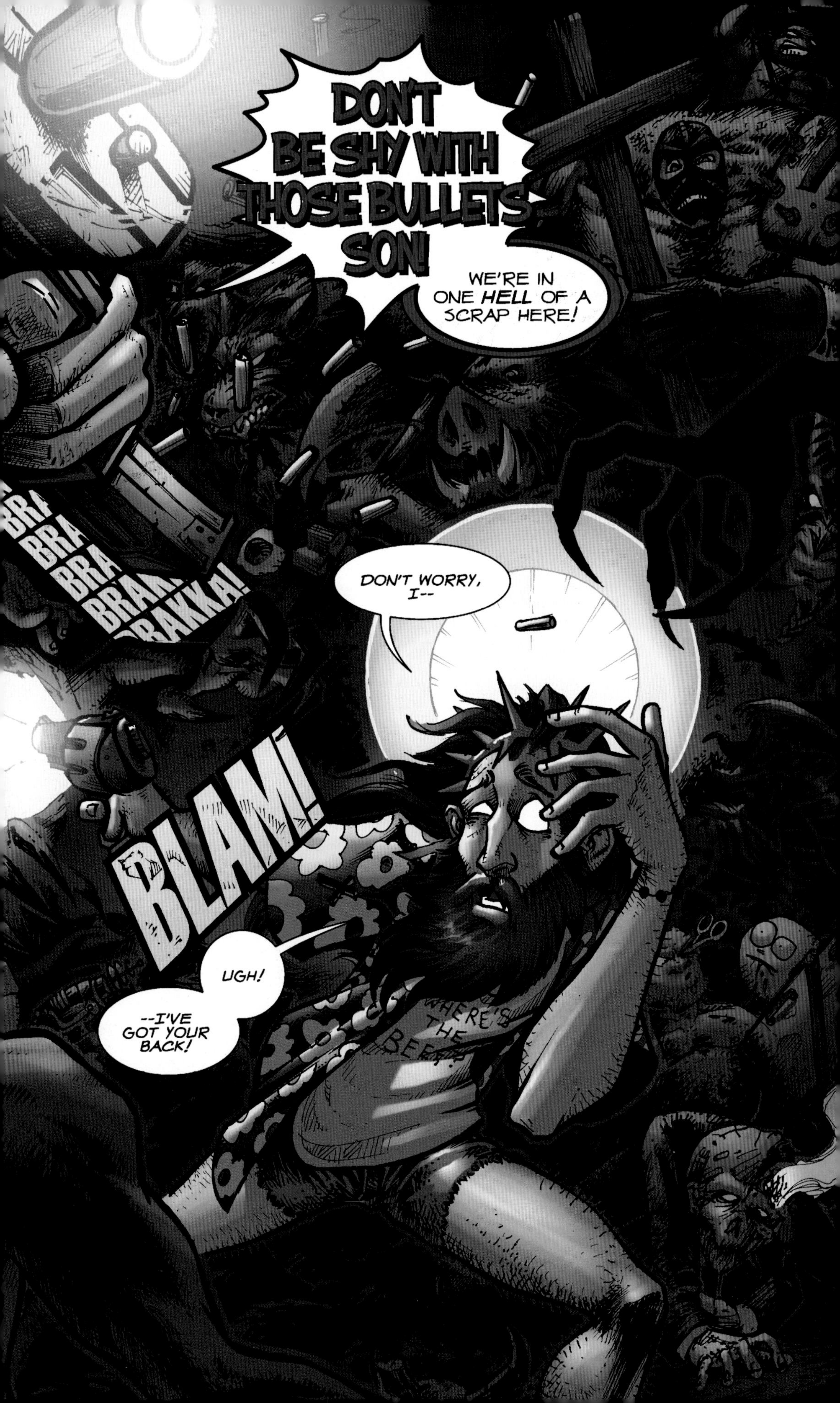
DON'T BE SHY WITH THOSE BULLETS SON!
WE'RE IN ONE HELL OF A SCRAP HERE!
BRA BRA BRA BRAK BRAKKA!
DON'T WORRY, I--
BLAM!
UGH!
--I'VE GOT YOUR BACK!
WHERE'S THE BEER?

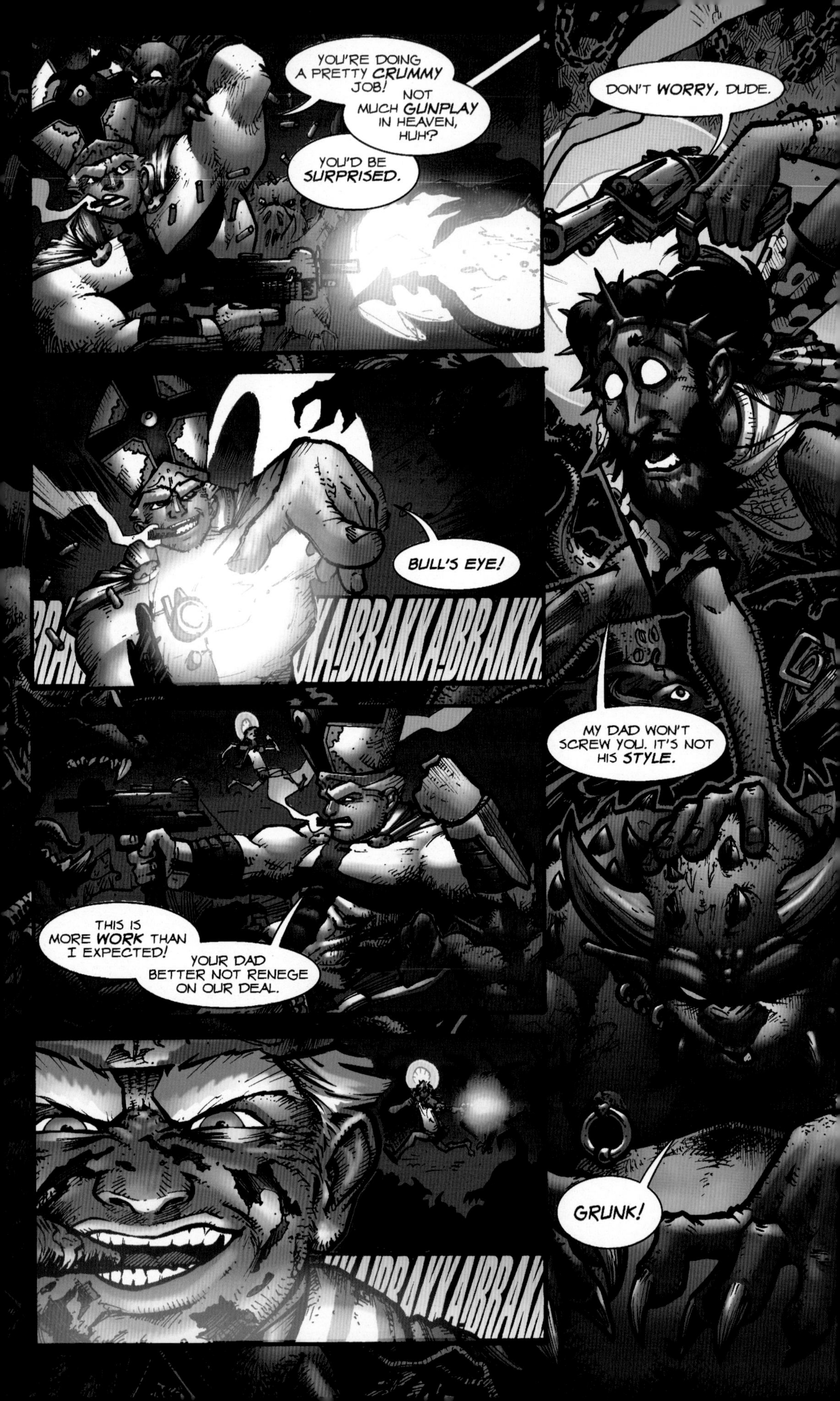
YOU'RE DOING A PRETTY CRUMMY JOB!
NOT MUCH GUNPLAY IN HEAVEN, HUH?
YOU'D BE SURPRISED.
DON'T WORRY, DUDE.
BULL'S EYE!
BRAKKA!BRAKKA!BRAKKA!
MY DAD WON'T SCREW YOU. IT'S NOT HIS STYLE.
THIS IS MORE WORK THAN I EXPECTED!
YOUR DAD BETTER NOT RENEGE ON OUR DEAL.
GRUNK!
BRAKKA!BRAKKA!BRAKK

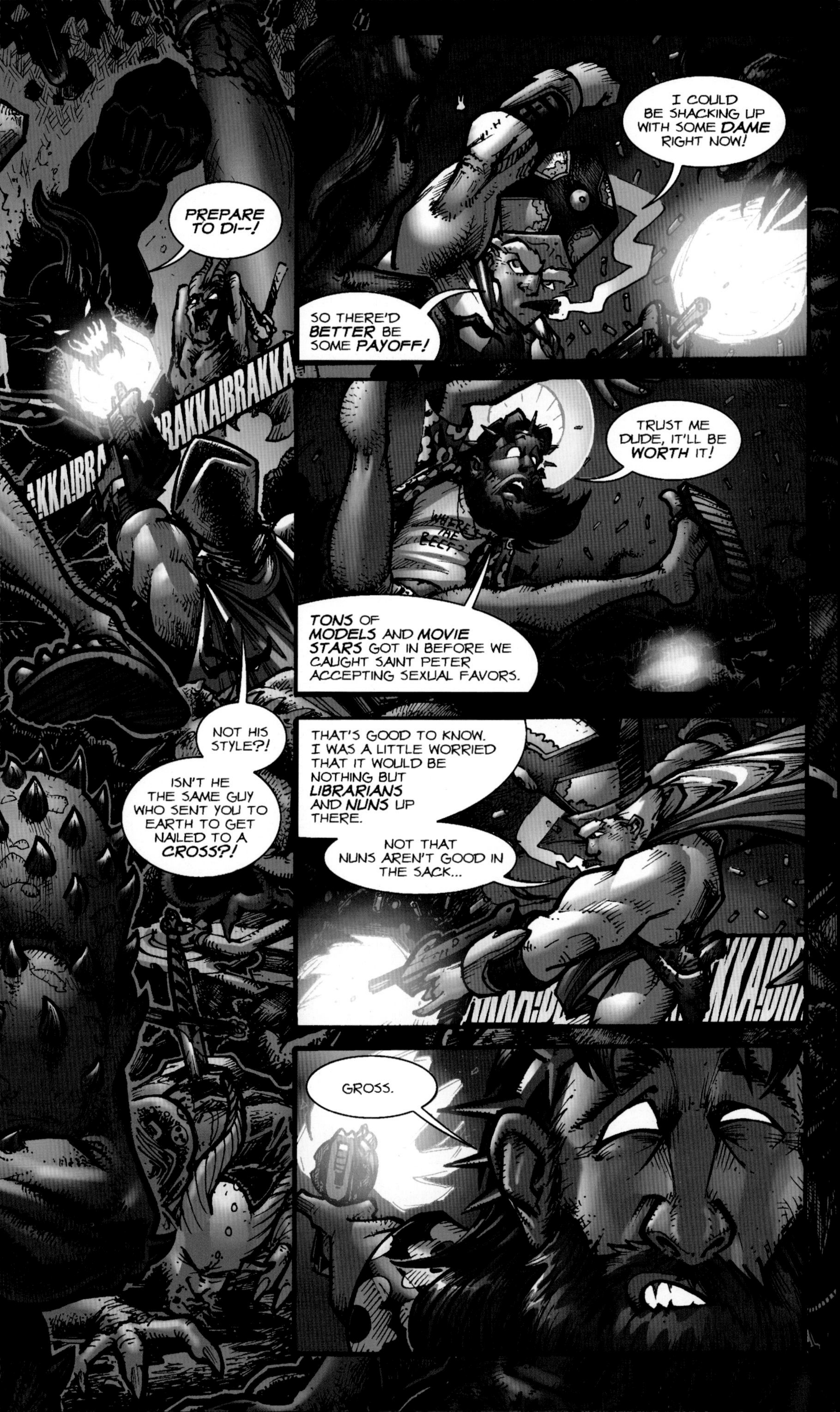
PREPARE TO DI--!
BRAKKA!BRAKKA!BRAKKA!
I COULD BE SHACKING UP WITH SOME DAME RIGHT NOW!
SO THERE'D BETTER BE SOME PAYOFF!
TRUST ME DUDE, IT'LL BE WORTH IT!
TONS OF MODELS AND MOVIE STARS GOT IN BEFORE WE CAUGHT SAINT PETER ACCEPTING SEXUAL FAVORS.
NOT HIS STYLE?!
ISN'T HE THE SAME GUY WHO SENT YOU TO EARTH TO GET NAILED TO A CROSS?!
THAT'S GOOD TO KNOW. I WAS A LITTLE WORRIED THAT IT WOULD BE NOTHING BUT LIBRARIANS AND NUNS UP THERE.
NOT THAT NUNS AREN'T GOOD IN THE SACK...
GROSS.

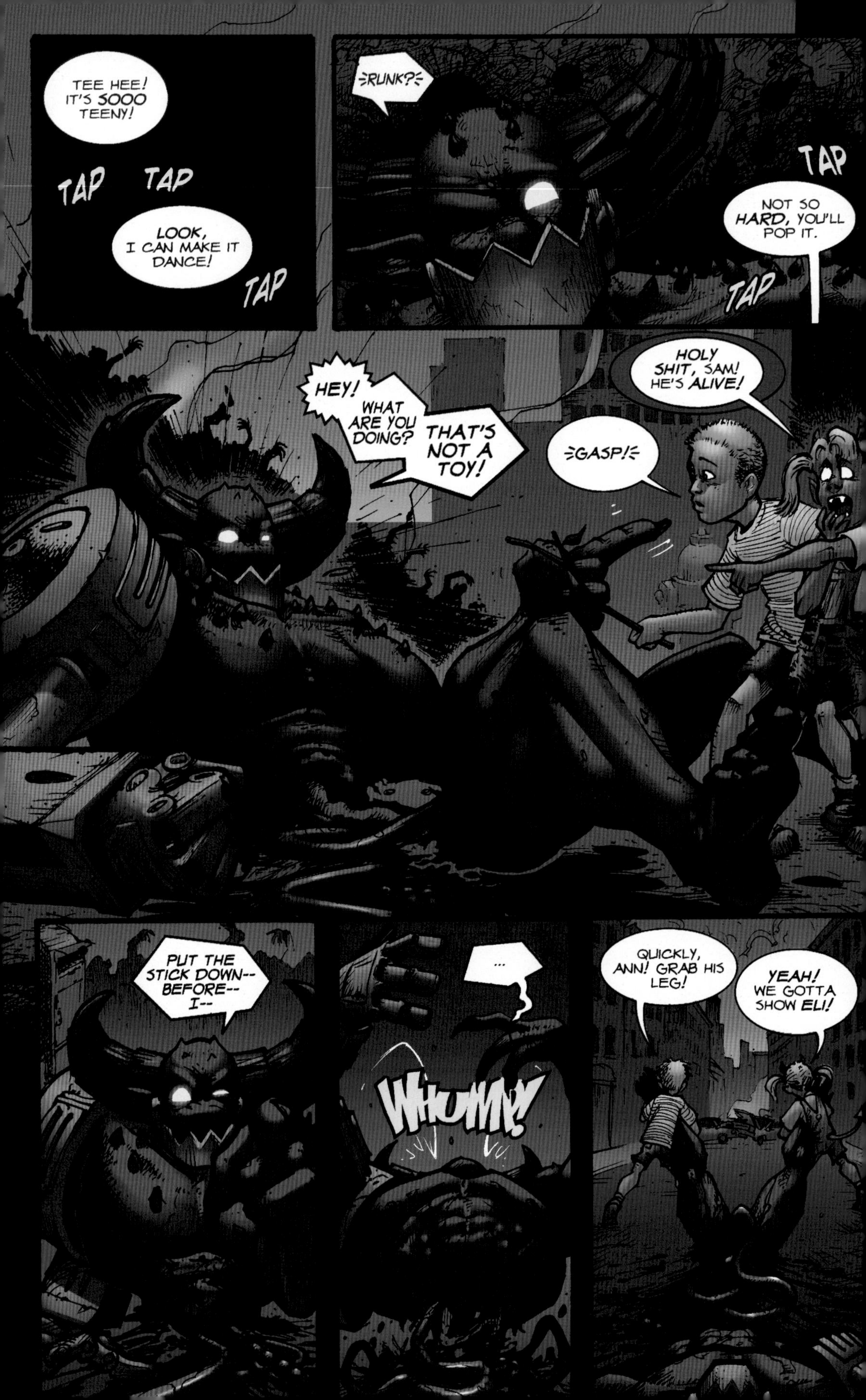
TEE HEE! IT'S SOOO TEENY!
TAP TAP
LOOK, I CAN MAKE IT DANCE!
TAP
=RUNK?=
TAP
NOT SO HARD, YOU'LL POP IT.
TAP
HEY!
WHAT ARE YOU DOING?
THAT'S NOT A TOY!
HOLY SHIT, SAM! HE'S ALIVE!
=GASP!=
PUT THE STICK DOWN-- BEFORE-- I--
...
WHUMP!
QUICKLY, ANN! GRAB HIS LEG!
YEAH! WE GOTTA SHOW ELI!

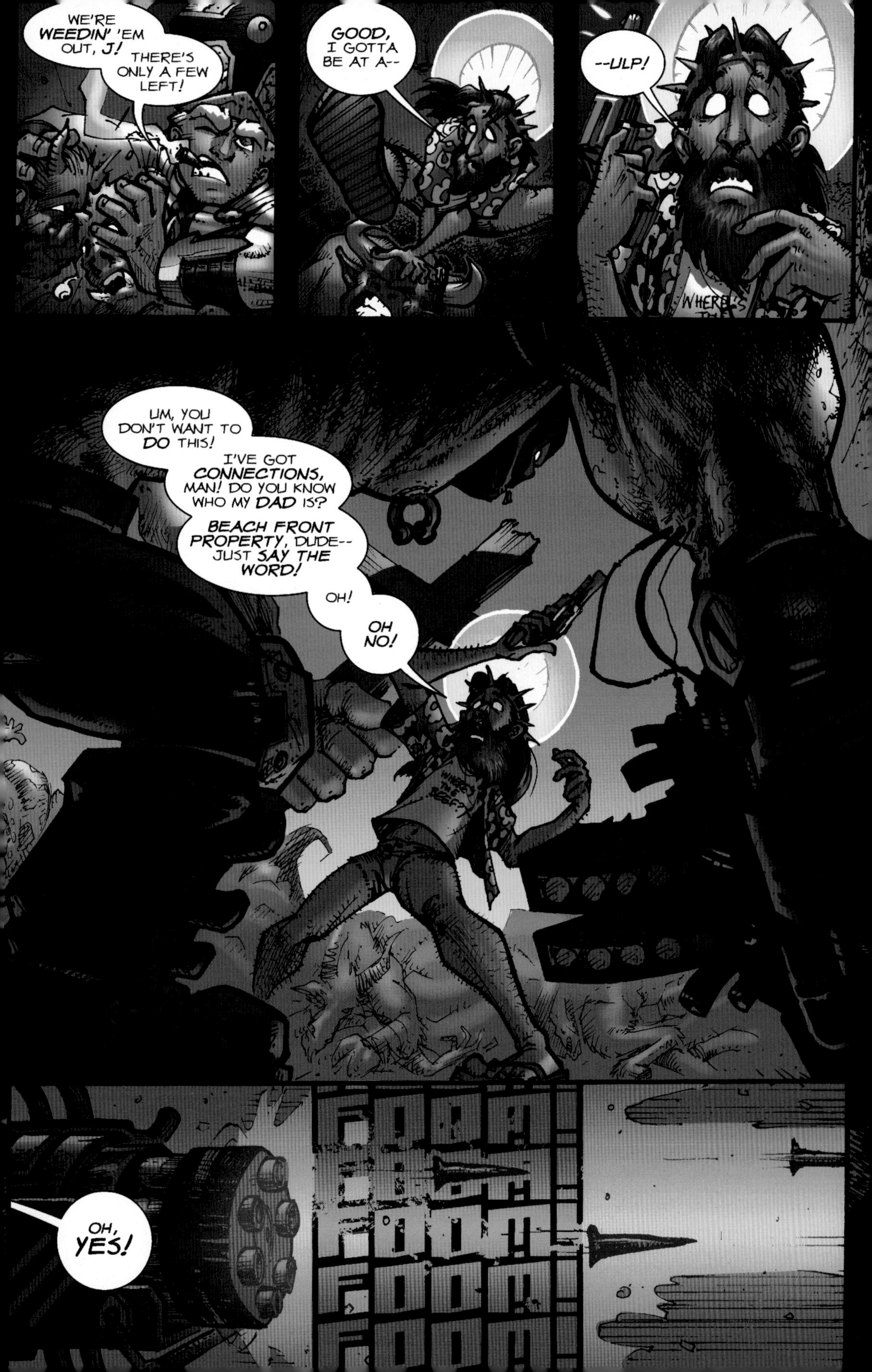

WE'RE WEEDIN' 'EM OUT, J!
THERE'S ONLY A FEW LEFT!
GOOD, I GOTTA BE AT A--
--ULP!
UM, YOU DON'T WANT TO DO THIS!
I'VE GOT CONNECTIONS, MAN! DO YOU KNOW WHO MY DAD IS?
BEACH FRONT PROPERTY, DUDE-- JUST SAY THE WORD!
OH!
OH NO!
OH, YES!

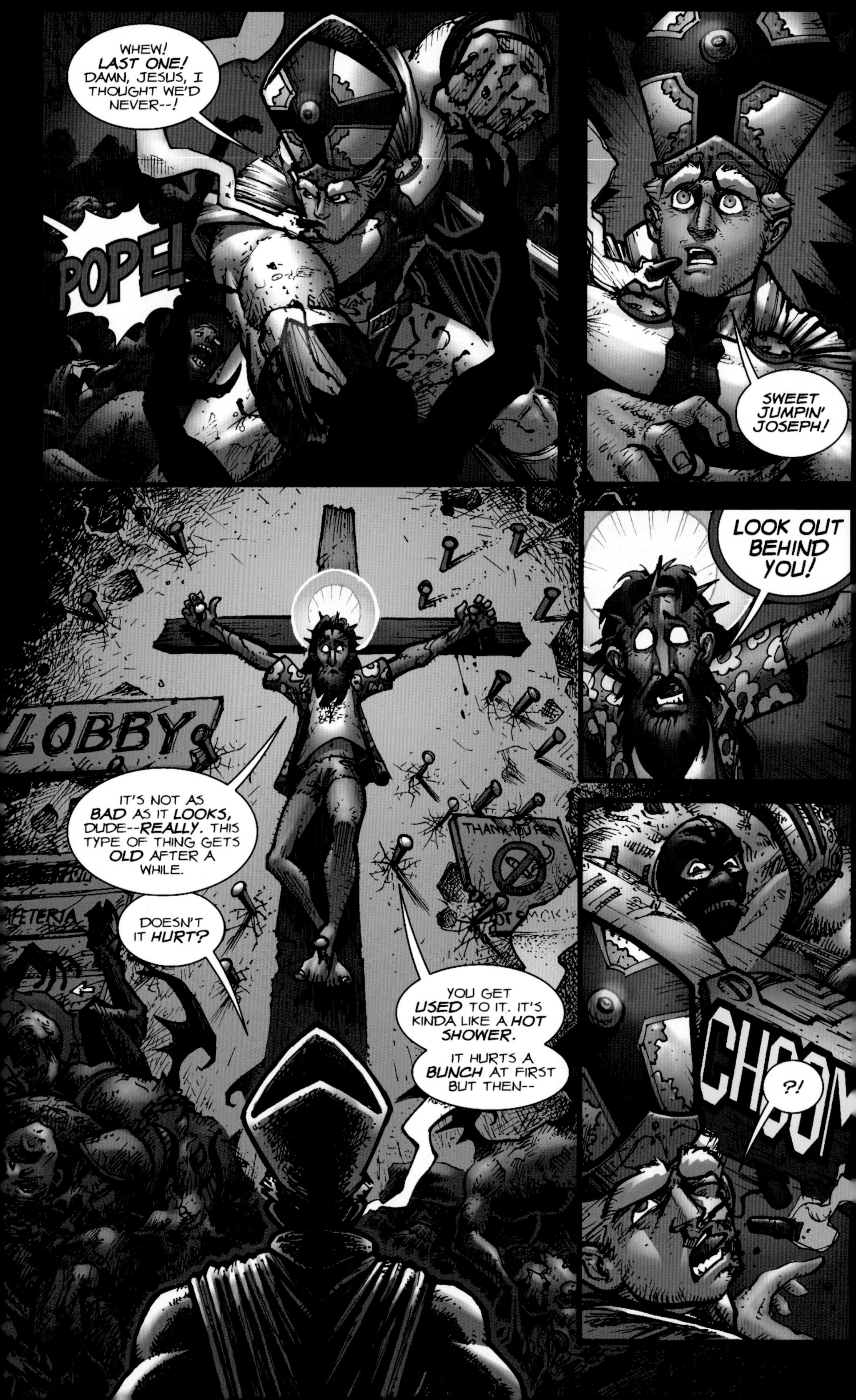
WHEW! LAST ONE! DAMN, JESUS, I THOUGHT WE'D NEVER--!
POPE!
SWEET JUMPIN' JOSEPH!
LOBBY
IT'S NOT AS BAD AS IT LOOKS, DUDE--REALLY. THIS TYPE OF THING GETS OLD AFTER A WHILE.
DOESN'T IT HURT?
YOU GET USED TO IT. IT'S KINDA LIKE A HOT SHOWER.
IT HURTS A BUNCH AT FIRST BUT THEN--
LOOK OUT BEHIND YOU!
CHOOM
?!

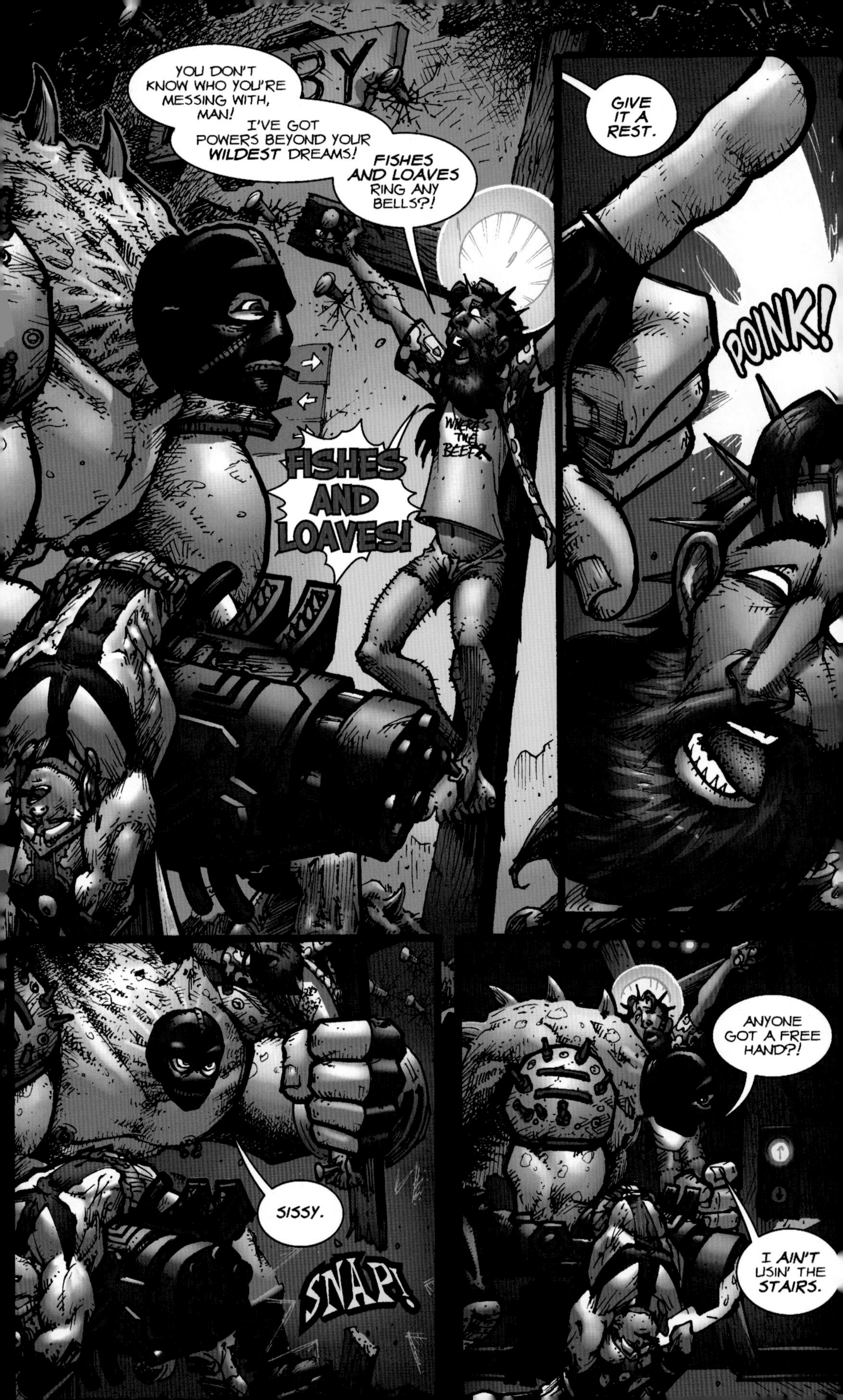

YOU DON'T KNOW WHO YOU'RE MESSING WITH, MAN!
I'VE GOT POWERS BEYOND YOUR WILDEST DREAMS!
FISHES AND LOAVES RING ANY BELLS?!
FISHES AND LOAVES!
GIVE IT A REST.
POINK!
SISSY.
SNAP!
ANYONE GOT A FREE HAND?!
I AIN'T USIN' THE STAIRS.

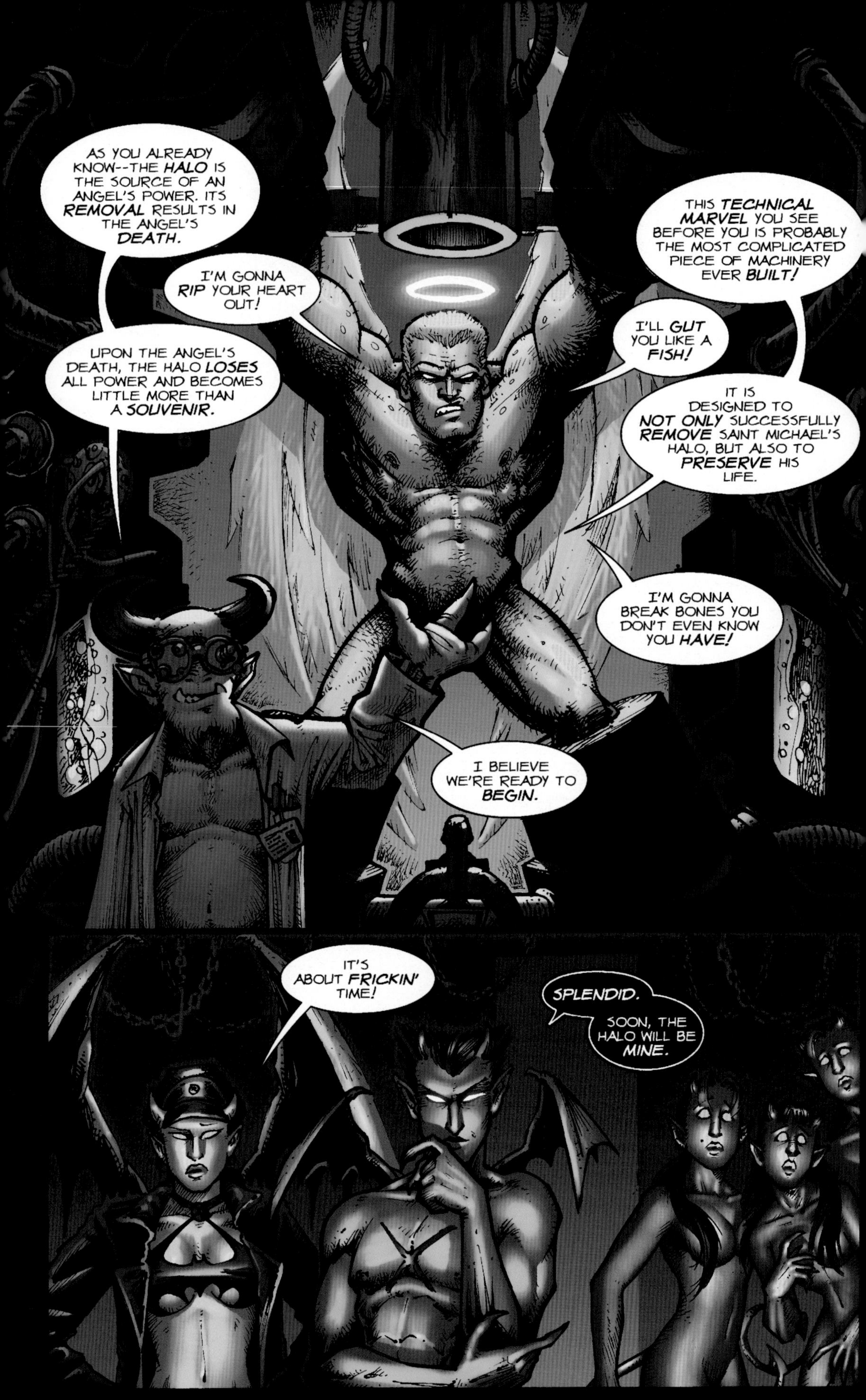
AS YOU ALREADY KNOW--THE HALO IS THE SOURCE OF AN ANGEL'S POWER. ITS REMOVAL RESULTS IN THE ANGEL'S DEATH.
I'M GONNA RIP YOUR HEART OUT!
UPON THE ANGEL'S DEATH, THE HALO LOSES ALL POWER AND BECOMES LITTLE MORE THAN A SOUVENIR.
THIS TECHNICAL MARVEL YOU SEE BEFORE YOU IS PROBABLY THE MOST COMPLICATED PIECE OF MACHINERY EVER BUILT!
I'LL GUT YOU LIKE A FISH!
IT IS DESIGNED TO NOT ONLY SUCCESSFULLY REMOVE SAINT MICHAEL'S HALO, BUT ALSO TO PRESERVE HIS LIFE.
I'M GONNA BREAK BONES YOU DON'T EVEN KNOW YOU HAVE!
I BELIEVE WE'RE READY TO BEGIN.
IT'S ABOUT FRICKIN' TIME!
SPLENDID.
SOON, THE HALO WILL BE MINE.

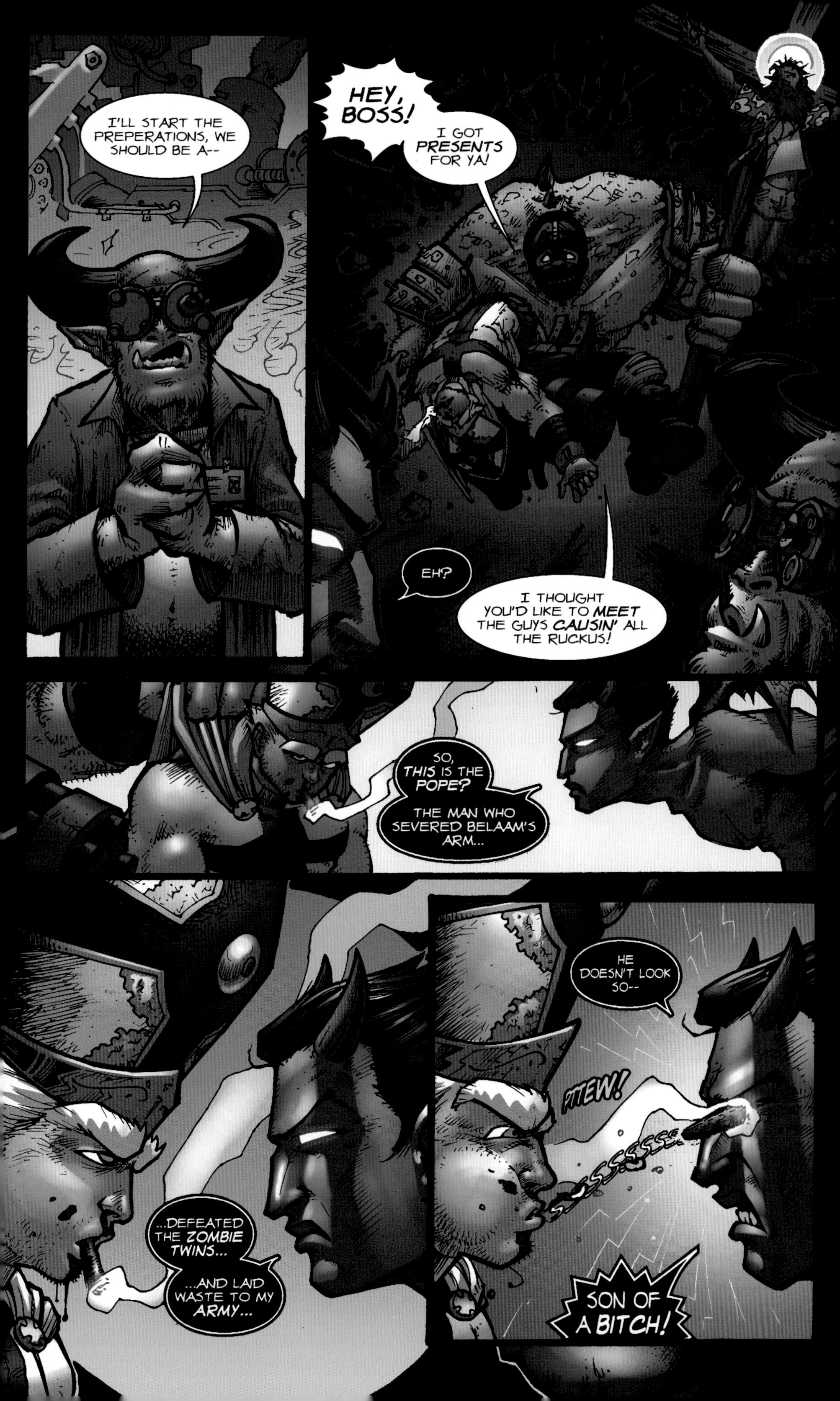
I'LL START THE PREPERATIONS, WE SHOULD BE A--
HEY, BOSS!
I GOT PRESENTS FOR YA!
EH?
I THOUGHT YOU'D LIKE TO MEET THE GUYS CAUSIN' ALL THE RUCKUS!
SO, THIS IS THE POPE?
THE MAN WHO SEVERED BELAAM'S ARM...
...DEFEATED THE ZOMBIE TWINS...
...AND LAID WASTE TO MY ARMY...
HE DOESN'T LOOK SO--
PTTEW!
SSSSSSSSS
SON OF A BITCH!

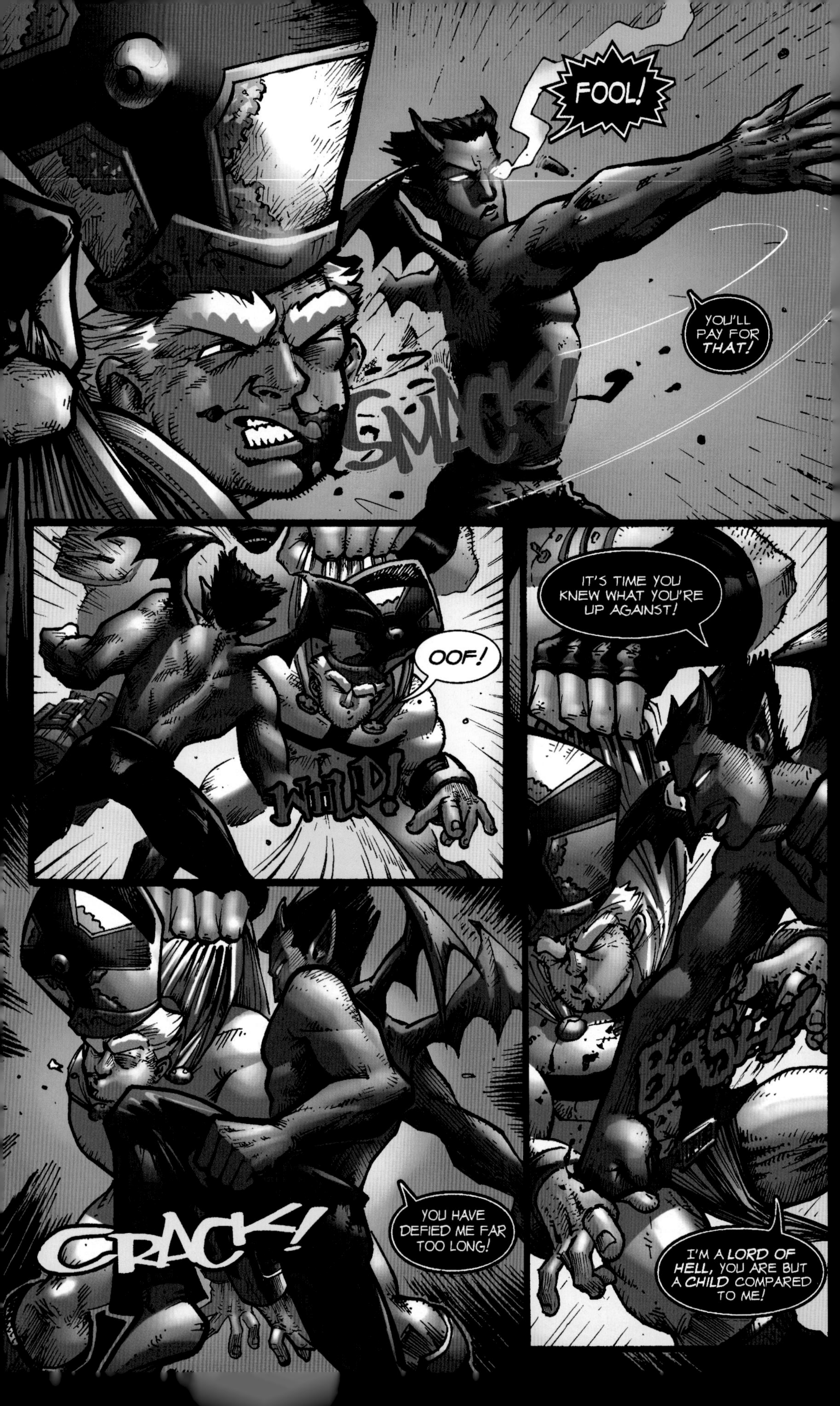
FOOL!
SMACK!
YOU'LL PAY FOR *THAT!*
OOF!
IT'S TIME YOU KNEW WHAT YOU'RE UP AGAINST!
CRACK!
YOU HAVE DEFIED ME FAR TOO LONG!
BASH!
I'M A **LORD OF HELL,** YOU ARE BUT A **CHILD** COMPARED TO ME!

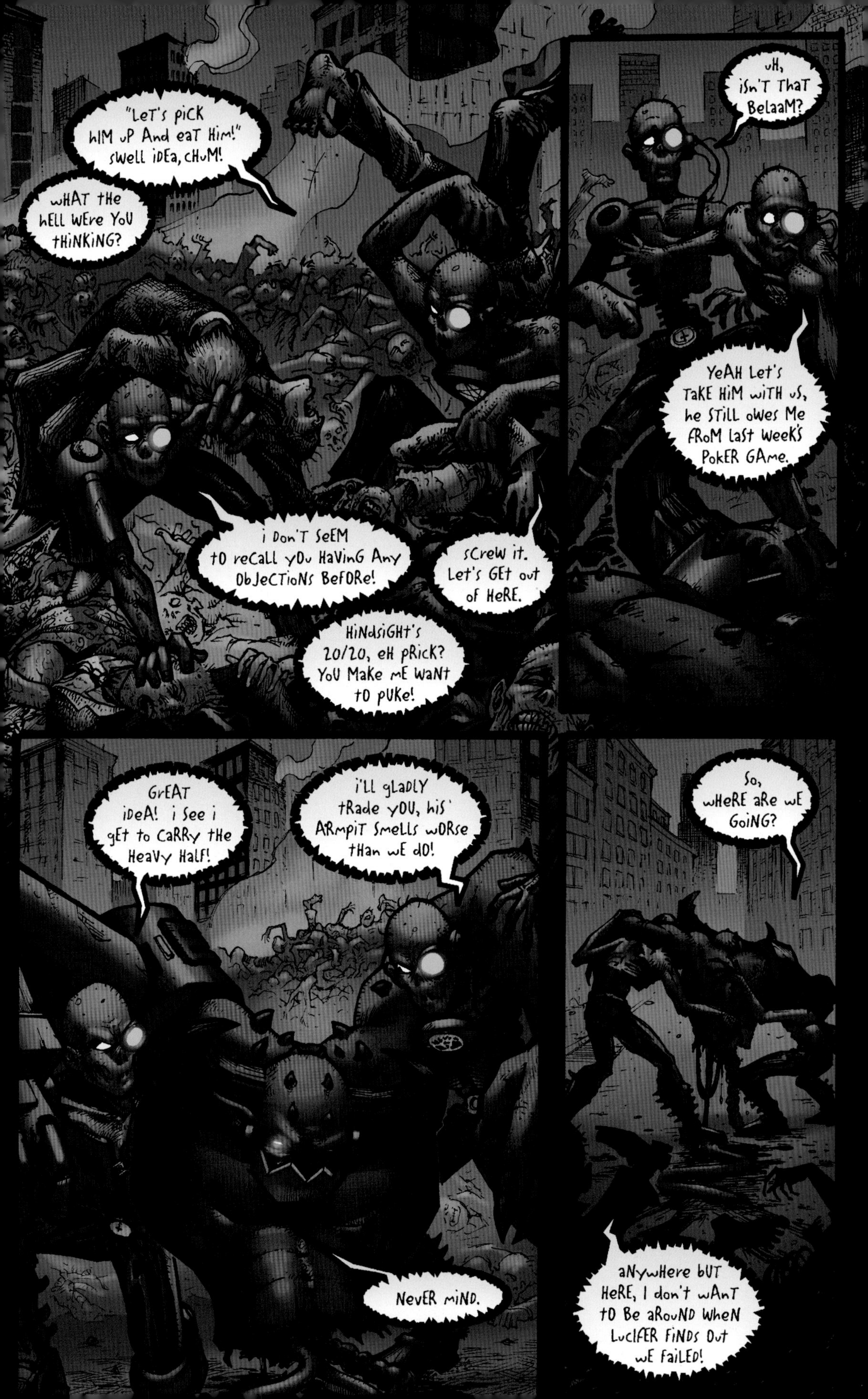
"LET'S PICK HIM UP AND EAT HIM!" SWELL IDEA, CHUM!
WHAT THE HELL WERE YOU THINKING?
I DON'T SEEM TO RECALL YOU HAVING ANY OBJECTIONS BEFORE!
SCREW IT. LET'S GET OUT OF HERE.
HINDSIGHT'S 20/20, EH PRICK? YOU MAKE ME WANT TO PUKE!
UH, ISN'T THAT BELAAM?
YEAH LET'S TAKE HIM WITH US, HE STILL OWES ME FROM LAST WEEK'S POKER GAME.
GREAT IDEA! I SEE I GET TO CARRY THE HEAVY HALF!
I'LL GLADLY TRADE YOU, HIS' ARMPIT SMELLS WORSE THAN WE DO!
NEVER MIND.
SO, WHERE ARE WE GOING?
ANYWHERE BUT HERE, I DON'T WANT TO BE AROUND WHEN LUCIFER FINDS OUT WE FAILED!

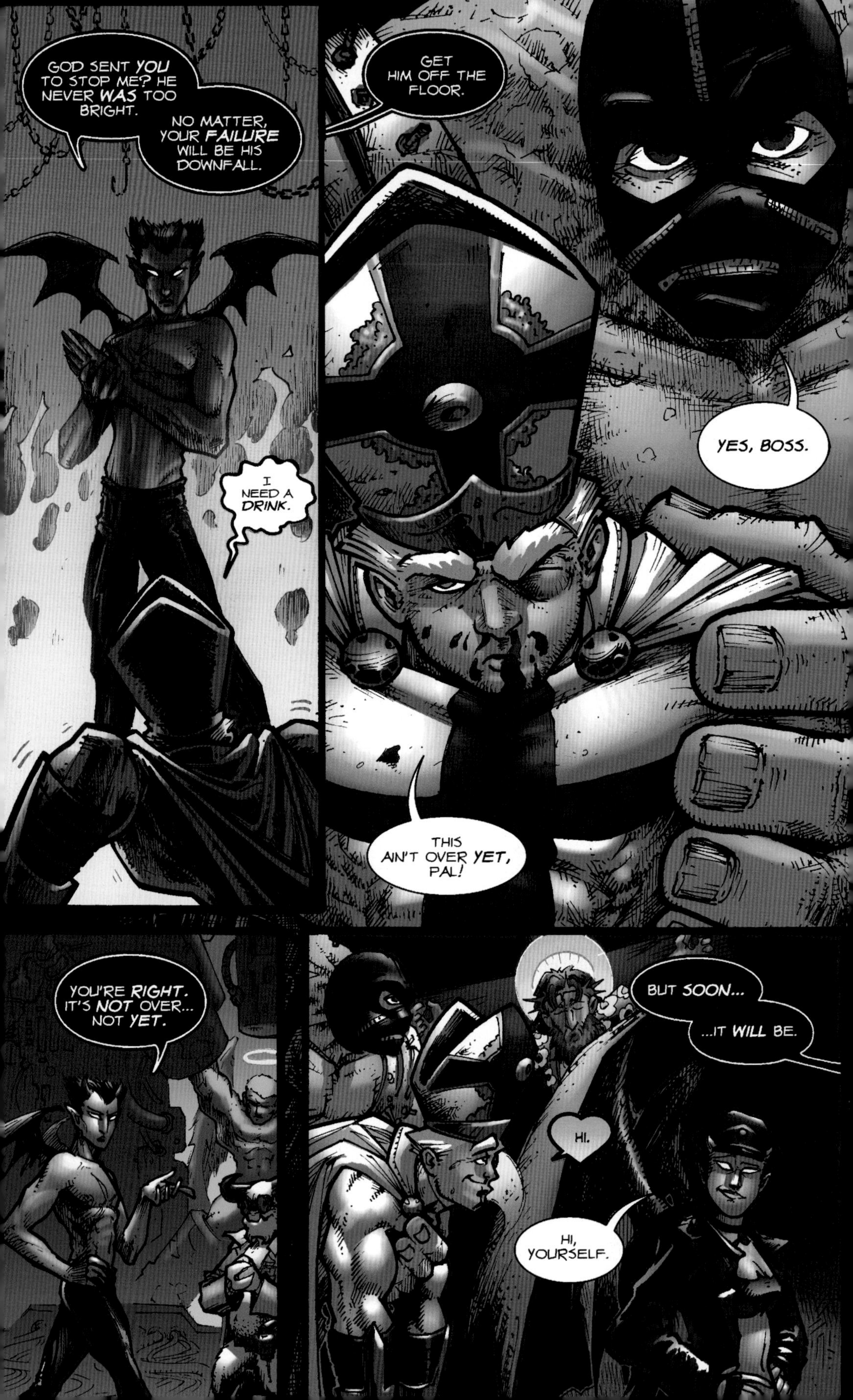
GOD SENT YOU TO STOP ME? HE NEVER WAS TOO BRIGHT.
NO MATTER, YOUR FAILURE WILL BE HIS DOWNFALL.
I NEED A DRINK.
GET HIM OFF THE FLOOR.
YES, BOSS.
THIS AIN'T OVER YET, PAL!
YOU'RE RIGHT. IT'S NOT OVER... NOT YET.
BUT SOON...
...IT WILL BE.
HI.
HI, YOURSELF.

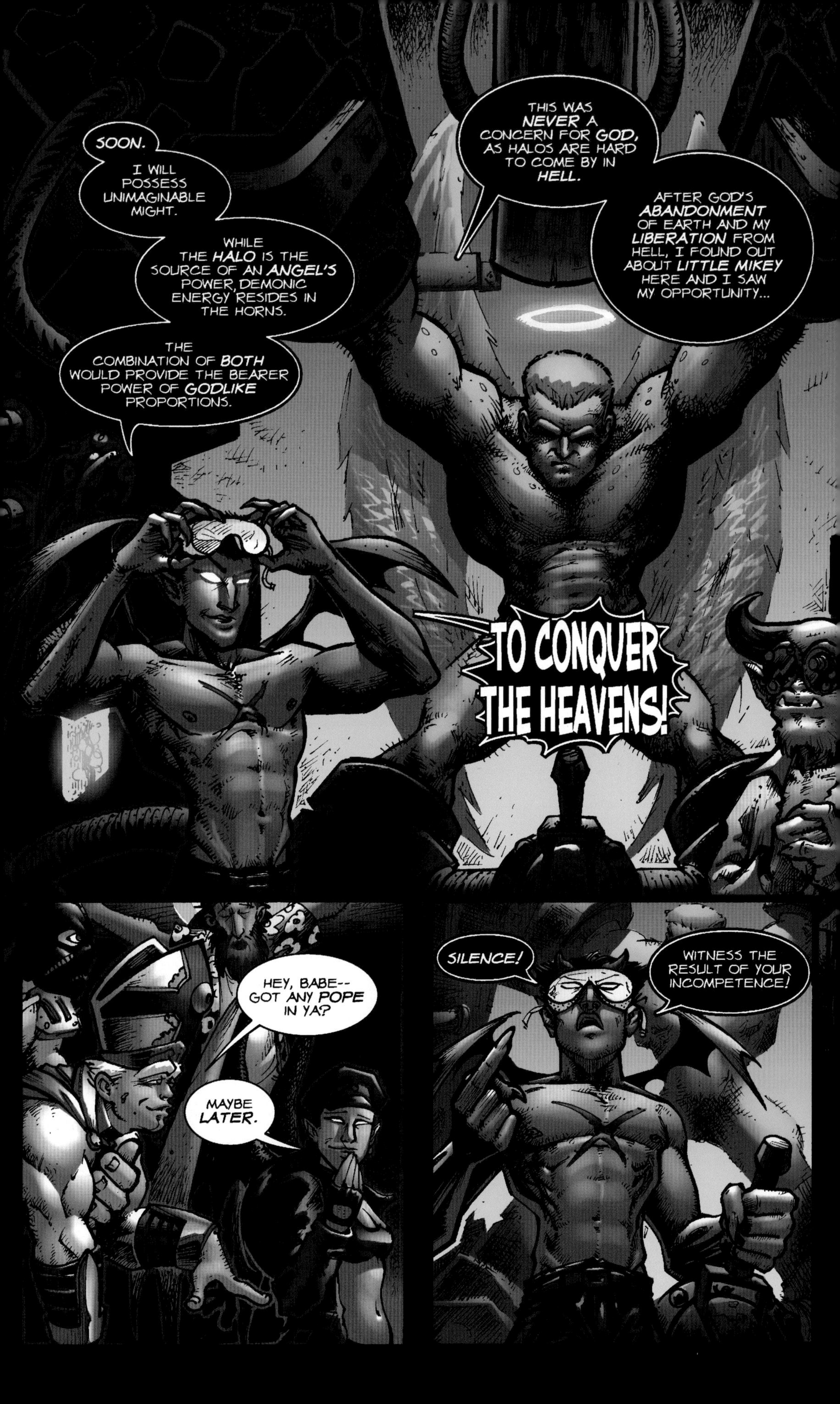

SOON.
I WILL POSSESS UNIMAGINABLE MIGHT.
WHILE THE HALO IS THE SOURCE OF AN ANGEL'S POWER, DEMONIC ENERGY RESIDES IN THE HORNS.
THE COMBINATION OF BOTH WOULD PROVIDE THE BEARER POWER OF GODLIKE PROPORTIONS.
THIS WAS NEVER A CONCERN FOR GOD, AS HALOS ARE HARD TO COME BY IN HELL.
AFTER GOD'S ABANDONMENT OF EARTH AND MY LIBERATION FROM HELL, I FOUND OUT ABOUT LITTLE MIKEY HERE AND I SAW MY OPPORTUNITY...
TO CONQUER THE HEAVENS!
HEY, BABE-- GOT ANY POPE IN YA?
MAYBE LATER.
SILENCE!
WITNESS THE RESULT OF YOUR INCOMPETENCE!

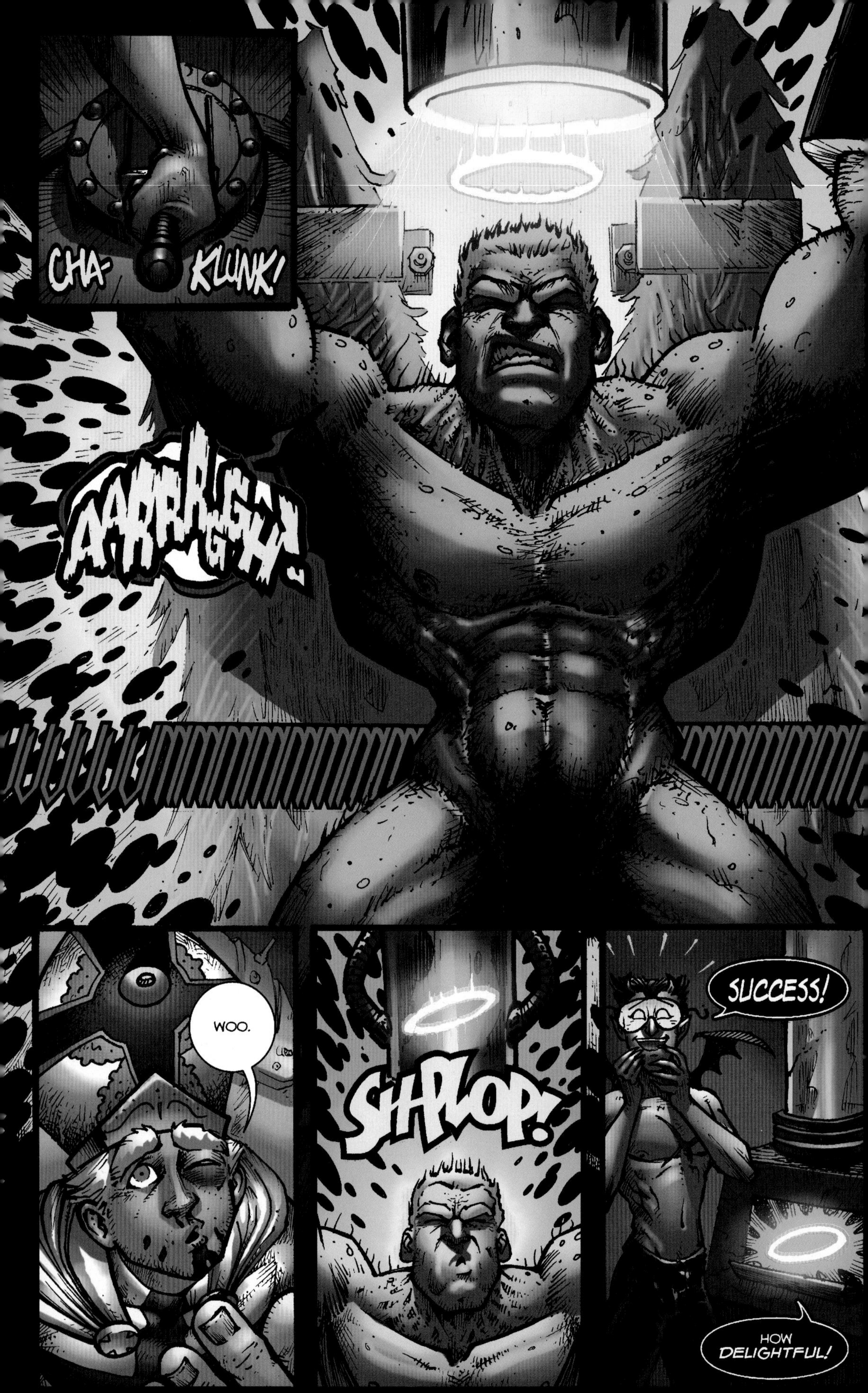
CHA-
KLUNK!
AARRRGGH!
WOO.
SHPLOP!
SUCCESS!
HOW DELIGHTFUL!

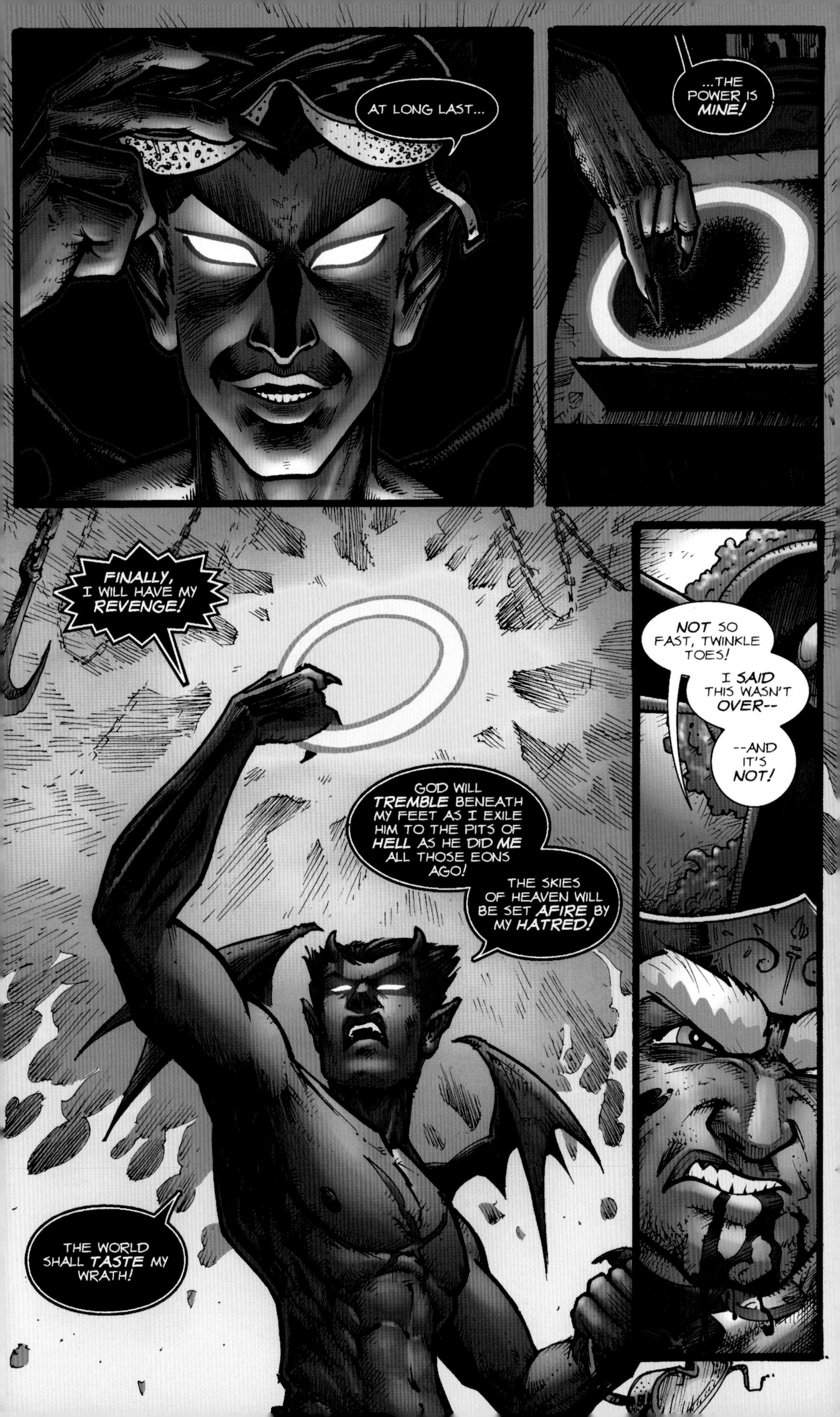
AT LONG LAST...
...THE POWER IS MINE!
FINALLY, I WILL HAVE MY REVENGE!
GOD WILL TREMBLE BENEATH MY FEET AS I EXILE HIM TO THE PITS OF HELL AS HE DID ME ALL THOSE EONS AGO!
THE SKIES OF HEAVEN WILL BE SET AFIRE BY MY HATRED!
THE WORLD SHALL TASTE MY WRATH!
NOT SO FAST, TWINKLE TOES!
I SAID THIS WASN'T OVER--
--AND IT'S NOT!

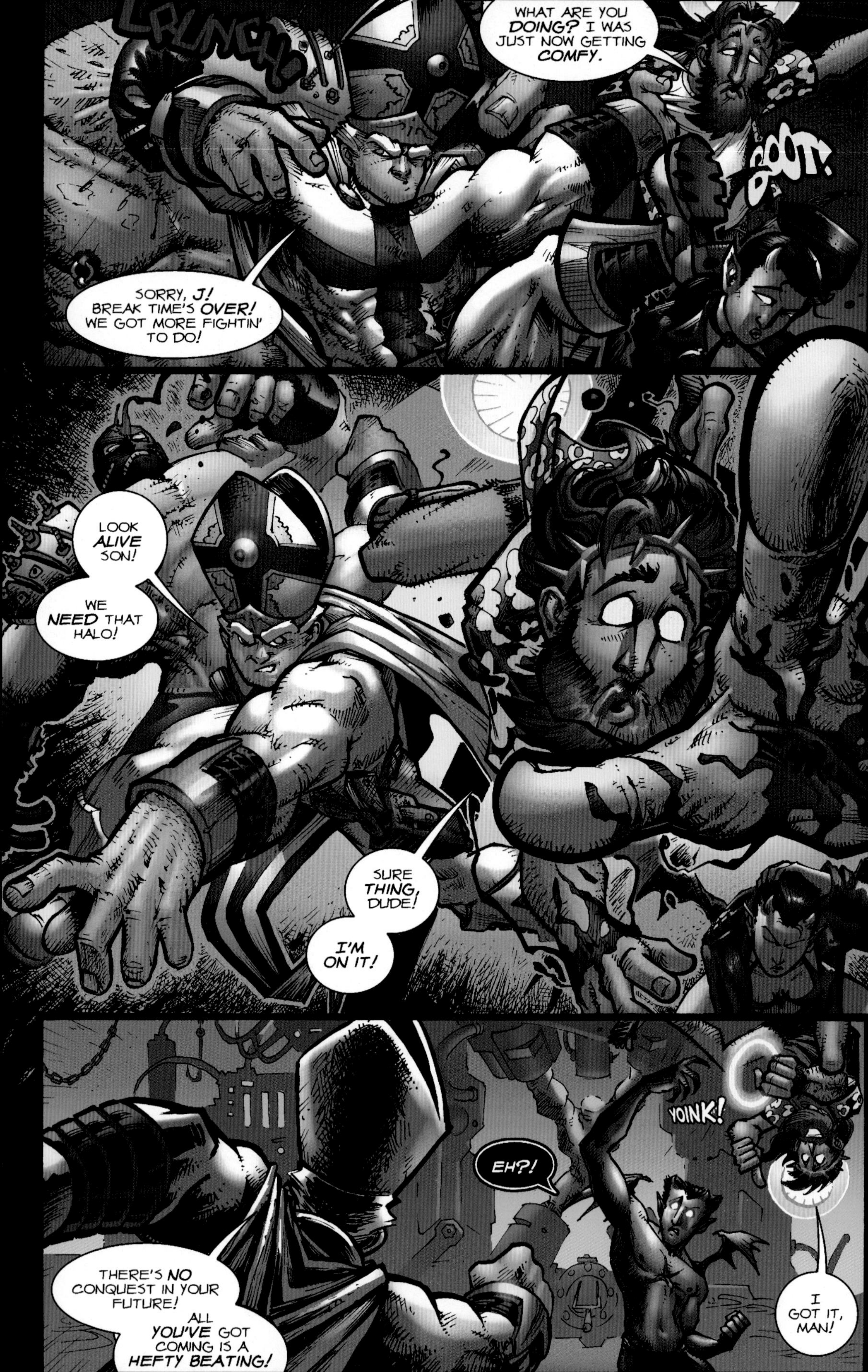
CRUNCH!
WHAT ARE YOU DOING? I WAS JUST NOW GETTING COMFY.
SORRY, J! BREAK TIME'S OVER! WE GOT MORE FIGHTIN' TO DO!
BOOT!
LOOK ALIVE SON!
WE NEED THAT HALO!
SURE THING, DUDE!
I'M ON IT!
YOINK!
EH?!
THERE'S NO CONQUEST IN YOUR FUTURE!
ALL YOU'VE GOT COMING IS A HEFTY BEATING!
I GOT IT, MAN!

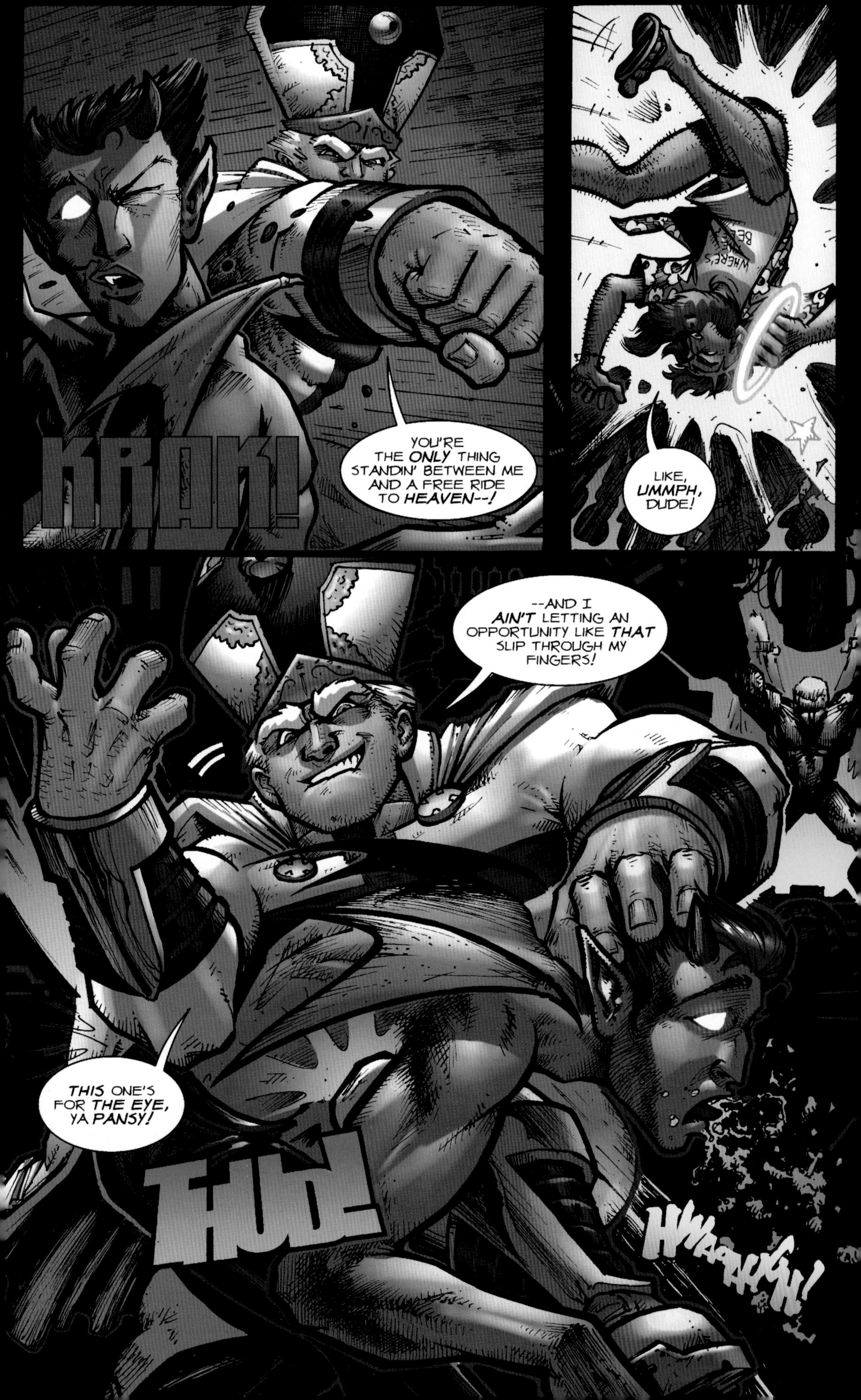
KRAK!
YOU'RE THE ONLY THING STANDIN' BETWEEN ME AND A FREE RIDE TO HEAVEN--!
LIKE, UMMPH, DUDE!
--AND I AIN'T LETTING AN OPPORTUNITY LIKE THAT SLIP THROUGH MY FINGERS!
THIS ONE'S FOR THE EYE, YA PANSY!
THUD!
HWAAAUGH!

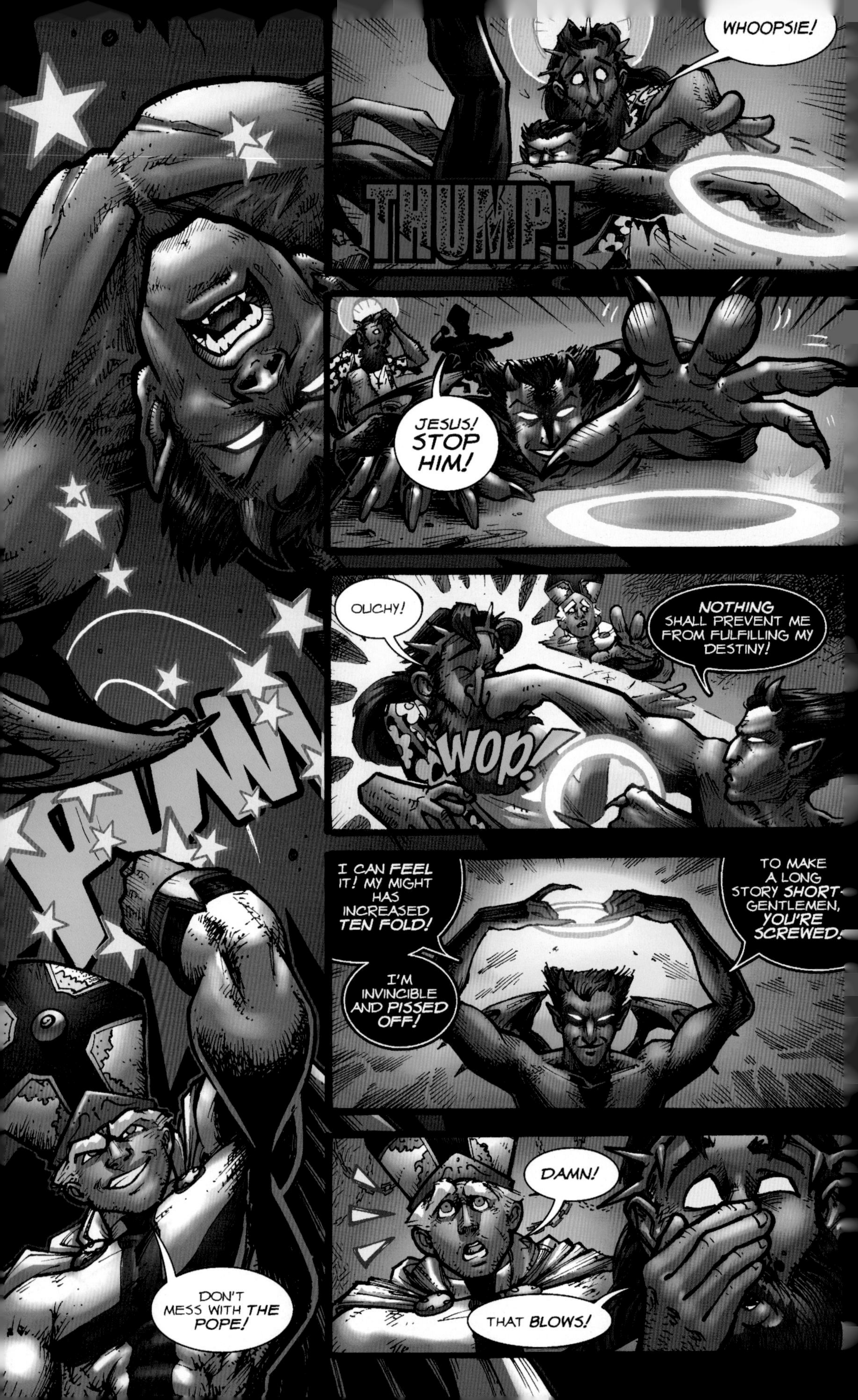
WHOOPSIE!
THUMP!
JESUS! STOP HIM!
OUCHY!
NOTHING SHALL PREVENT ME FROM FULFILLING MY DESTINY!
WOP!
I CAN FEEL IT! MY MIGHT HAS INCREASED TEN FOLD!
I'M INVINCIBLE AND PISSED OFF!
TO MAKE A LONG STORY SHORT-- GENTLEMEN, YOU'RE SCREWED.
DAMN!
THAT BLOWS!
DON'T MESS WITH THE POPE!

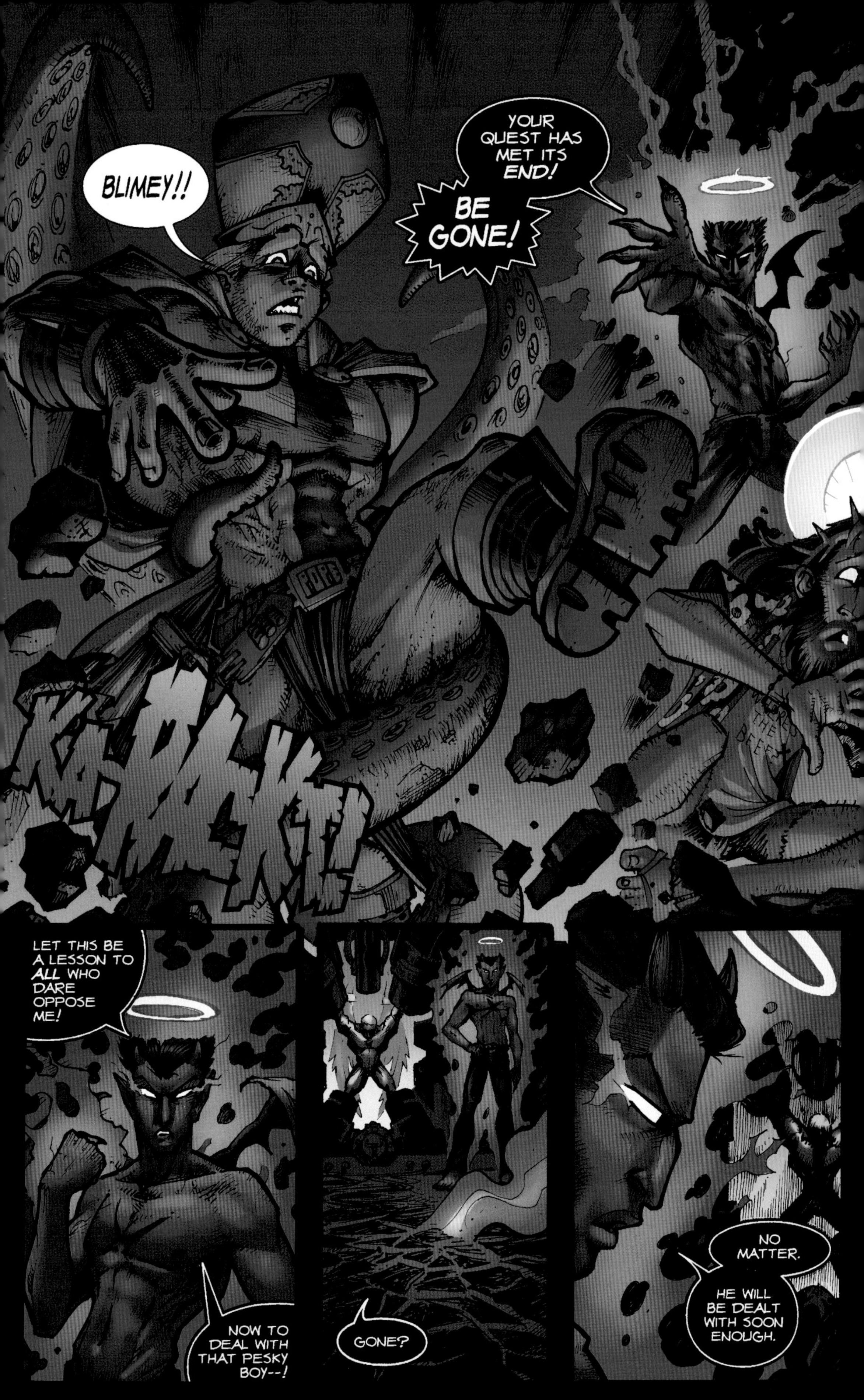
BLIMEY!!
YOUR QUEST HAS MET ITS END!
BE GONE!
LET THIS BE A LESSON TO ALL WHO DARE OPPOSE ME!
NOW TO DEAL WITH THAT PESKY BOY--!
GONE?
NO MATTER.
HE WILL BE DEALT WITH SOON ENOUGH.

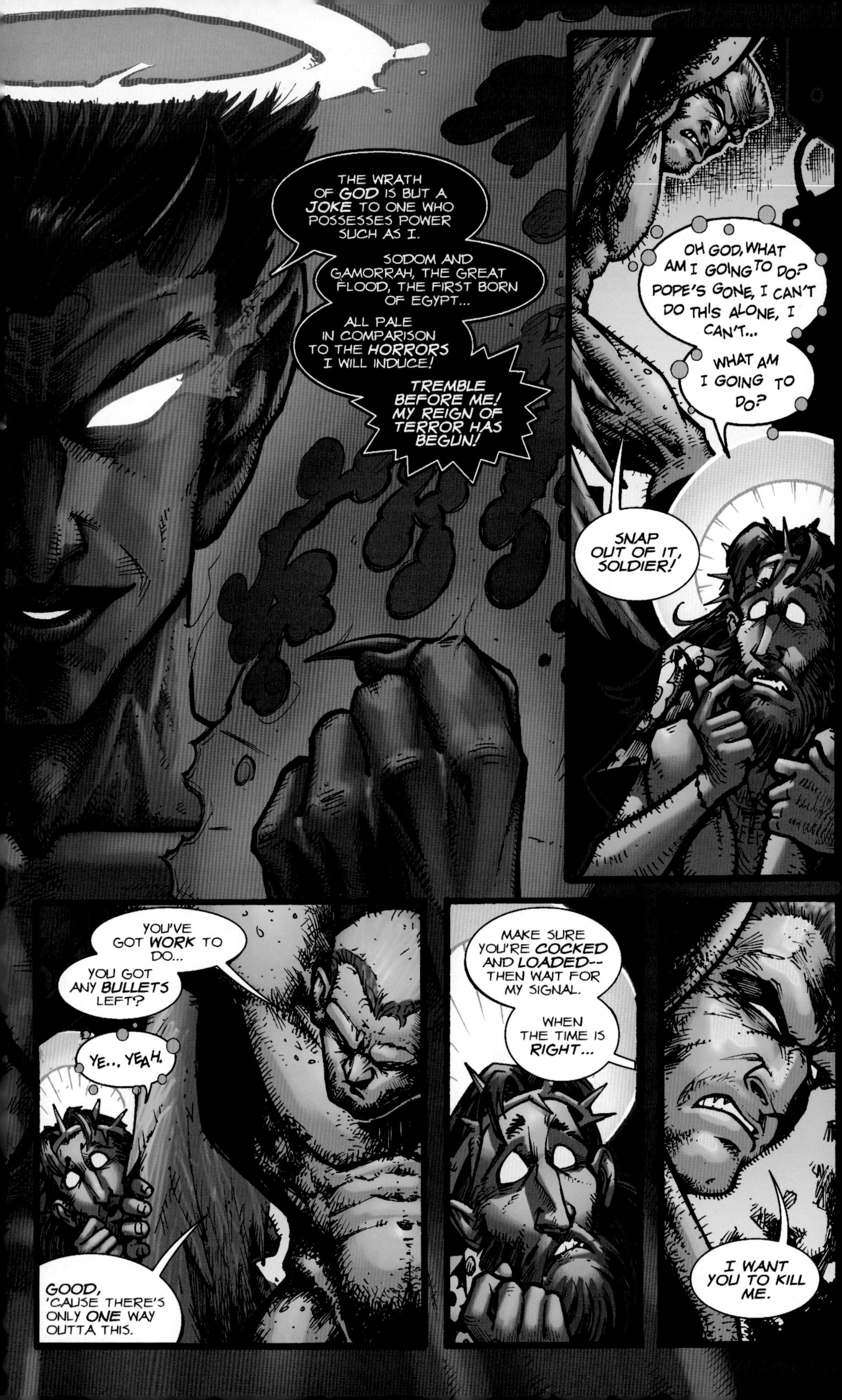
THE WRATH OF GOD IS BUT A JOKE TO ONE WHO POSSESSES POWER SUCH AS I.
SODOM AND GAMORRAH, THE GREAT FLOOD, THE FIRST BORN OF EGYPT...
ALL PALE IN COMPARISON TO THE HORRORS I WILL INDUCE!
TREMBLE BEFORE ME! MY REIGN OF TERROR HAS BEGUN!
OH GOD, WHAT AM I GOING TO DO? POPE'S GONE, I CAN'T DO THIS ALONE, I CAN'T...
WHAT AM I GOING TO DO?
SNAP OUT OF IT, SOLDIER!
YOU'VE GOT WORK TO DO...
YOU GOT ANY BULLETS LEFT?
YE... YEAH.
GOOD, 'CAUSE THERE'S ONLY ONE WAY OUTTA THIS.
MAKE SURE YOU'RE COCKED AND LOADED-- THEN WAIT FOR MY SIGNAL.
WHEN THE TIME IS RIGHT...
I WANT YOU TO KILL ME.

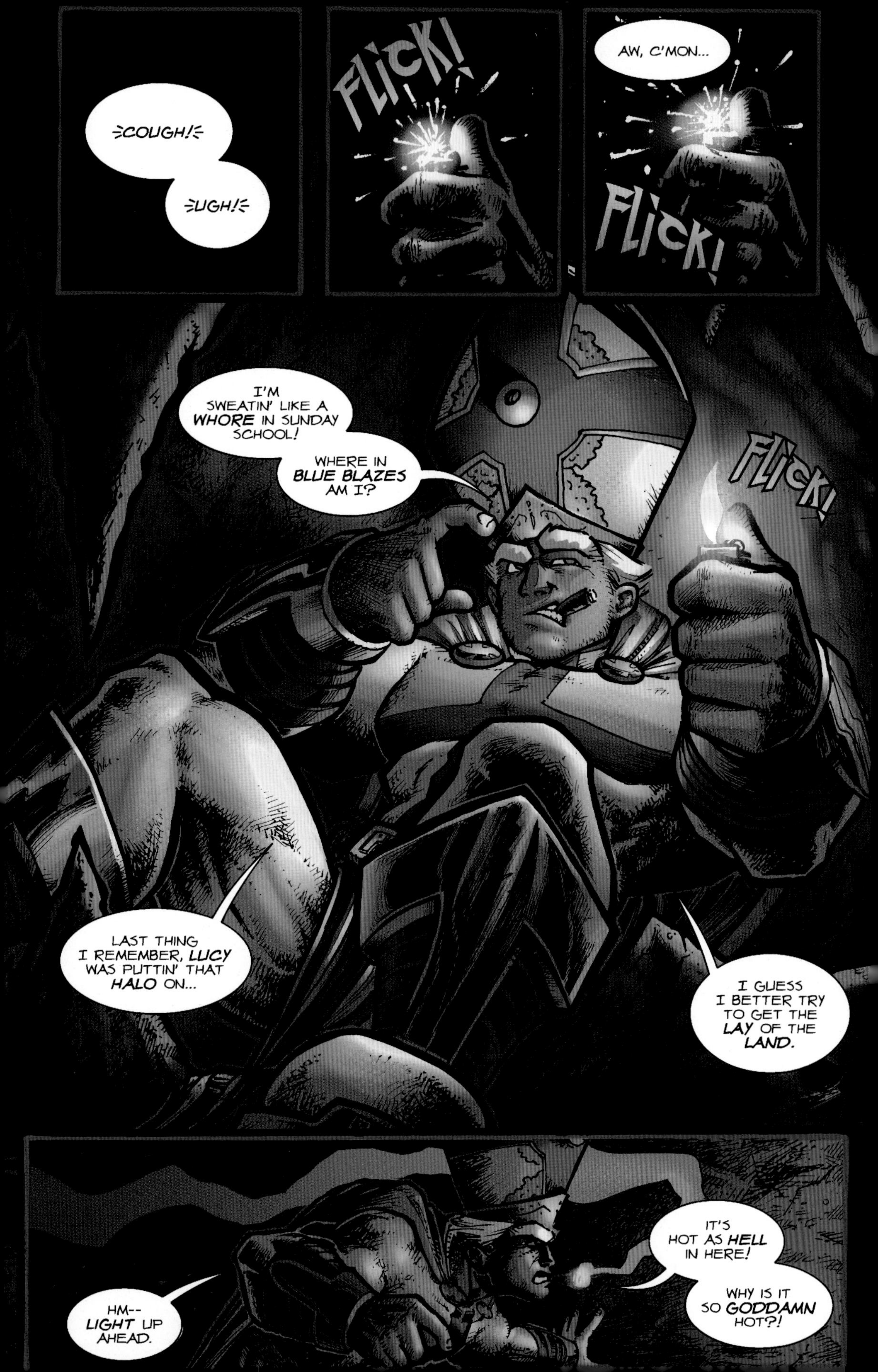

COUGH!
UGH!
FLICK!
AW, C'MON...
FLICK!
I'M SWEATIN' LIKE A WHORE IN SUNDAY SCHOOL!
WHERE IN BLUE BLAZES AM I?
FLICK!
LAST THING I REMEMBER, LUCY WAS PUTTIN' THAT HALO ON...
I GUESS I BETTER TRY TO GET THE LAY OF THE LAND.
IT'S HOT AS HELL IN HERE!
WHY IS IT SO GODDAMN HOT?!
HM-- LIGHT UP AHEAD.

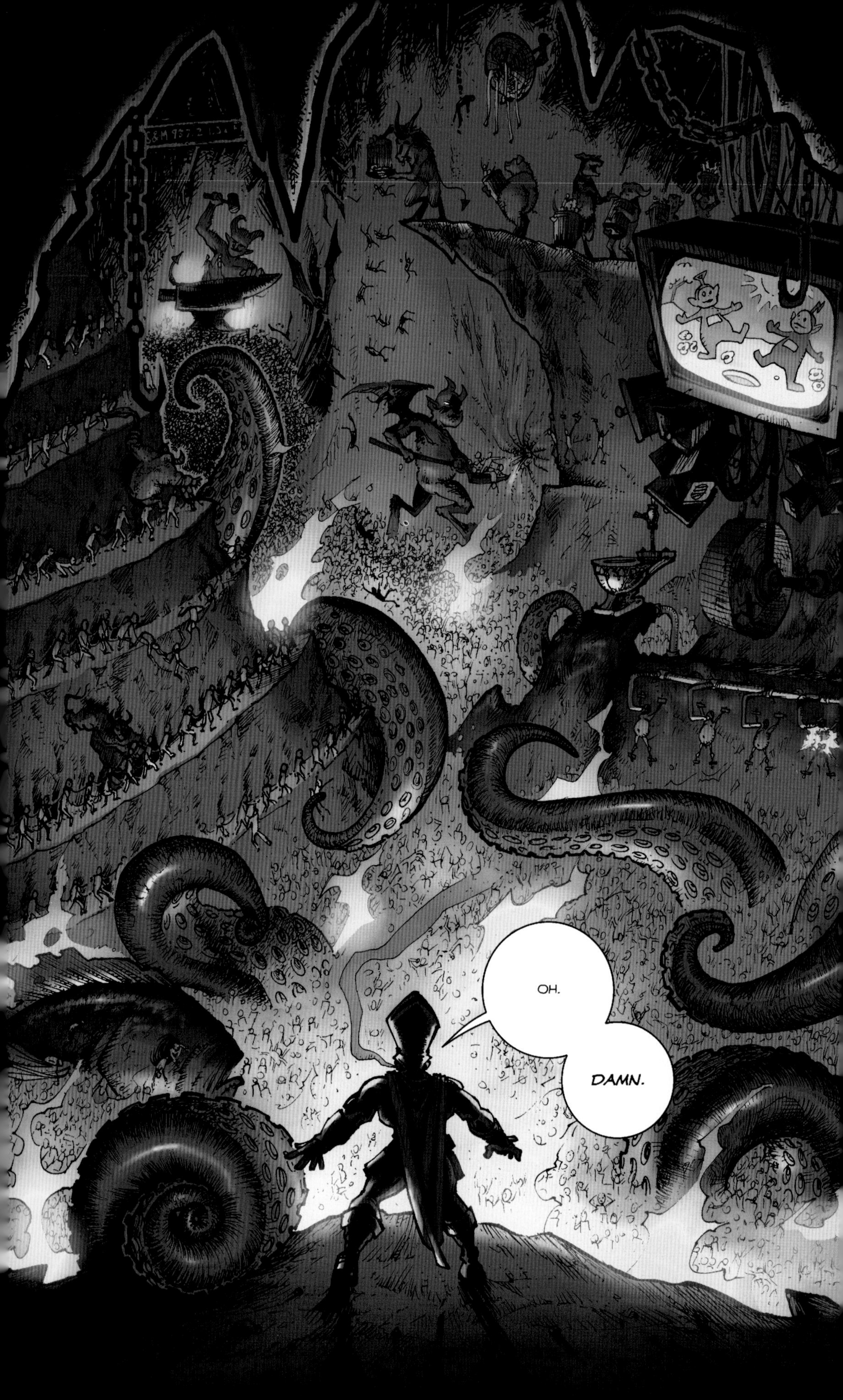
OH.
DAMN.

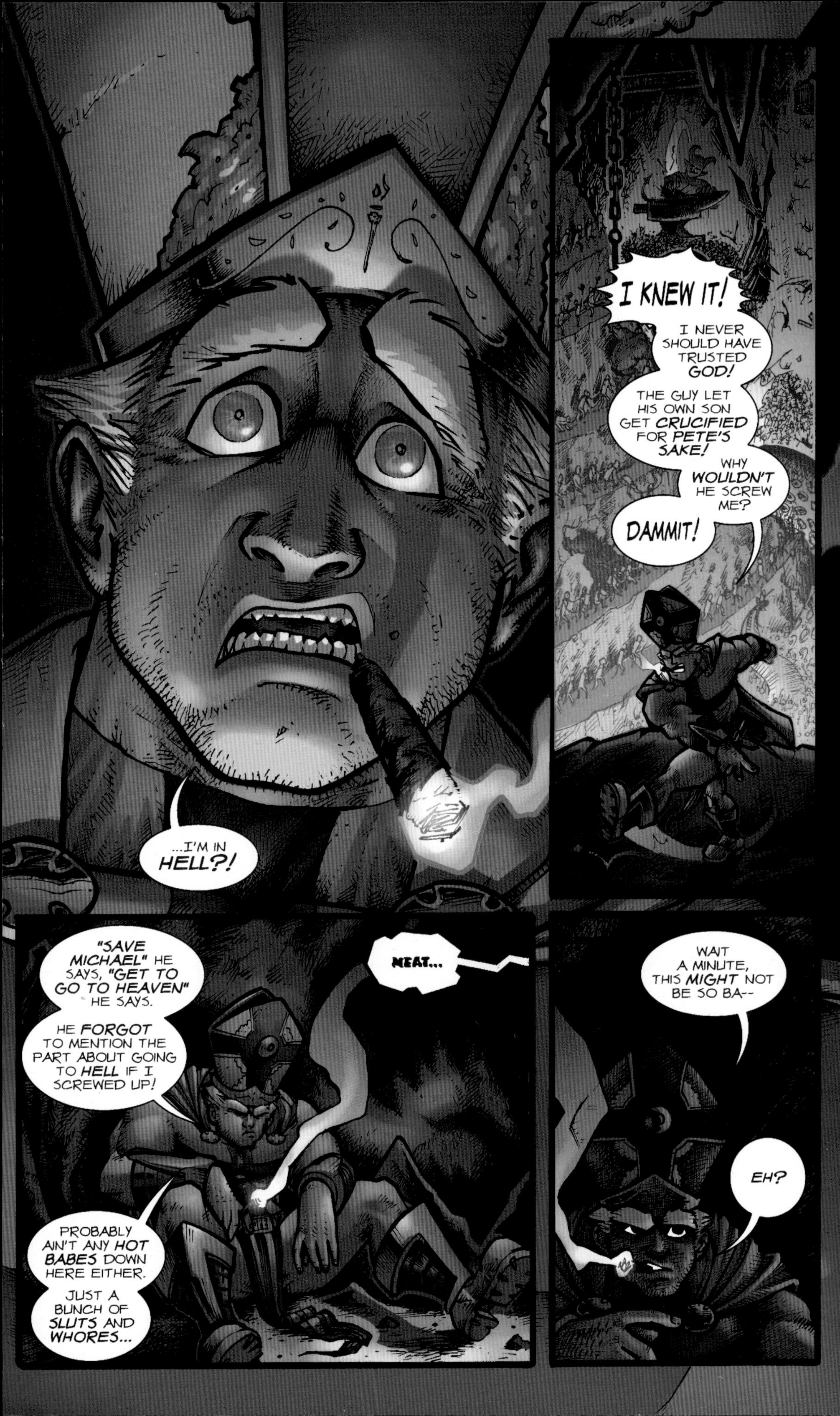

...I'M IN HELL?!
I KNEW IT!
I NEVER SHOULD HAVE TRUSTED GOD!
THE GUY LET HIS OWN SON GET CRUCIFIED FOR PETE'S SAKE!
WHY WOULDN'T HE SCREW ME?
DAMMIT!
"SAVE MICHAEL" HE SAYS, "GET TO GO TO HEAVEN" HE SAYS.
HE FORGOT TO MENTION THE PART ABOUT GOING TO HELL IF I SCREWED UP!
MEAT...
PROBABLY AIN'T ANY HOT BABES DOWN HERE EITHER.
JUST A BUNCH OF SLUTS AND WHORES...
WAIT A MINUTE, THIS MIGHT NOT BE SO BA--
EH?

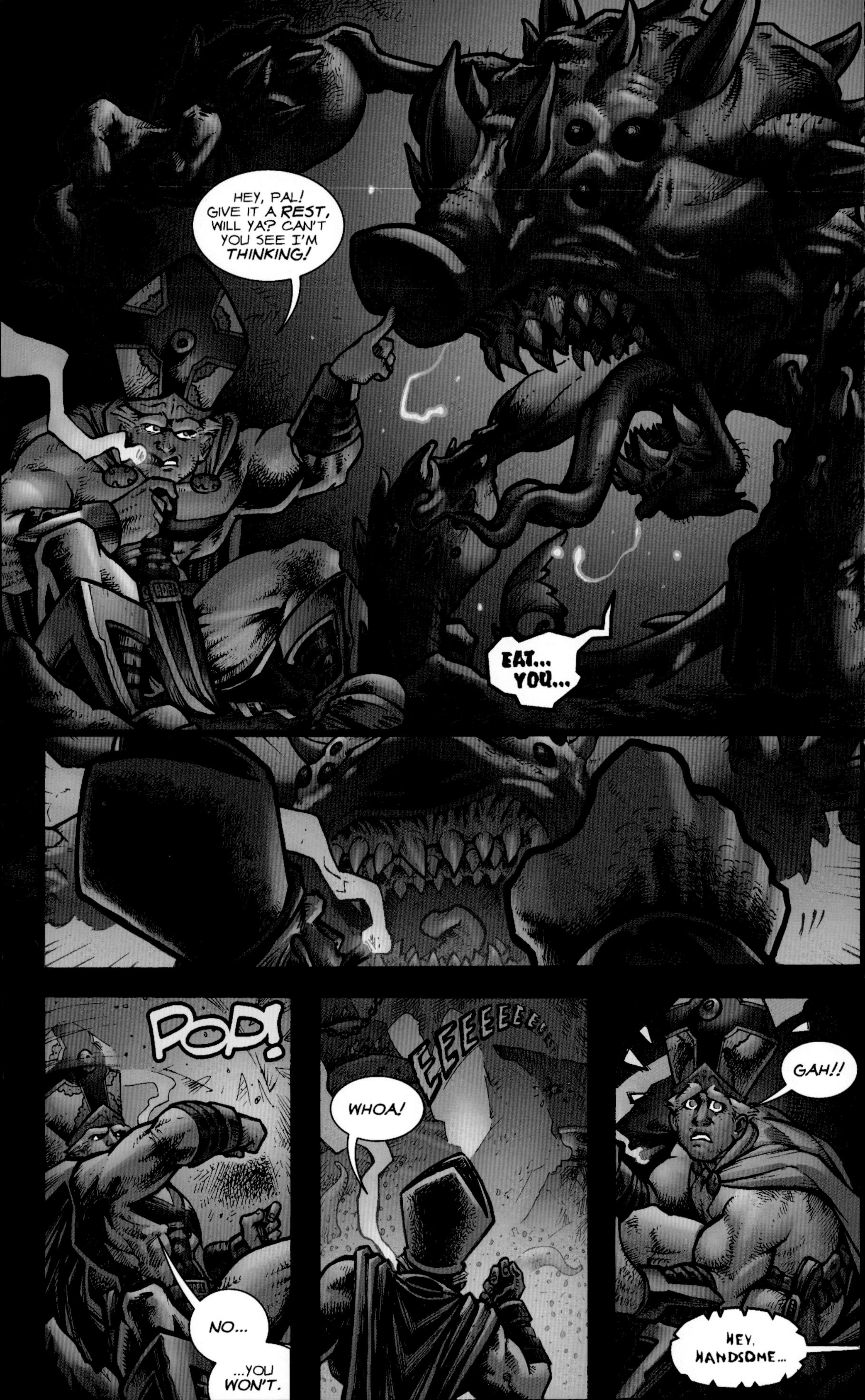
HEY, PAL! GIVE IT A REST, WILL YA? CAN'T YOU SEE I'M THINKING!
EAT... YOU...
POP!
NO...
...YOU WON'T.
EEEEEEEEEEE
WHOA!
GAH!!
HEY, HANDSOME...

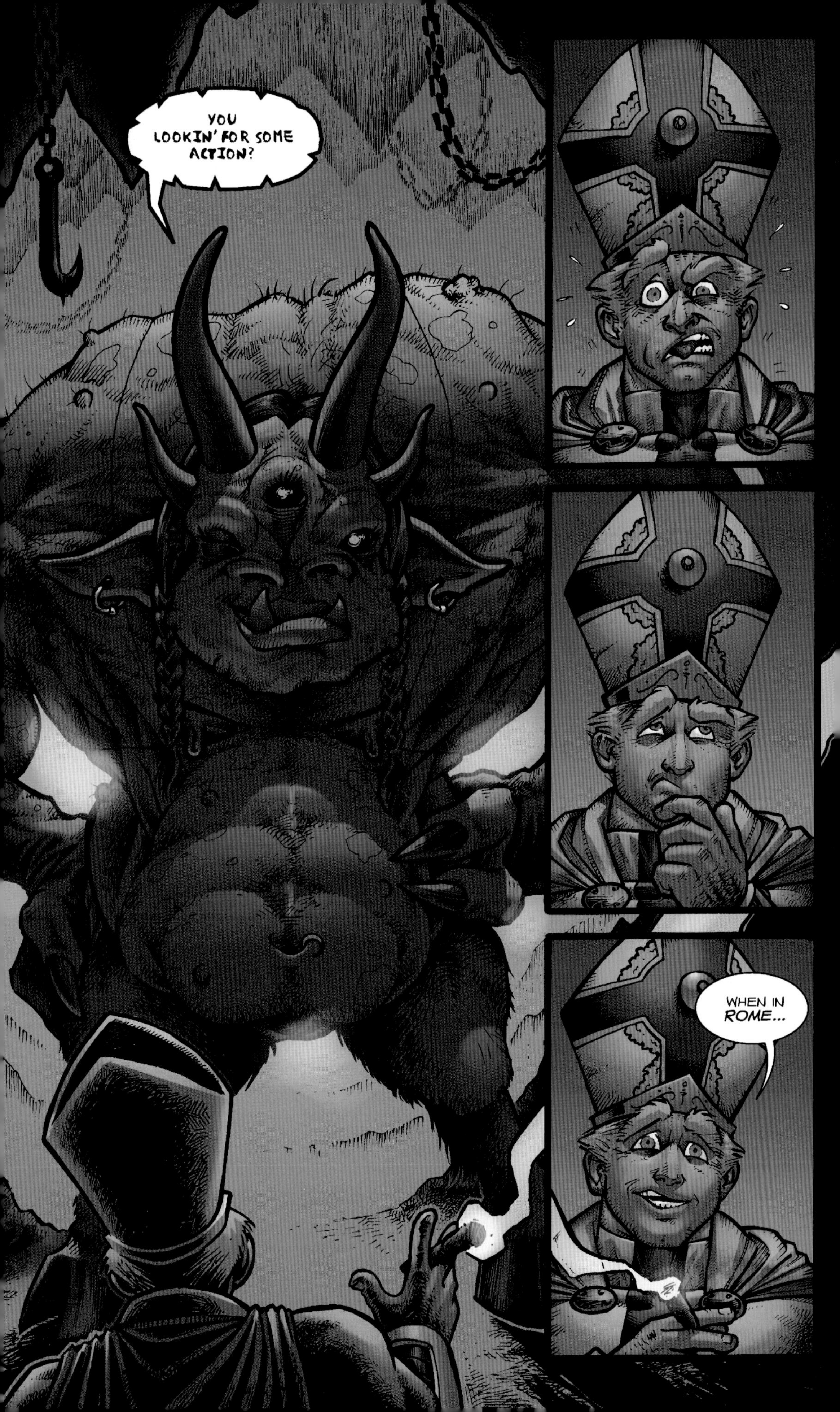
YOU LOOKIN' FOR SOME ACTION?
WHEN IN ROME...

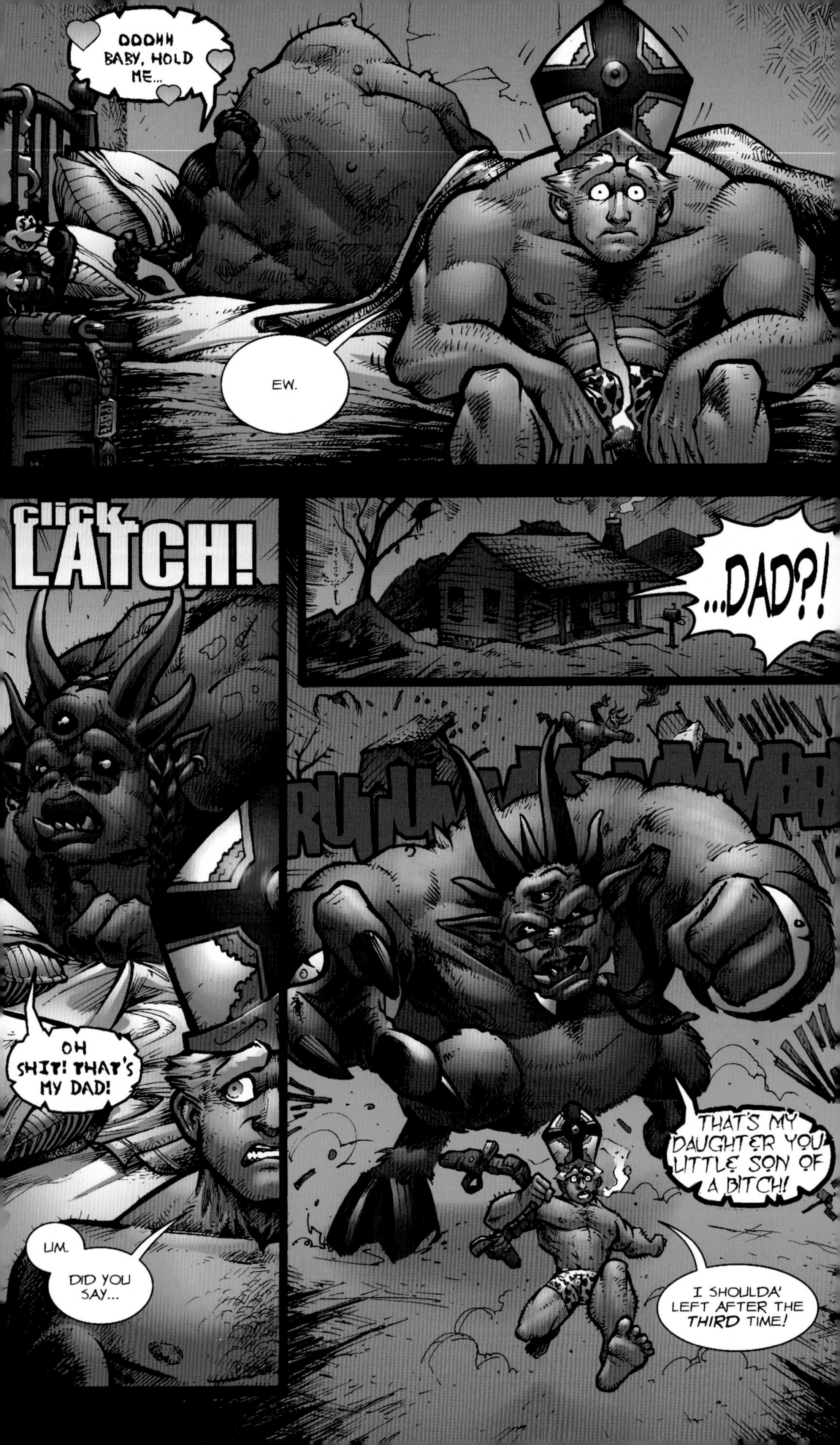
OOOHH BABY, HOLD ME...
EW.
click
LATCH!
...DAD?!
OH SHIT! THAT'S MY DAD!
UM.
DID YOU SAY...
THAT'S MY DAUGHTER YOU LITTLE SON OF A BITCH!
I SHOULDA' LEFT AFTER THE *THIRD* TIME!

SATANIC JAILBAIT... HOW WAS I SUPPOSED TO KNOW?!

IT TAKES A *WHILE* BUT I *FINALLY* LOSE HIM.

THAT TOOK A LOT OUT OF ME...

...AND SO DID RUNNING FROM HER DAD!

I SHOULDN'T HAVE SLEPT.

I'VE GOT TO START LOOKING FOR A WAY *OUT*.

THIS *ISN'T* GOING TO BE EASY.

HONEST DEMONS ARE HARD TO COME BY.

AND *POPE'S* AREN'T TOO *POPULAR* DOWN HERE.

LUCKILY, I'VE GOT TIME TO MAKE A FEW *FRIENDS*.

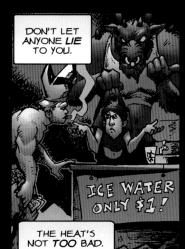

DON'T LET ANYONE *LIE* TO YOU.

ICE WATER ONLY $1!

THE HEAT'S NOT *TOO* BAD.

OF COURSE, IT AIN'T THE *HEAT* THAT GETS YA!

I NEED TO GET BACK *HOME*.

BUT *HUNGER* WAITS FOR NO MAN.

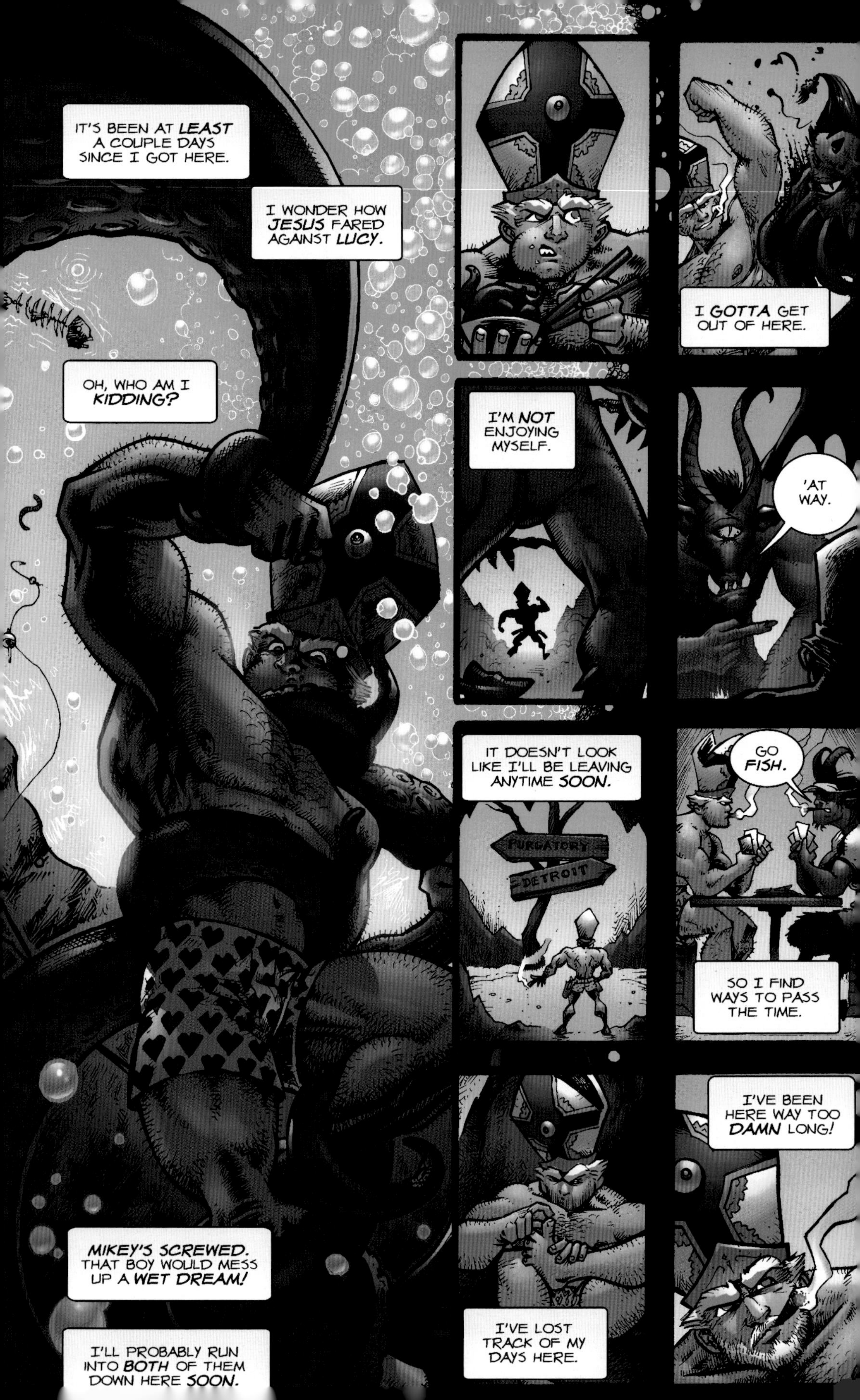
IT'S BEEN AT LEAST A COUPLE DAYS SINCE I GOT HERE.
I WONDER HOW JESUS FARED AGAINST LUCY.
OH, WHO AM I KIDDING?
MIKEY'S SCREWED. THAT BOY WOULD MESS UP A WET DREAM!
I'LL PROBABLY RUN INTO BOTH OF THEM DOWN HERE SOON.
I GOTTA GET OUT OF HERE.
I'M NOT ENJOYING MYSELF.
'AT WAY.
IT DOESN'T LOOK LIKE I'LL BE LEAVING ANYTIME SOON.
PURGATORY
DETROIT
GO FISH.
SO I FIND WAYS TO PASS THE TIME.
I'VE LOST TRACK OF MY DAYS HERE.
I'VE BEEN HERE WAY TOO DAMN LONG!

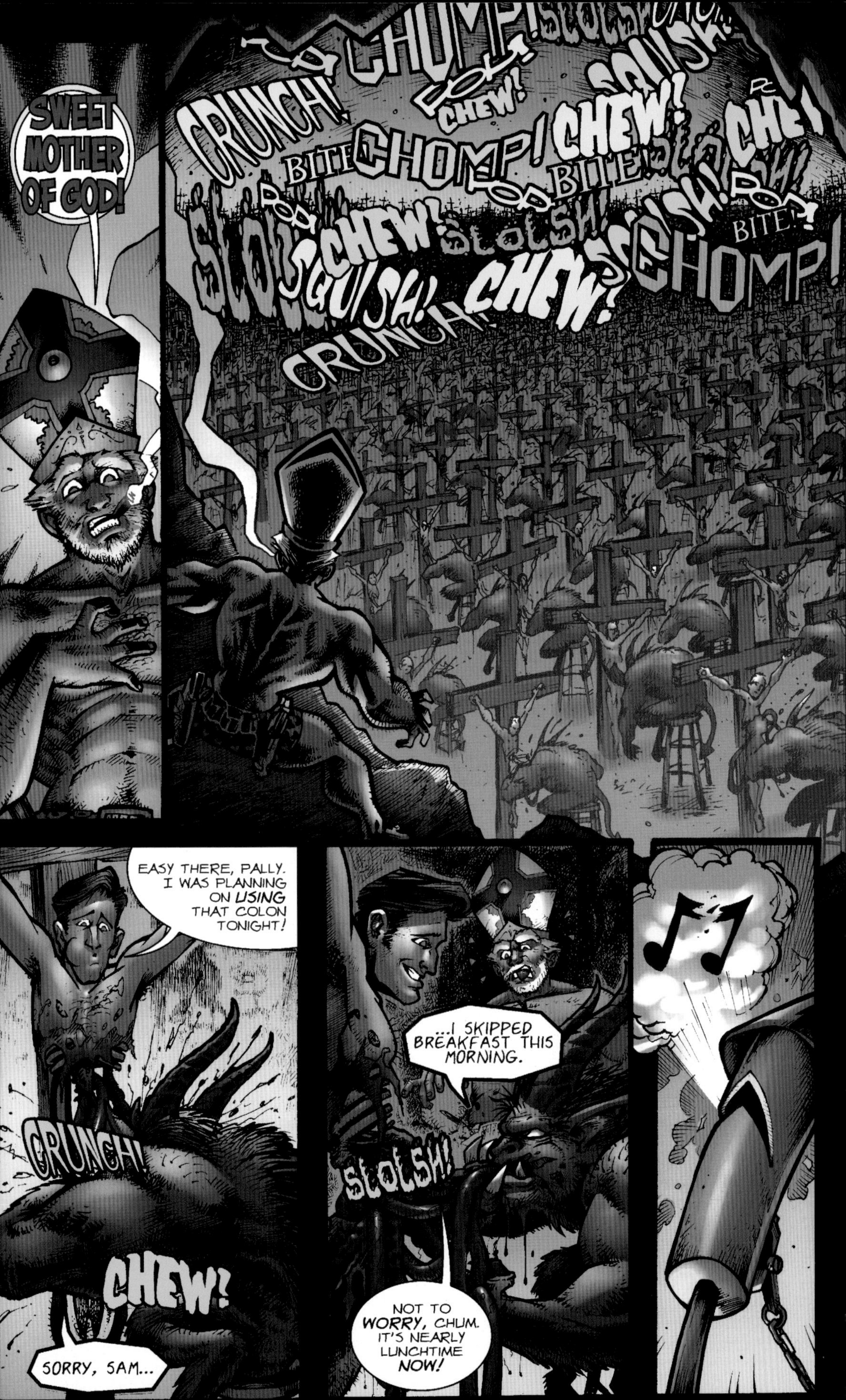
SWEET MOTHER OF GOD!
CRUNCH! CHOMP! CHEW! CHOMP! CHEW! BITE! BITE! CHEW! SQUISH! CHEW! BITE! CHOMP! CRUNCH!
EASY THERE, PALLY. I WAS PLANNING ON USING THAT COLON TONIGHT!
CRUNCH!
CHEW!
SORRY, SAM...
...I SKIPPED BREAKFAST THIS MORNING.
SLOSH!
NOT TO WORRY, CHUM. IT'S NEARLY LUNCHTIME NOW!

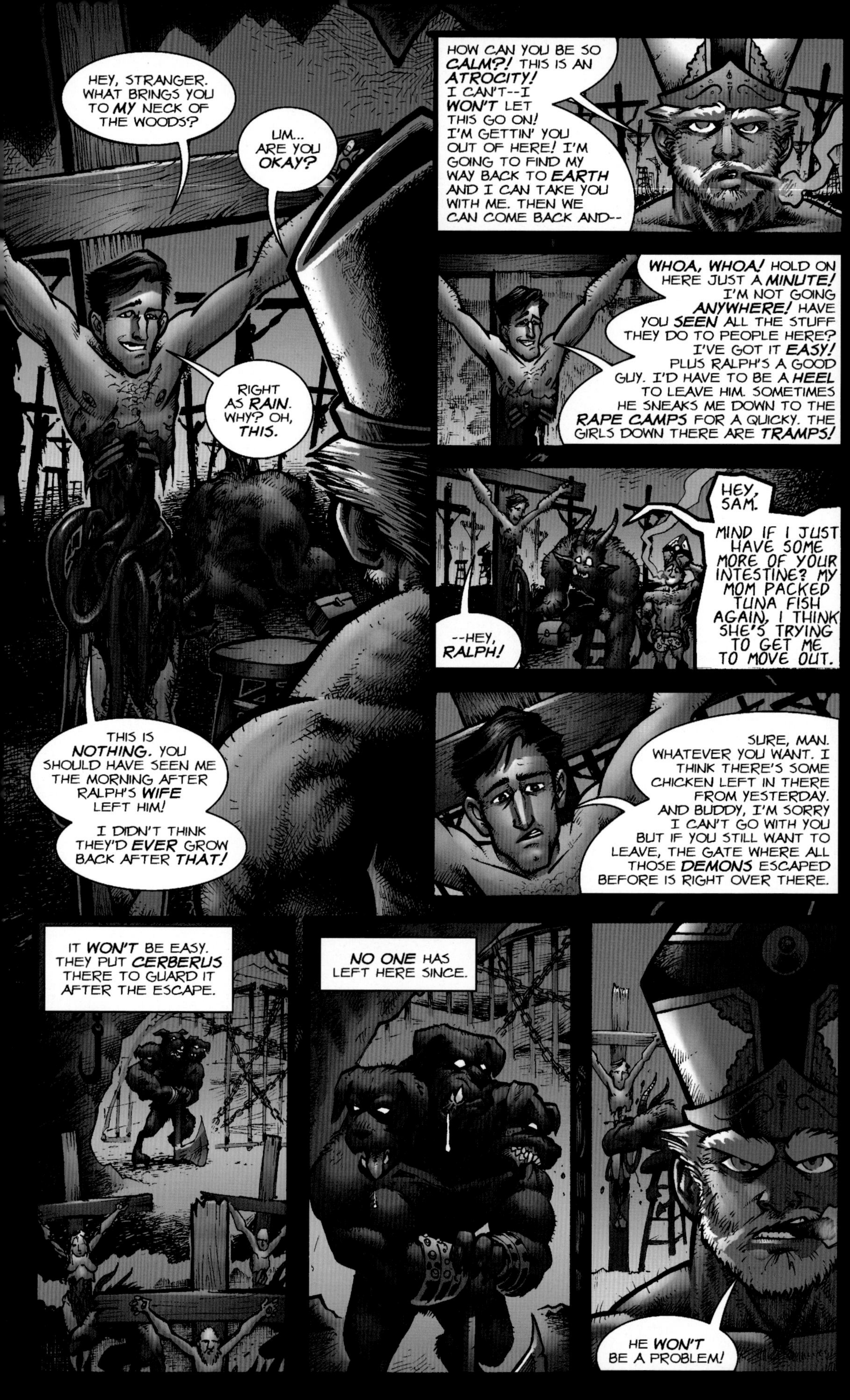
HEY, STRANGER. WHAT BRINGS YOU TO MY NECK OF THE WOODS?
UM... ARE YOU OKAY?
RIGHT AS RAIN. WHY? OH, THIS.
THIS IS NOTHING. YOU SHOULD HAVE SEEN ME THE MORNING AFTER RALPH'S WIFE LEFT HIM!
I DIDN'T THINK THEY'D EVER GROW BACK AFTER THAT!
HOW CAN YOU BE SO CALM?! THIS IS AN ATROCITY! I CAN'T--I WON'T LET THIS GO ON! I'M GETTIN' YOU OUT OF HERE! I'M GOING TO FIND MY WAY BACK TO EARTH AND I CAN TAKE YOU WITH ME. THEN WE CAN COME BACK AND--
WHOA, WHOA! HOLD ON HERE JUST A MINUTE! I'M NOT GOING ANYWHERE! HAVE YOU SEEN ALL THE STUFF THEY DO TO PEOPLE HERE? I'VE GOT IT EASY! PLUS RALPH'S A GOOD GUY. I'D HAVE TO BE A HEEL TO LEAVE HIM. SOMETIMES HE SNEAKS ME DOWN TO THE RAPE CAMPS FOR A QUICKY. THE GIRLS DOWN THERE ARE TRAMPS!
HEY, SAM.
MIND IF I JUST HAVE SOME MORE OF YOUR INTESTINE? MY MOM PACKED TUNA FISH AGAIN, I THINK SHE'S TRYING TO GET ME TO MOVE OUT.
--HEY, RALPH!
SURE, MAN. WHATEVER YOU WANT. I THINK THERE'S SOME CHICKEN LEFT IN THERE FROM YESTERDAY. AND BUDDY, I'M SORRY I CAN'T GO WITH YOU BUT IF YOU STILL WANT TO LEAVE, THE GATE WHERE ALL THOSE DEMONS ESCAPED BEFORE IS RIGHT OVER THERE.
IT WON'T BE EASY. THEY PUT CERBERUS THERE TO GUARD IT AFTER THE ESCAPE.
NO ONE HAS LEFT HERE SINCE.
HE WON'T BE A PROBLEM!

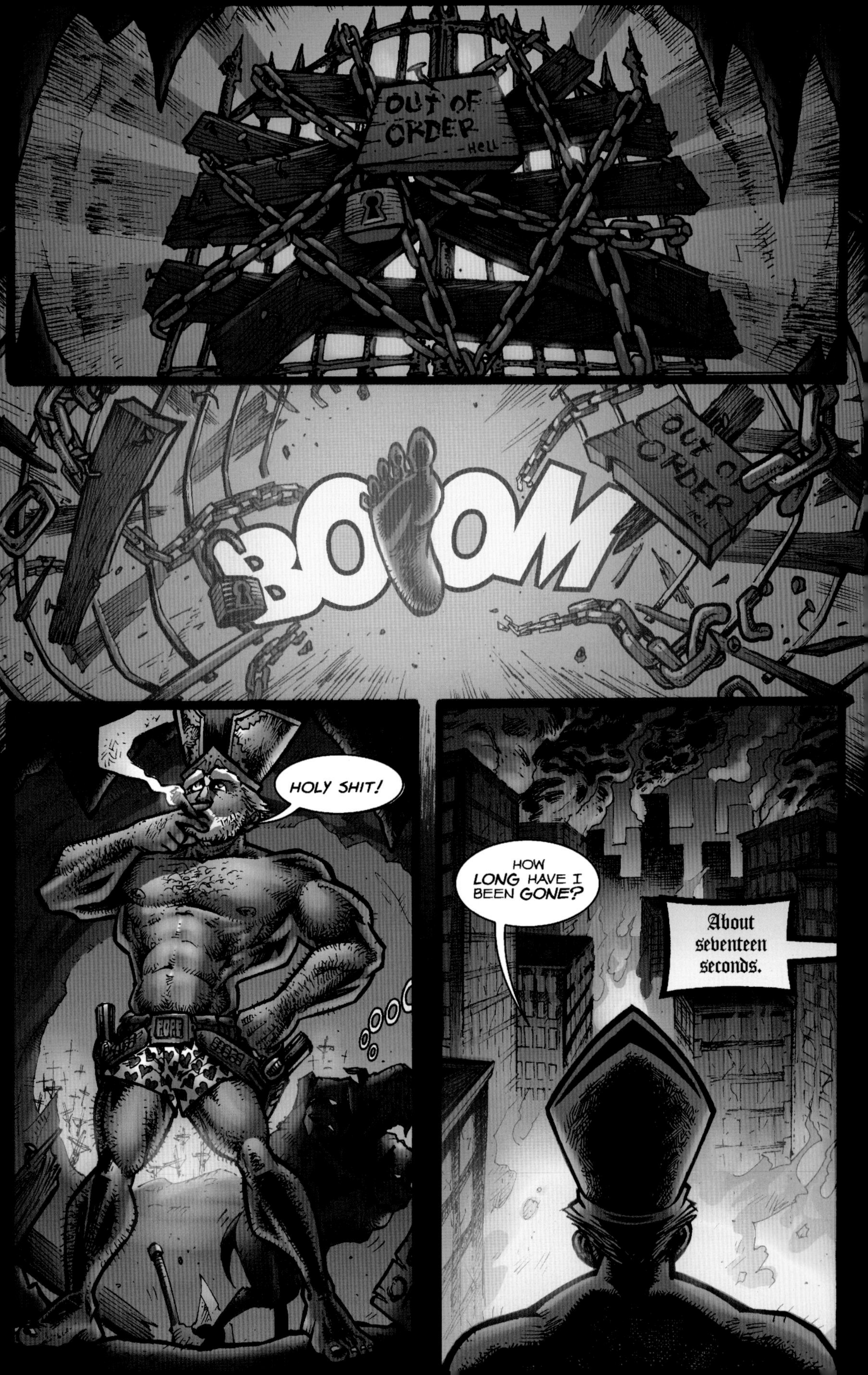
OUT OF ORDER -HELL
BOOM
HOLY SHIT!
HOW LONG HAVE I BEEN GONE?
About seventeen seconds.

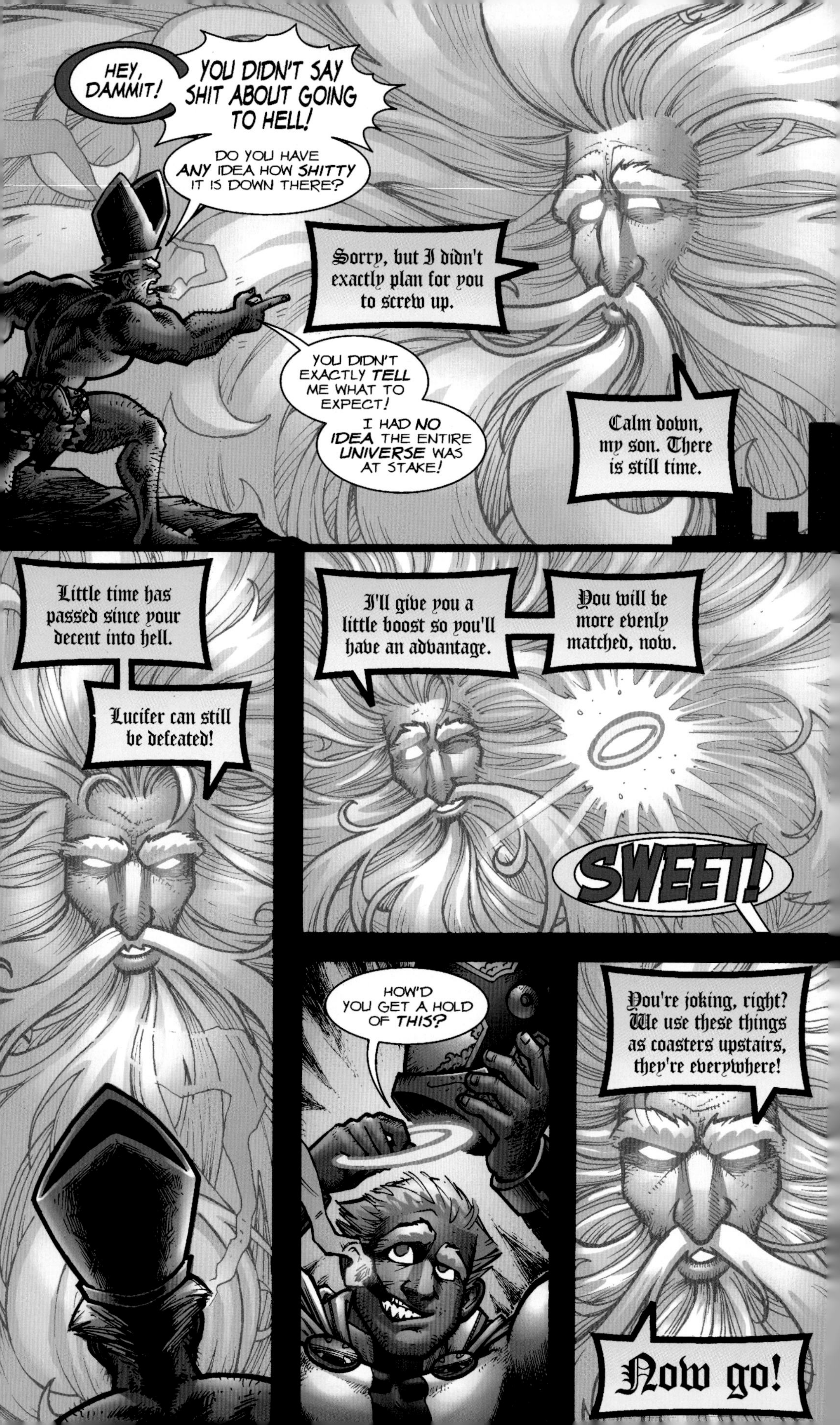
HEY, DAMMIT!
YOU DIDN'T SAY SHIT ABOUT GOING TO HELL!
DO YOU HAVE ANY IDEA HOW SHITTY IT IS DOWN THERE?
Sorry, but I didn't exactly plan for you to screw up.
YOU DIDN'T EXACTLY TELL ME WHAT TO EXPECT!
I HAD NO IDEA THE ENTIRE UNIVERSE WAS AT STAKE!
Calm down, my son. There is still time.
Little time has passed since your decent into hell.
Lucifer can still be defeated!
I'll give you a little boost so you'll have an advantage.
You will be more evenly matched, now.
SWEET!
HOW'D YOU GET A HOLD OF THIS?
You're joking, right? We use these things as coasters upstairs, they're everywhere!
Now go!

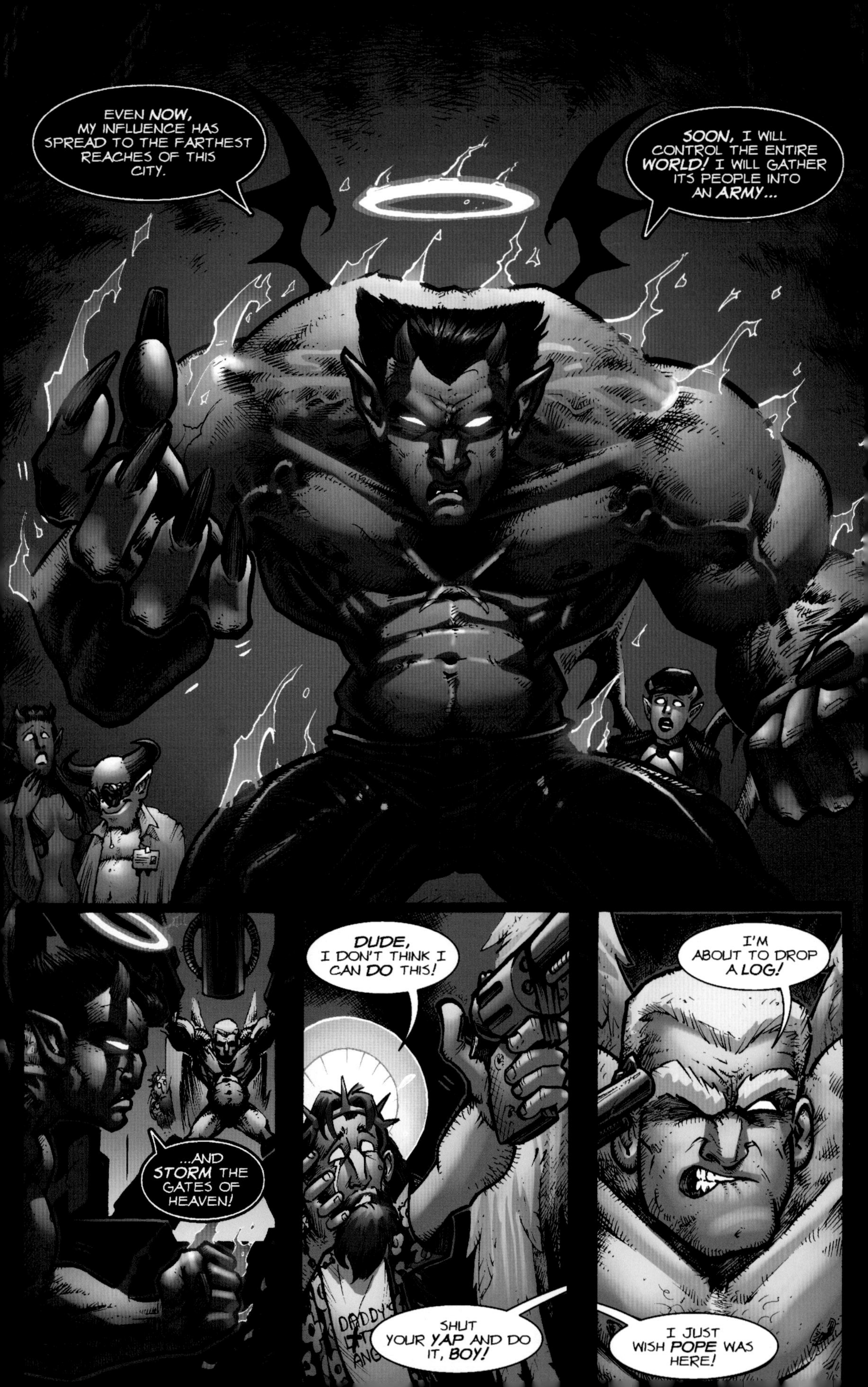
EVEN NOW, MY INFLUENCE HAS SPREAD TO THE FARTHEST REACHES OF THIS CITY.
SOON, I WILL CONTROL THE ENTIRE WORLD! I WILL GATHER ITS PEOPLE INTO AN ARMY...
...AND STORM THE GATES OF HEAVEN!
DUDE, I DON'T THINK I CAN DO THIS!
SHUT YOUR YAP AND DO IT, BOY!
I'M ABOUT TO DROP A LOG!
I JUST WISH POPE WAS HERE!

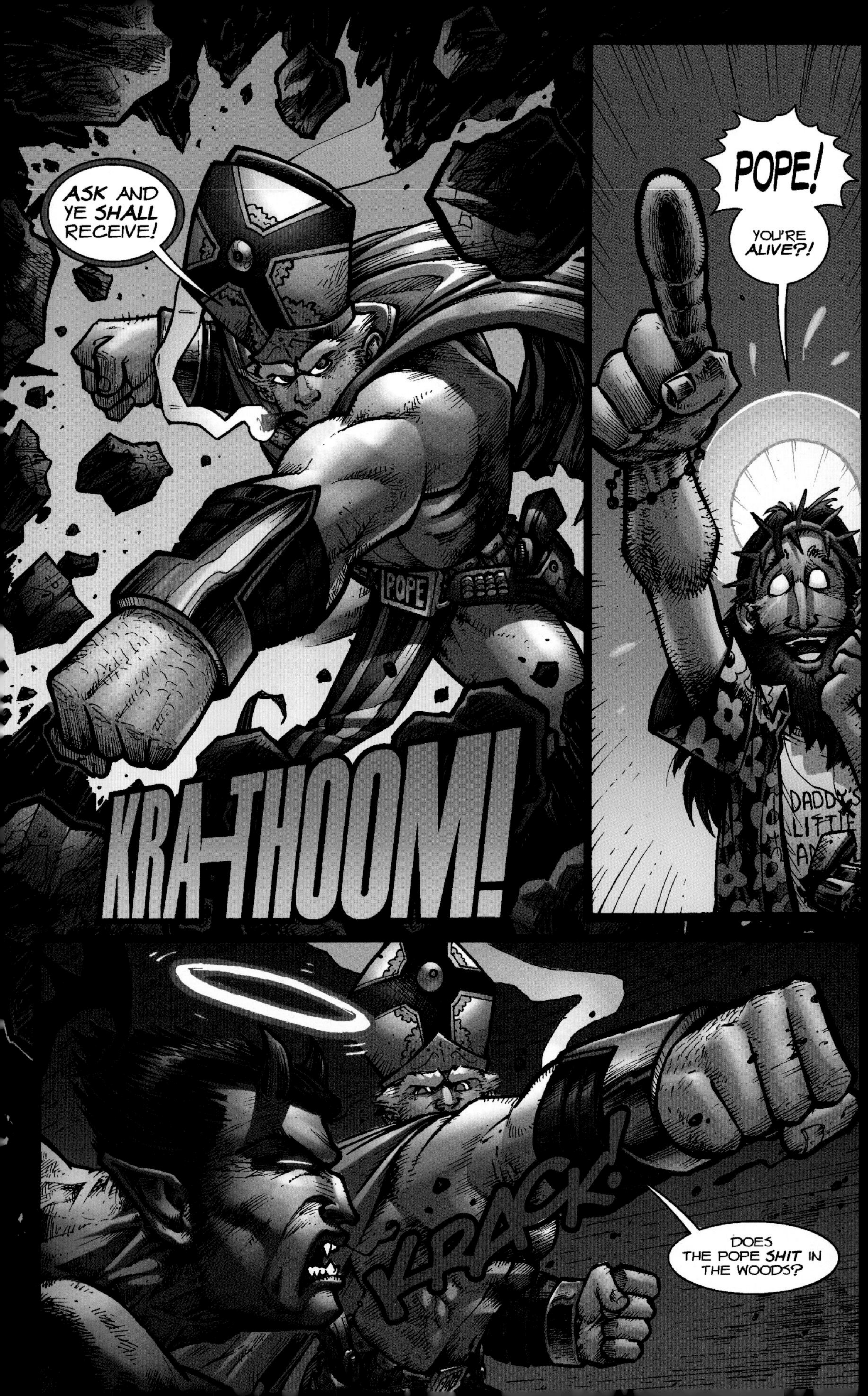
ASK AND YE SHALL RECEIVE!
KRA-THOOM!
POPE!
YOU'RE ALIVE?!
DOES THE POPE SHIT IN THE WOODS?
KRACK!

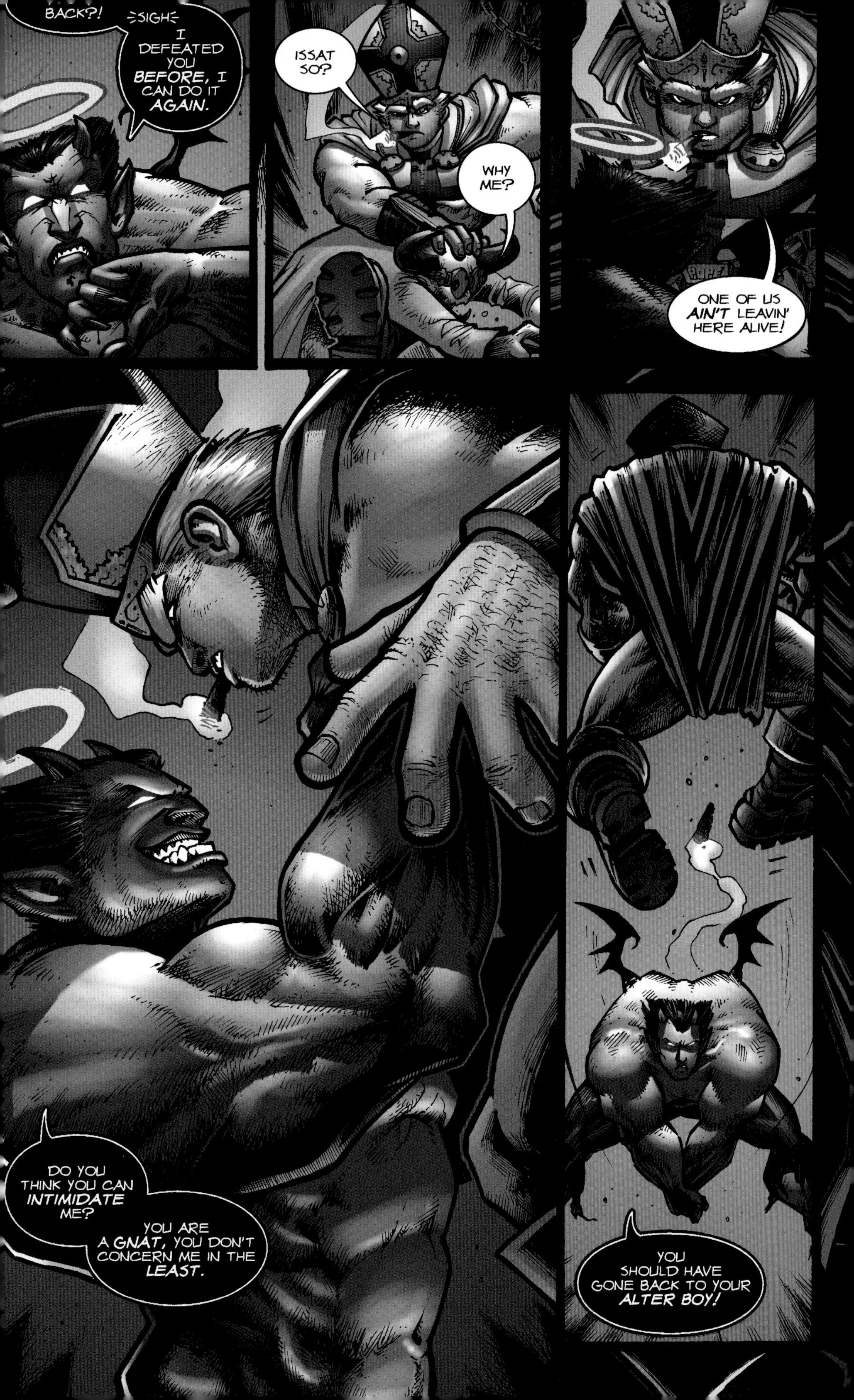
BACK?!
=SIGH=
I DEFEATED YOU BEFORE, I CAN DO IT AGAIN.
ISSAT SO?
WHY ME?
ONE OF US AIN'T LEAVIN' HERE ALIVE!
DO YOU THINK YOU CAN INTIMIDATE ME?
YOU ARE A GNAT, YOU DON'T CONCERN ME IN THE LEAST.
YOU SHOULD HAVE GONE BACK TO YOUR ALTER BOY!

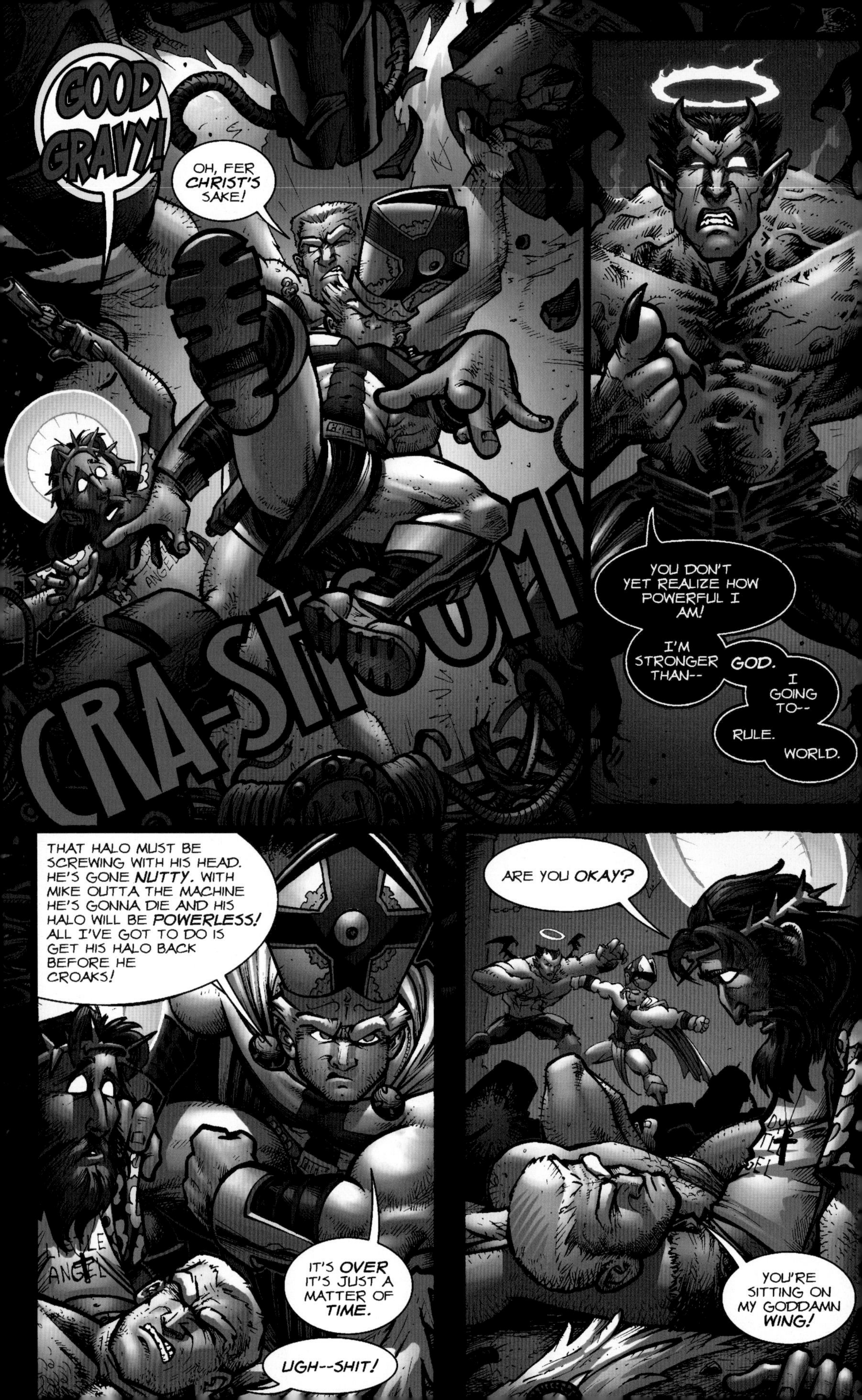
GOOD GRAVY!
OH, FER CHRIST'S SAKE!
CRA-SHOOM!
YOU DON'T YET REALIZE HOW POWERFUL I AM!
I'M STRONGER THAN--
GOD.
I GOING TO--
RULE.
WORLD.
THAT HALO MUST BE SCREWING WITH HIS HEAD. HE'S GONE NUTTY. WITH MIKE OUTTA THE MACHINE HE'S GONNA DIE AND HIS HALO WILL BE POWERLESS! ALL I'VE GOT TO DO IS GET HIS HALO BACK BEFORE HE CROAKS!
IT'S OVER IT'S JUST A MATTER OF TIME.
UGH--SHIT!
ARE YOU OKAY?
YOU'RE SITTING ON MY GODDAMN WING!

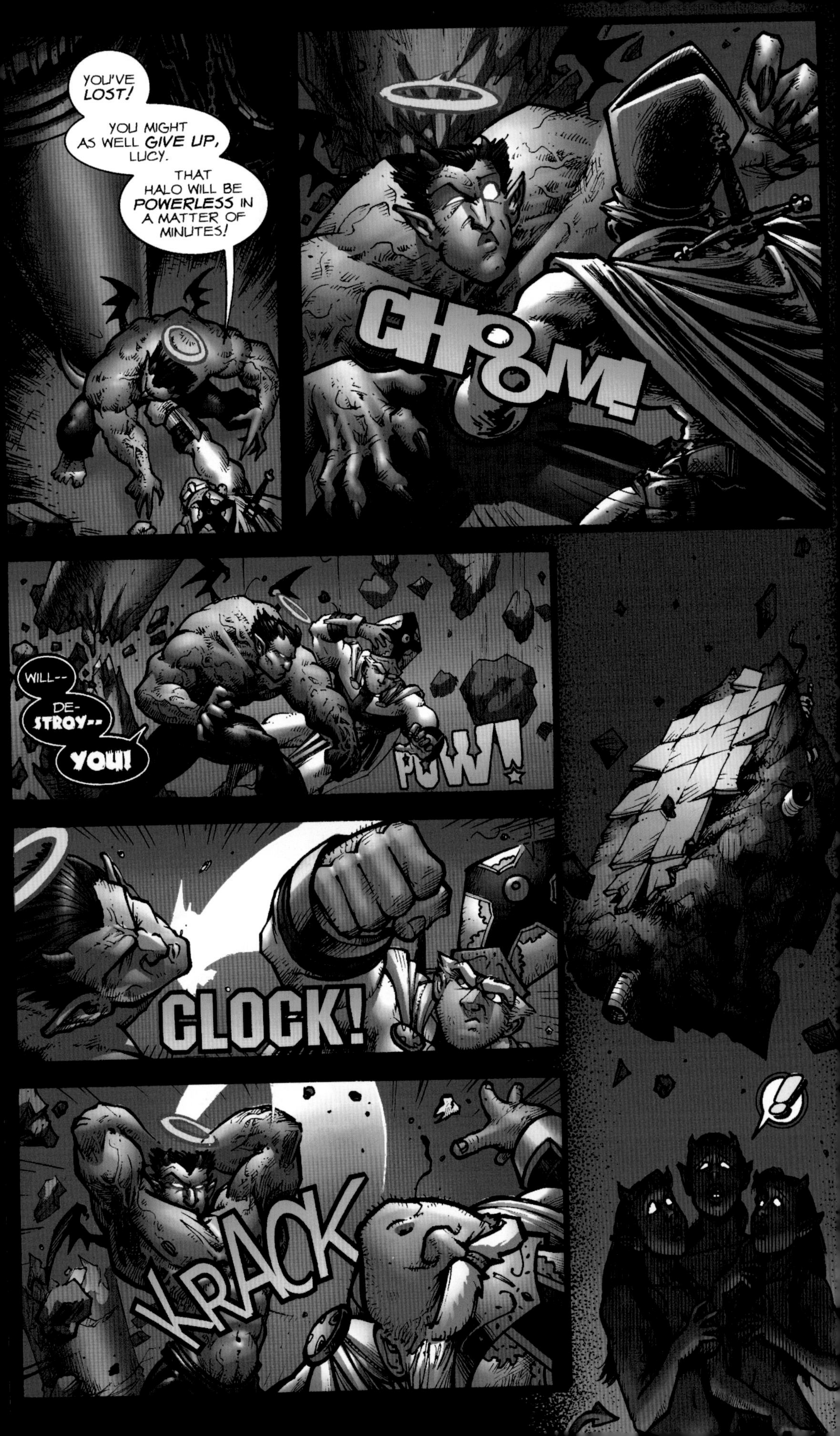

YOU'VE LOST!
YOU MIGHT AS WELL GIVE UP, LUCY.
THAT HALO WILL BE POWERLESS IN A MATTER OF MINUTES!
CHOOM!
WILL--
DE-STROY--
YOU!
POW!
CLOCK!
KRACK
!

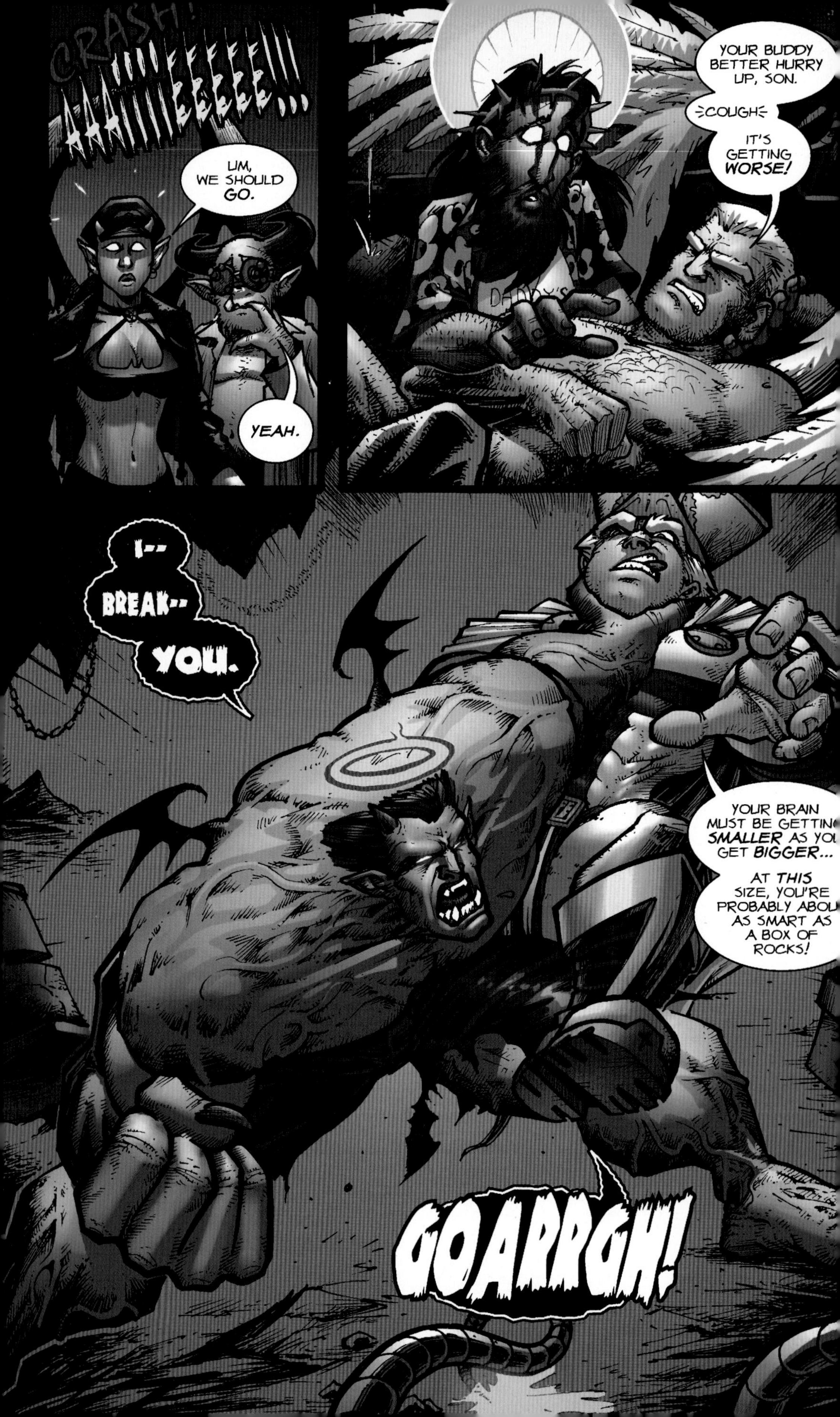
CRASH!
AAAIIIIEEEEE!!!
UM, WE SHOULD GO.
YEAH.
YOUR BUDDY BETTER HURRY UP, SON.
COUGH
IT'S GETTING WORSE!
I-- BREAK-- YOU.
YOUR BRAIN MUST BE GETTING SMALLER AS YOU GET BIGGER...
AT THIS SIZE, YOU'RE PROBABLY ABOUT AS SMART AS A BOX OF ROCKS!
GOARRGH!

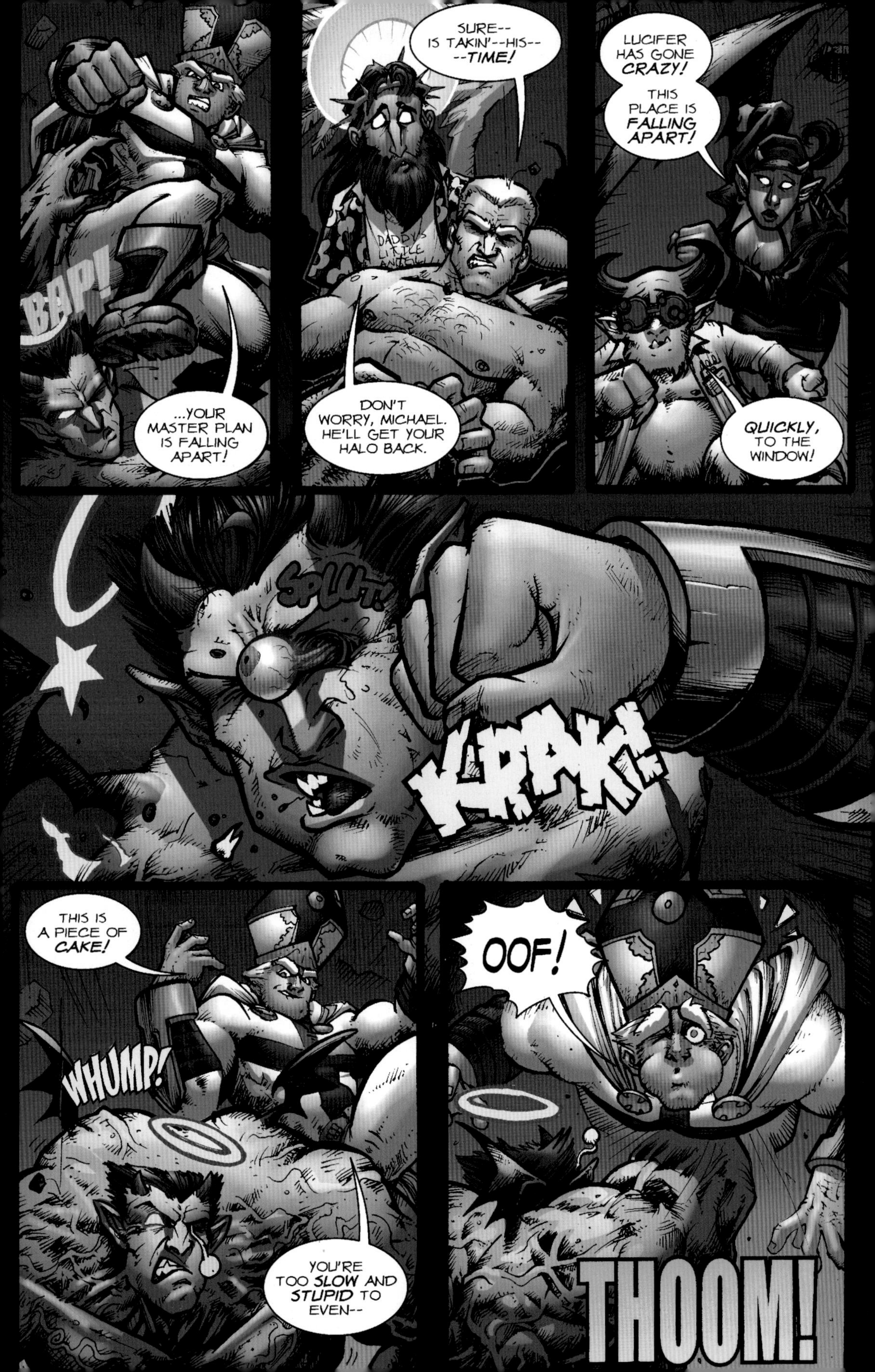
BAP!
...YOUR MASTER PLAN IS FALLING APART!
SURE-- IS TAKIN'--HIS-- --TIME!
DON'T WORRY, MICHAEL. HE'LL GET YOUR HALO BACK.
LUCIFER HAS GONE CRAZY!
THIS PLACE IS FALLING APART!
QUICKLY, TO THE WINDOW!
SPLUT!
KRAK!
THIS IS A PIECE OF CAKE!
WHUMP!
YOU'RE TOO SLOW AND STUPID TO EVEN--
OOF!
THOOM!

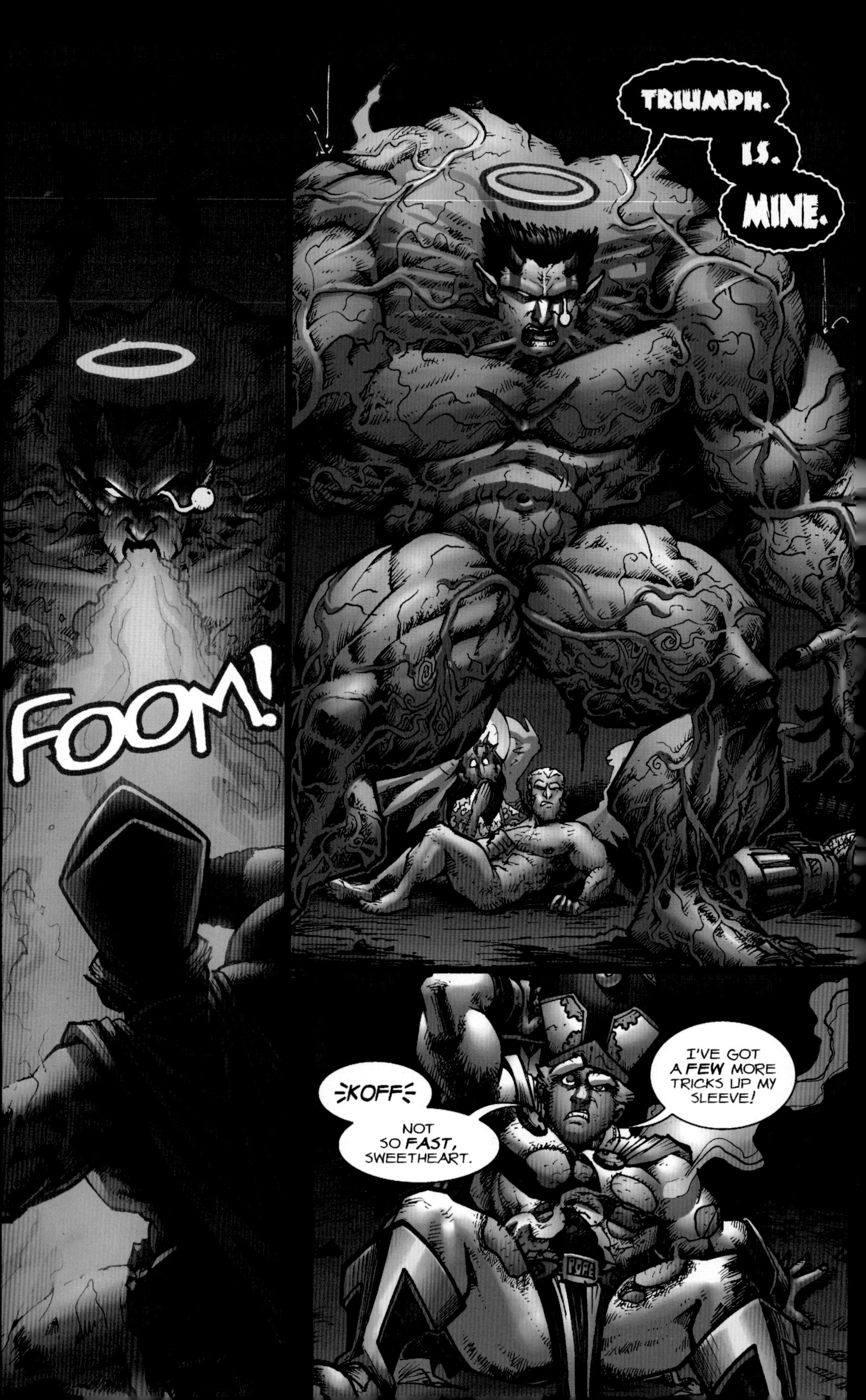
FOOM!
TRIUMPH.
IS.
MINE.
≶KOFF≶
NOT SO FAST, SWEETHEART.
I'VE GOT A FEW MORE TRICKS UP MY SLEEVE!

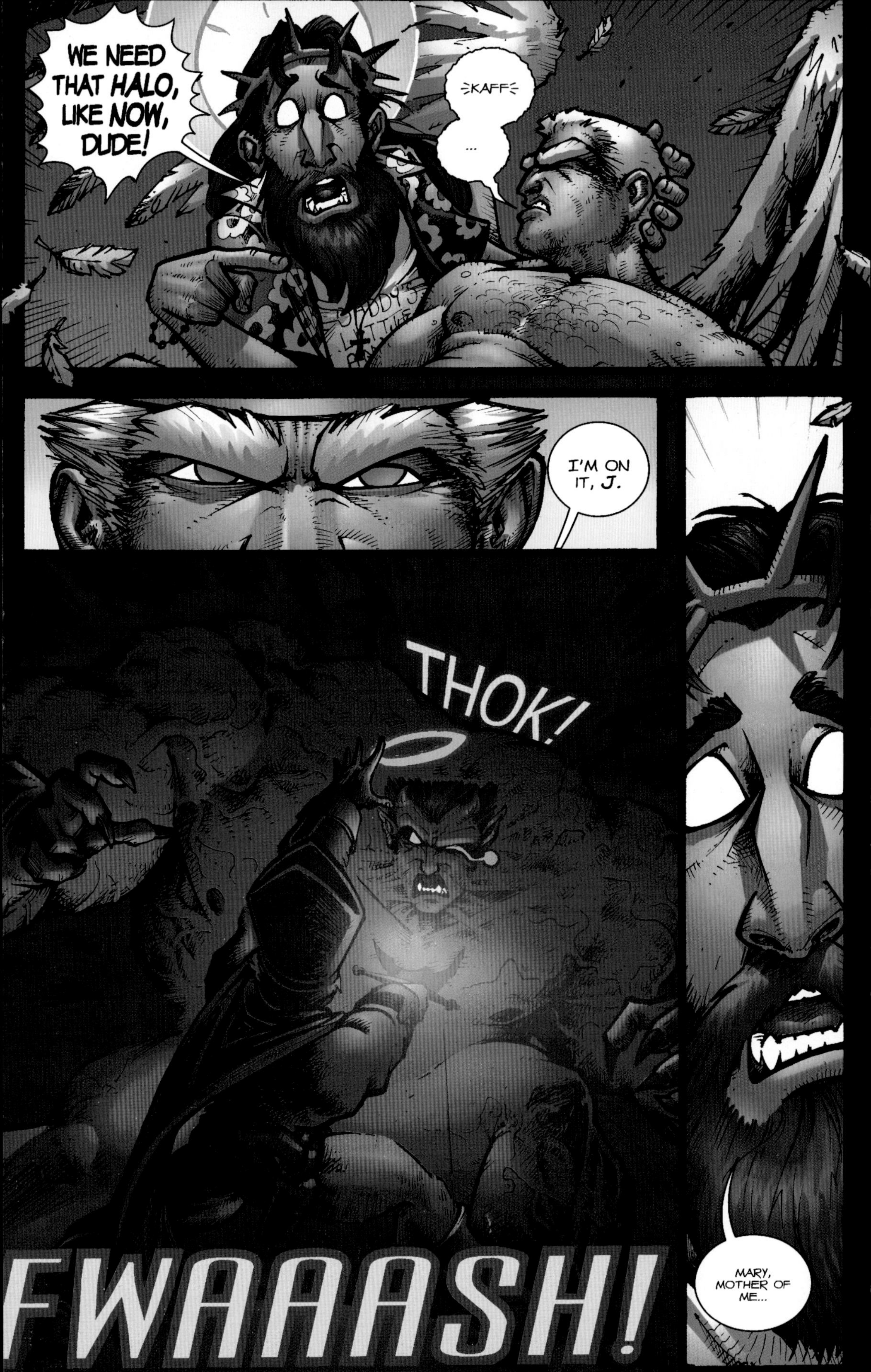
WE NEED THAT HALO, LIKE NOW, DUDE!
KAFF
...
I'M ON IT, J.
THOK!
FWAAASH!
MARY, MOTHER OF ME...

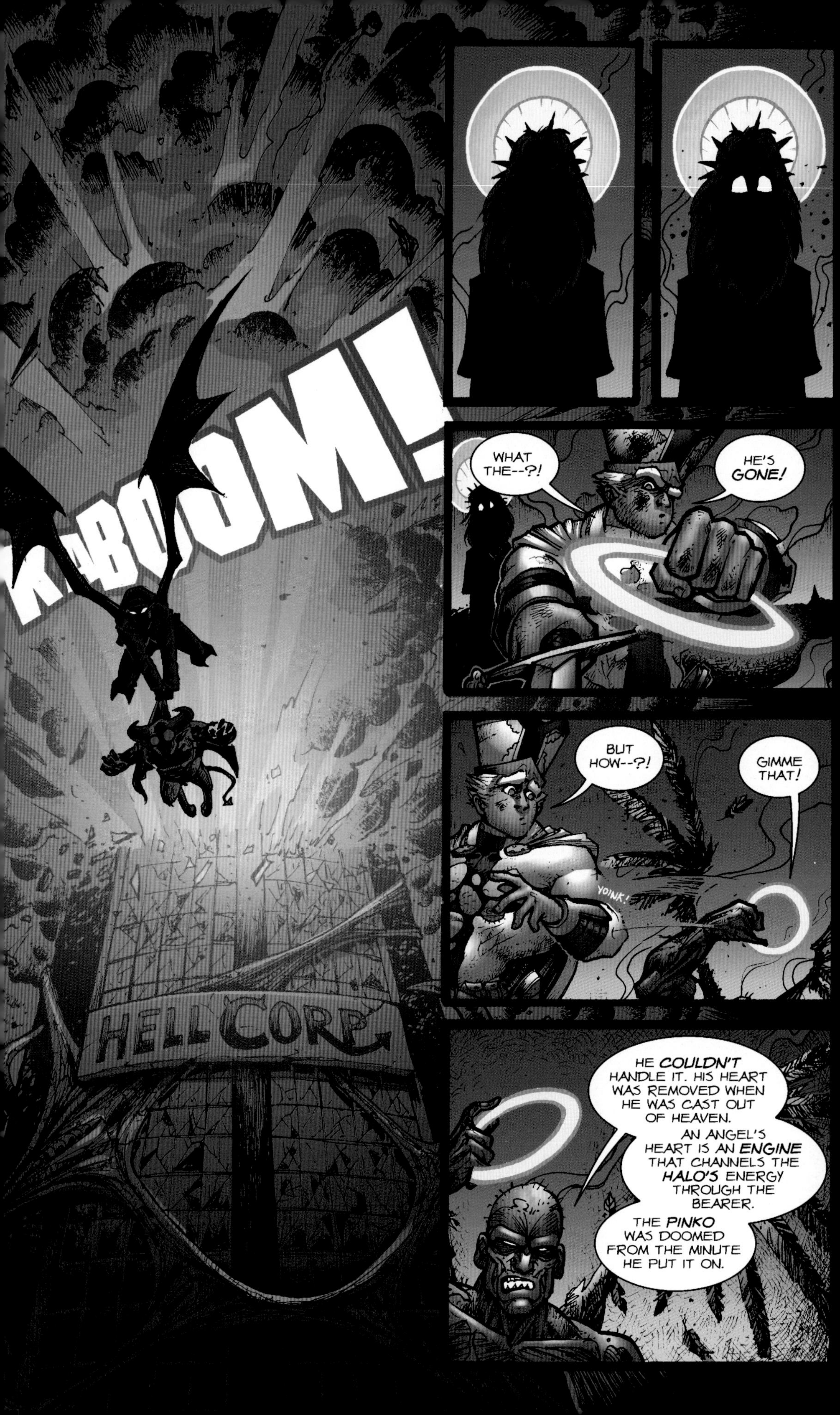
KABOOM!
HELL CORP
WHAT THE--?!
HE'S GONE!
BUT HOW--?!
GIMME THAT!
YOINK!
HE COULDN'T HANDLE IT. HIS HEART WAS REMOVED WHEN HE WAS CAST OUT OF HEAVEN.
AN ANGEL'S HEART IS AN ENGINE THAT CHANNELS THE HALO'S ENERGY THROUGH THE BEARER.
THE PINKO WAS DOOMED FROM THE MINUTE HE PUT IT ON.

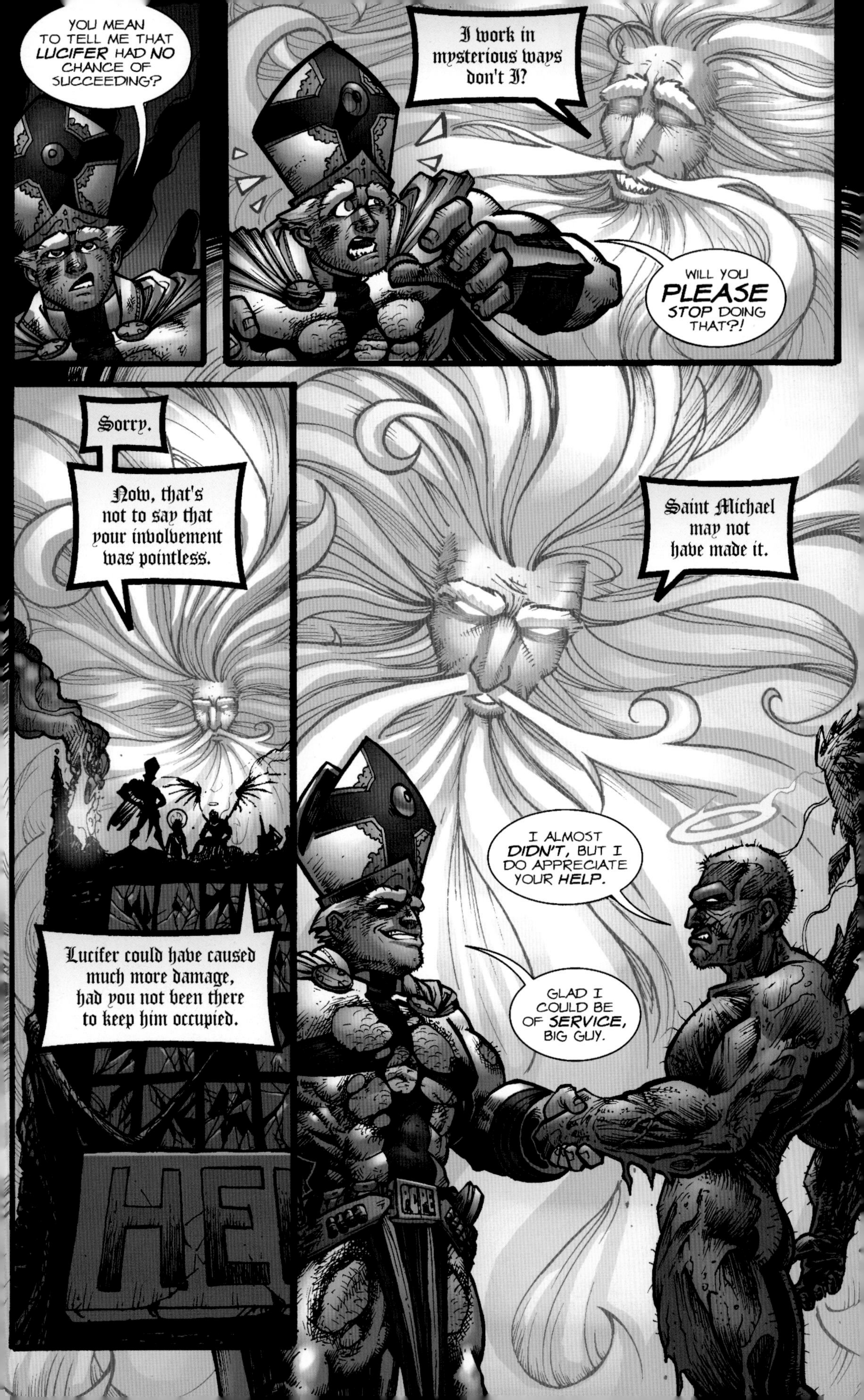
YOU MEAN TO TELL ME THAT LUCIFER HAD NO CHANCE OF SUCCEEDING?
I work in mysterious ways don't I?
WILL YOU PLEASE STOP DOING THAT?!
Sorry.
Now, that's not to say that your involvement was pointless.
Lucifer could have caused much more damage, had you not been there to keep him occupied.
Saint Michael may not have made it.
I ALMOST DIDN'T, BUT I DO APPRECIATE YOUR HELP.
GLAD I COULD BE OF SERVICE, BIG GUY.

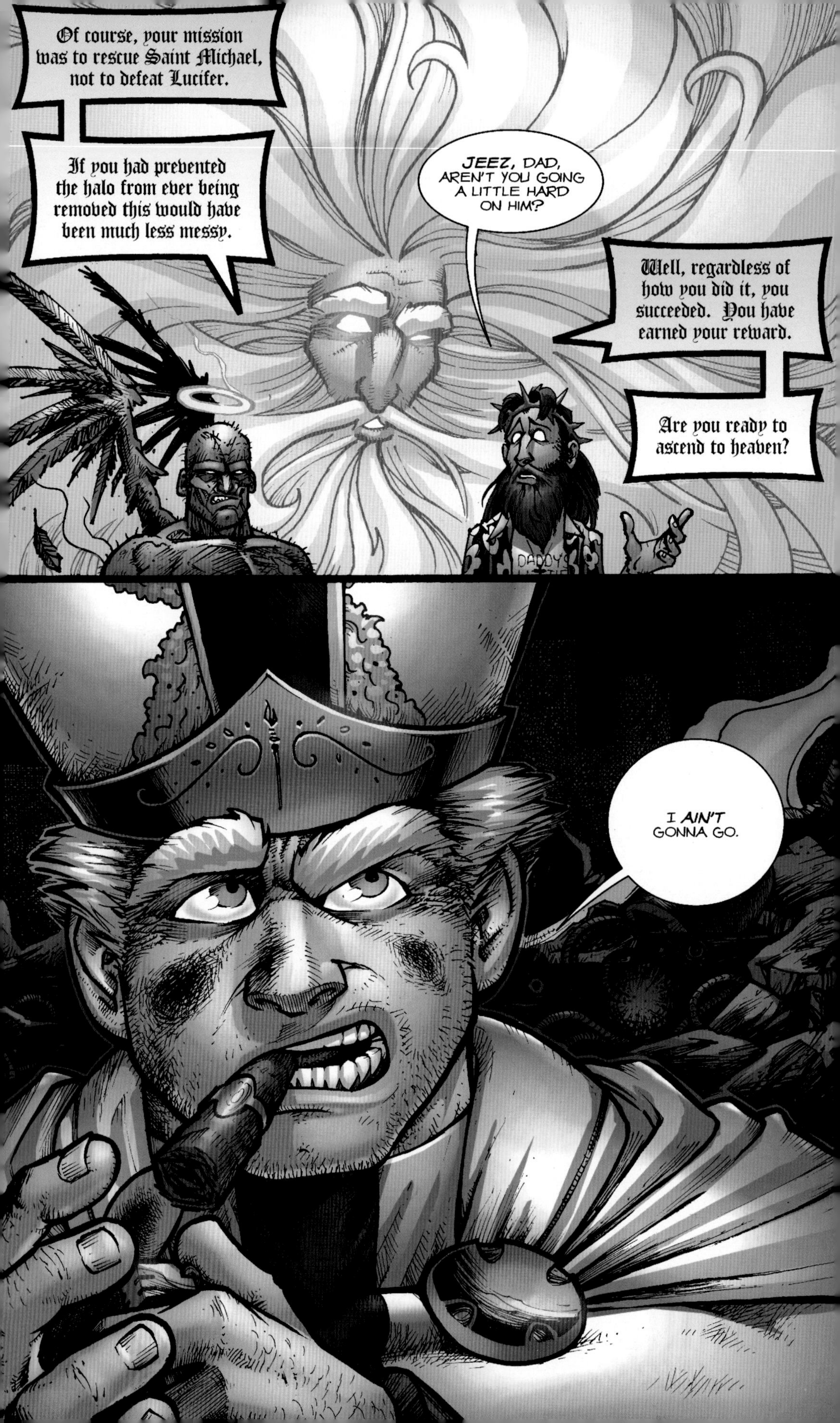
Of course, your mission was to rescue Saint Michael, not to defeat Lucifer.
If you had prevented the halo from ever being removed this would have been much less messy.
JEEZ, DAD, AREN'T YOU GOING A LITTLE HARD ON HIM?
Well, regardless of how you did it, you succeeded. You have earned your reward.
Are you ready to ascend to heaven?
DADDY'S
I AIN'T GONNA GO.

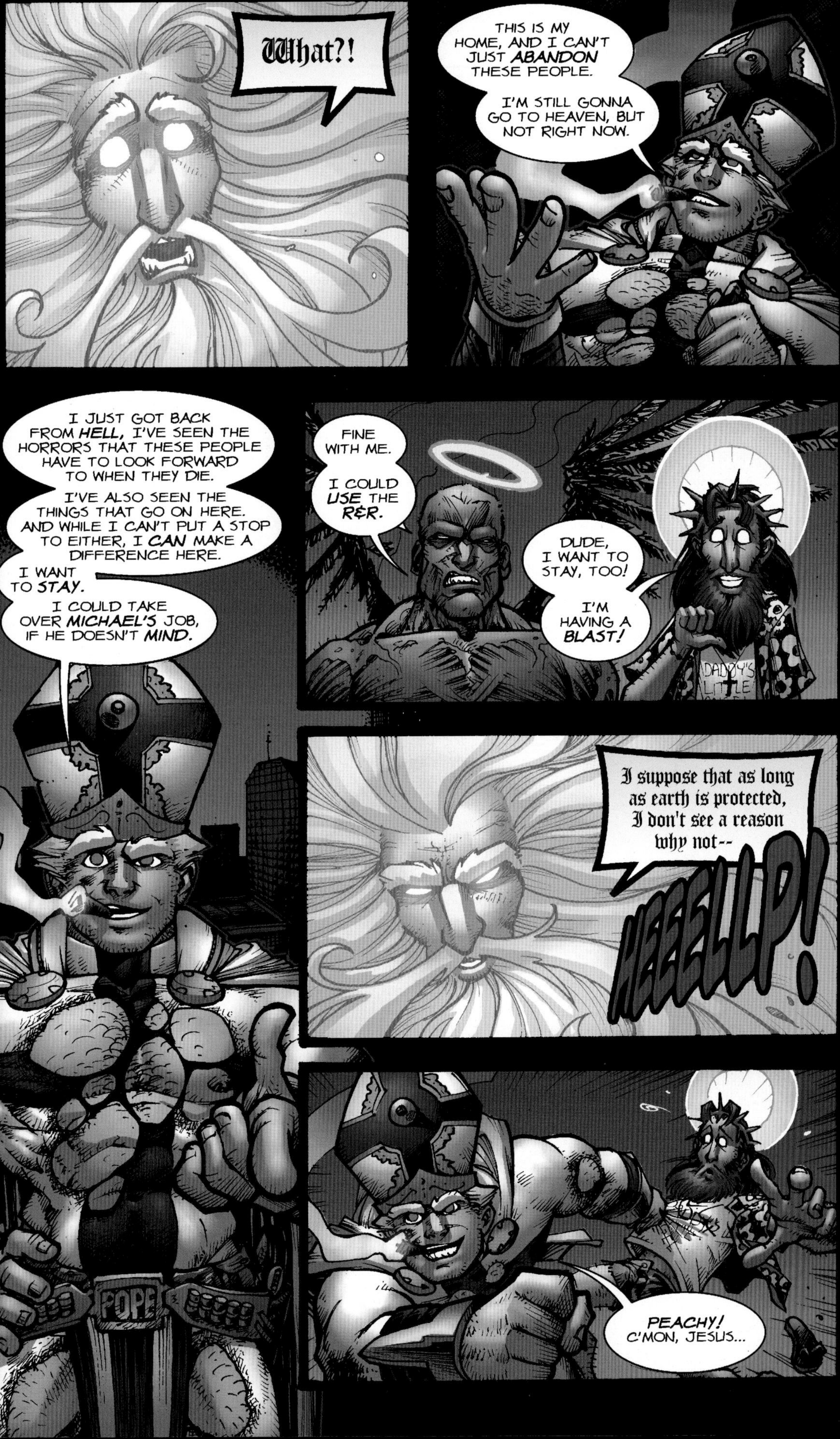
What?!
THIS IS MY HOME, AND I CAN'T JUST ABANDON THESE PEOPLE.
I'M STILL GONNA GO TO HEAVEN, BUT NOT RIGHT NOW.
I JUST GOT BACK FROM HELL, I'VE SEEN THE HORRORS THAT THESE PEOPLE HAVE TO LOOK FORWARD TO WHEN THEY DIE.
I'VE ALSO SEEN THE THINGS THAT GO ON HERE. AND WHILE I CAN'T PUT A STOP TO EITHER, I CAN MAKE A DIFFERENCE HERE.
I WANT TO STAY.
I COULD TAKE OVER MICHAEL'S JOB, IF HE DOESN'T MIND.
FINE WITH ME.
I COULD USE THE R&R.
DUDE, I WANT TO STAY, TOO!
I'M HAVING A BLAST!
DADDY'S LITTLE
I suppose that as long as earth is protected, I don't see a reason why not--
HEEELLP!
POPE
PEACHY! C'MON, JESUS...

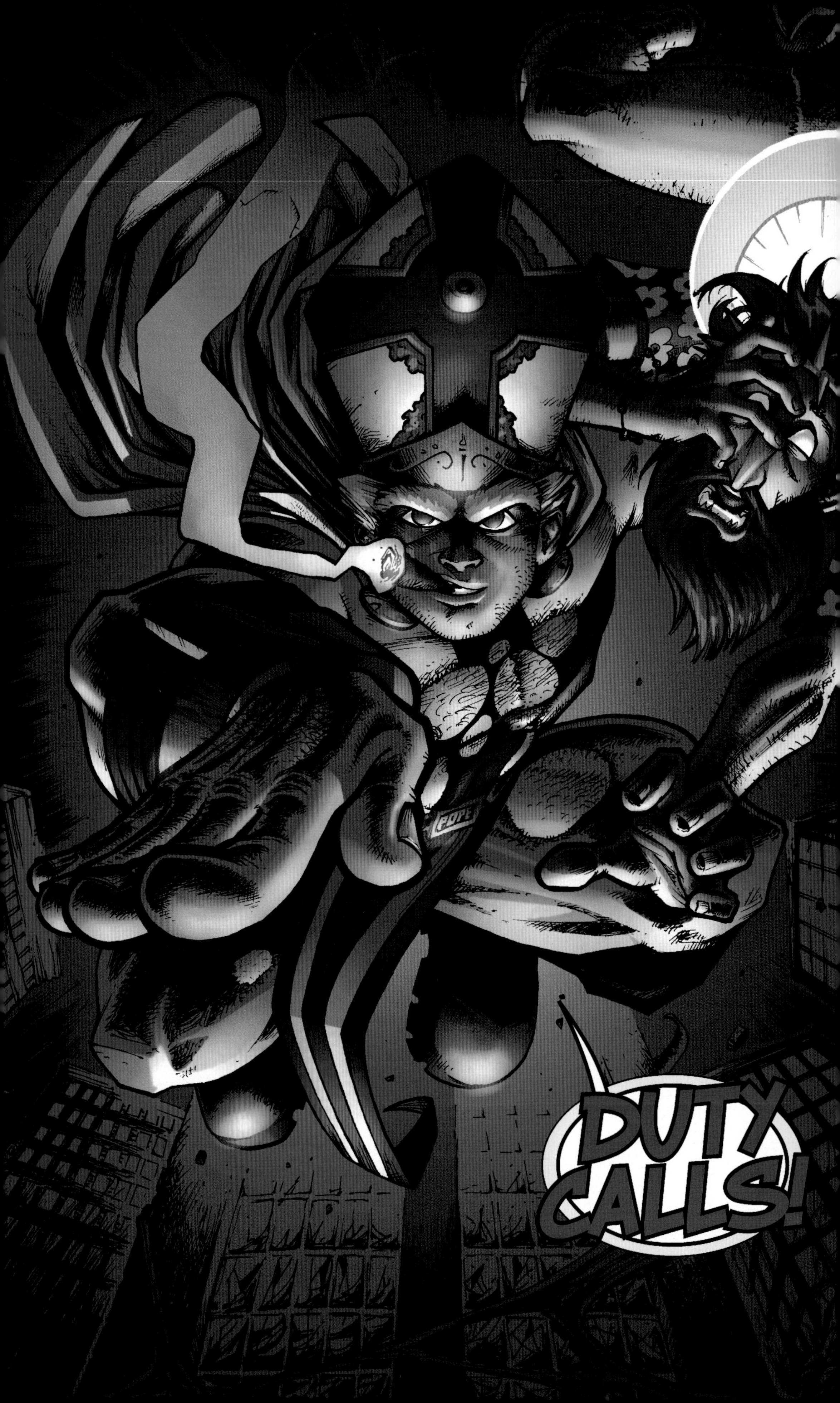
DUTY CALLS!

Sketchbook

Welcome to the Battle Pope Volume 1 sketchbook. As I'm sure most of you know this is a color reprint of an old black and white series Tony Moore and I did way back in the year 2000. We also did a trade paperback then. All the sketches and most of the commentary seen here are from that old volume (I wouldn't have remembered all this stuff).

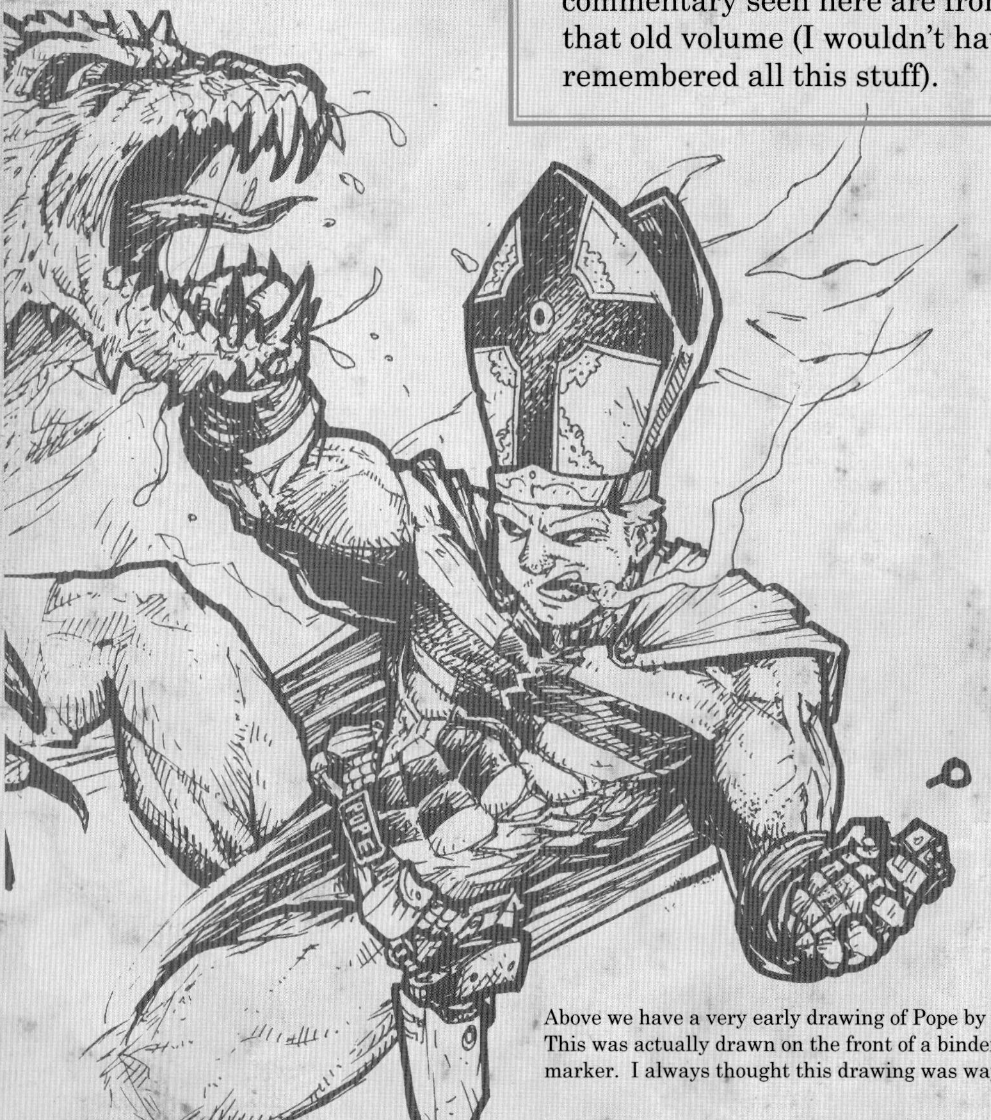

POPE

Above we have a very early drawing of Pope by Tony. This was actually drawn on the front of a binder in marker. I always thought this drawing was way cool

This is a page from Tony's sketchbook featuring art used in the original Battle Pope Website. The whole site was done before the first issue was started so it's no surprise it looks almost nothing like the Pope we all know and love today.

A lot of time and effort was put into that old Battle Pope Website. To my knowledge, the sketches here are all that remain of it.

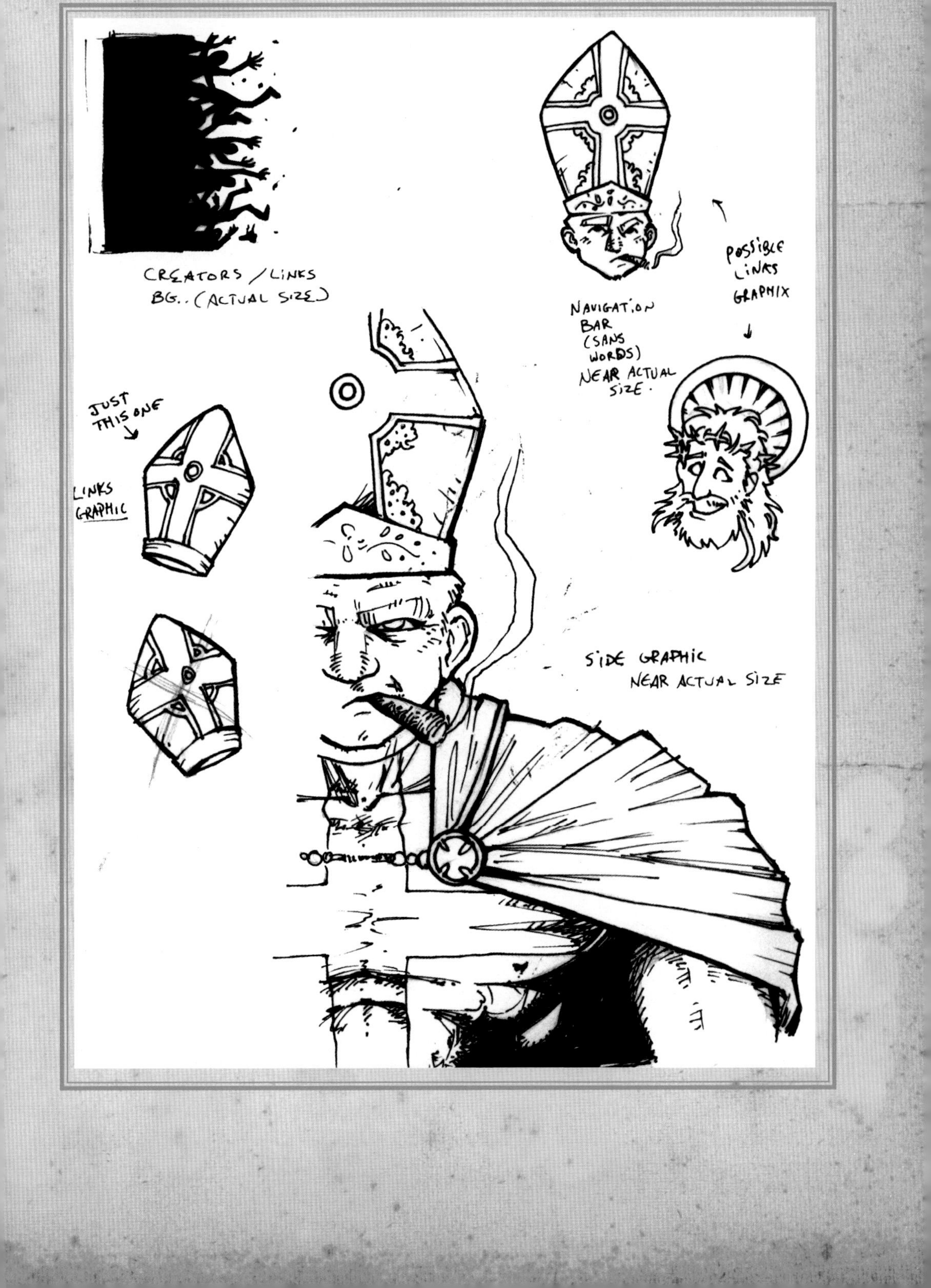

CREATORS / LINKS
BG.. (ACTUAL SIZE)
NAVIGATION BAR (SANS WORDS) NEAR ACTUAL SIZE.
POSSIBLE LINKS GRAPHIX
JUST THIS ONE
LINKS GRAPHIC
SIDE GRAPHIC
NEAR ACTUAL SIZE

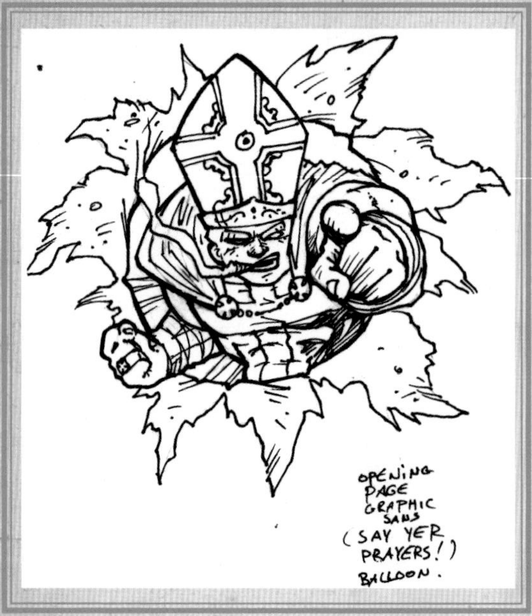
OPENING PAGE GRAPHIC SANS (SAY YER PRAYERS!) BALLOON.

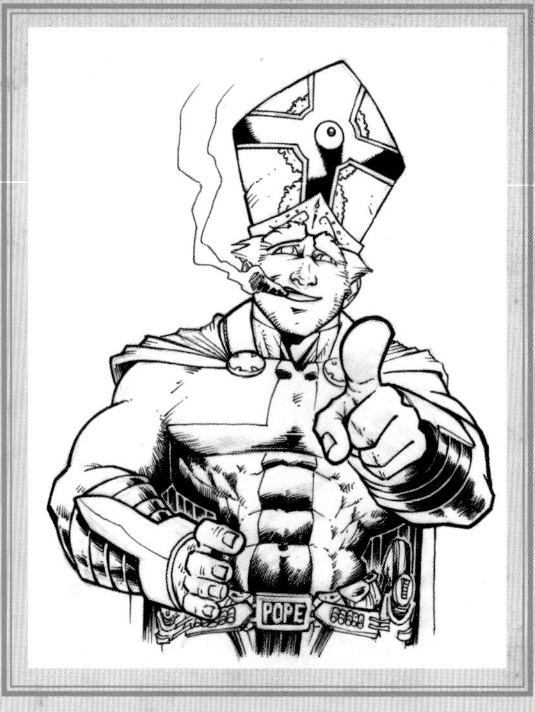
POPE

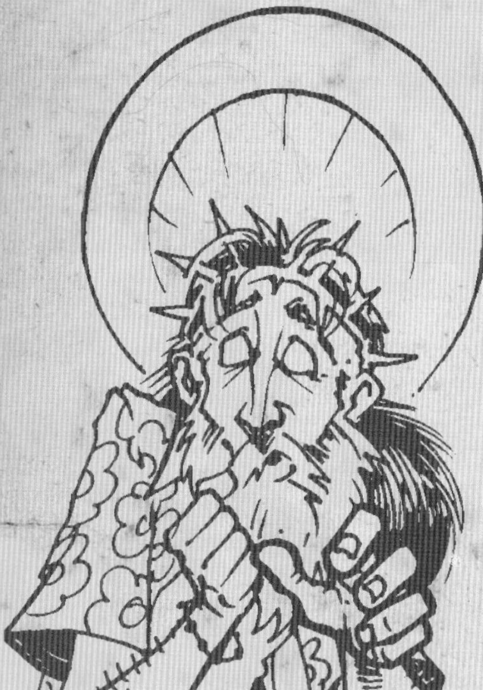

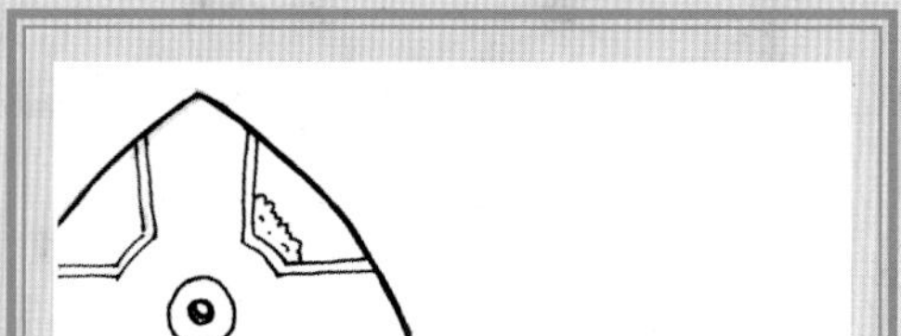

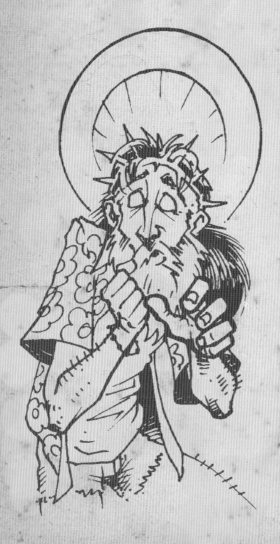

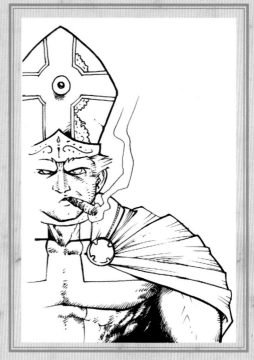

Here you'll see an illustration of Pope used for the opening page of the Website. Also, we have new art used for the updated Battle Pope Website (one of many). Note the smaller nose and the miter's more stylish fit, bringing Pope closer to how he actually looked in the comic. The Jesus drawing here was slotted behind Pope on the main page of the Website. I thought it would be negligent to leave the Son of God off the main page.

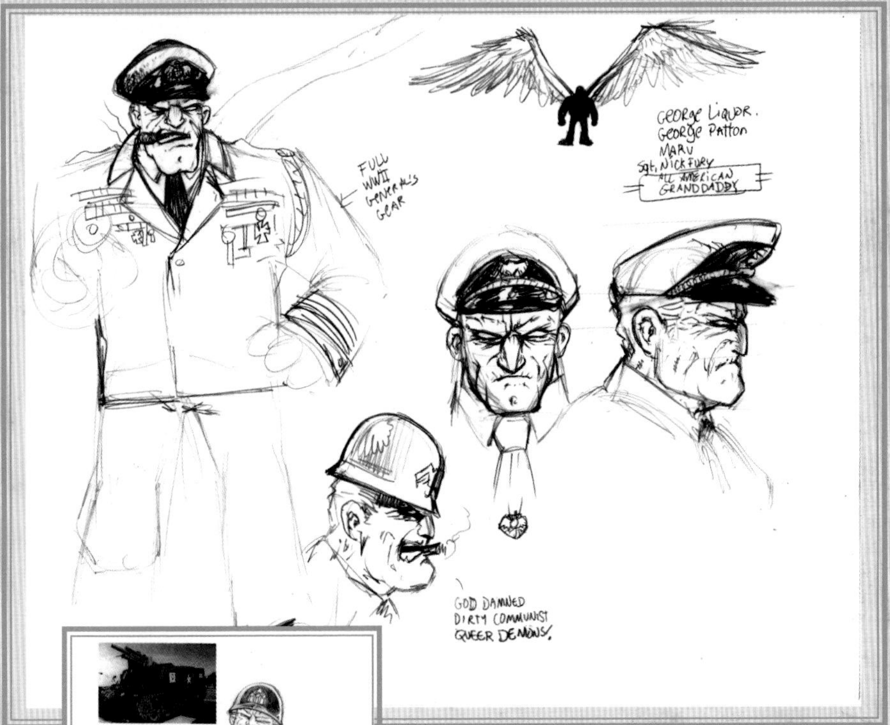
FULL WWII GENERAL'S GEAR
GEORGE LIQUOR.
GEORGE PATTON
MARV
Sgt. NICK FURY
ALL AMERICAN GRANDDADDY
GOD DAMNED DIRTY COMMUNIST QUEER DEMONS!

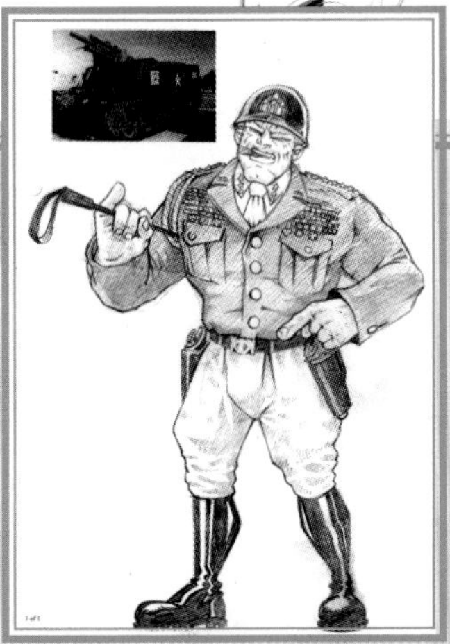

Some early style sheets for Pope and Michael here. Mike was changed pretty drastically before appearing in the book. Hell, so was Pope... look at those ears! Mike was created completely by Tony, also on this page is an early drawing of what Tony thought he should look like. He's a lot thinner and younger in the book. When we started on Pope I had the rough outline of the story ready. It was "Pope and Jesus are sent by God to fight Lucifer--who's on Earth for some reason." When Tony created Saint Michael... that was the missing piece I needed to give the story purpose. I came up with a back-story for Mike and the rescue mission story was complete.

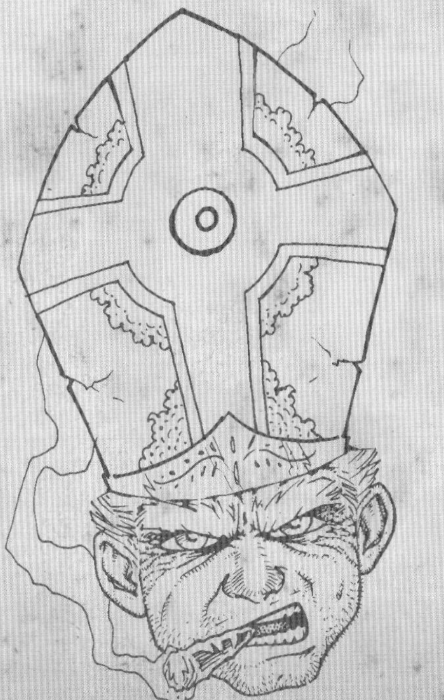

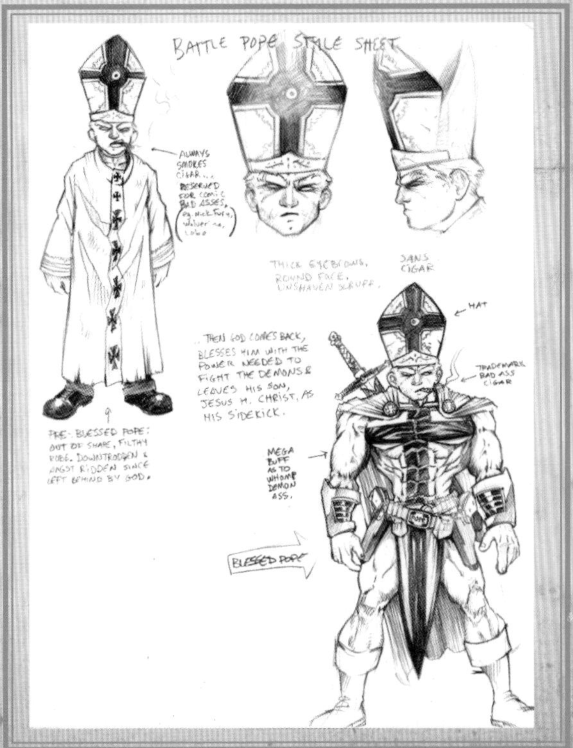
BATTLE POPE STYLE SHEET
ALWAYS SMOKES CIGAR... RESERVED FOR COMIC BAD ASSES, (eg. Nick Fury, Wolverine, Lobo)
THICK EYEBROWS, ROUND FACE, UNSHAVEN SCRUFF.
SANS CIGAR
HAT
THEN GOD COMES BACK, BLESSES HIM WITH THE POWER NEEDED TO FIGHT THE DEMONS & LEAVES HIS SON, JESUS H. CHRIST, AS HIS SIDEKICK.
TRADEMARK BAD ASS CIGAR
PRE-BLESSED POPE: OUT OF SHAPE, FILTHY ROBE. DOWNTRODDEN & ANGST RIDDEN SINCE LEFT BEHIND BY GOD.
MEGA BUFF AS TO WHOMP DEMON ASS.
BLESSED POPE

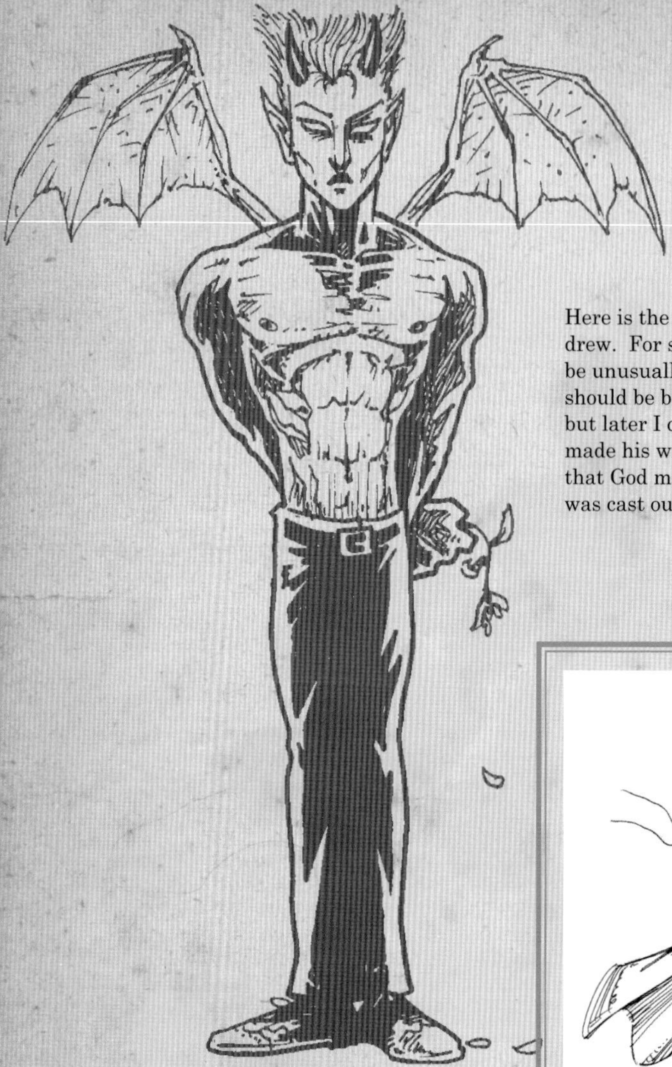

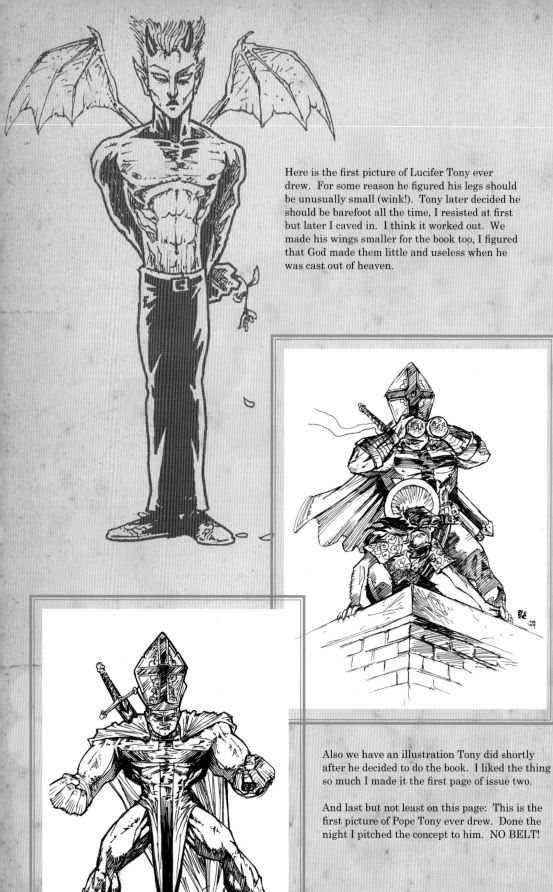

Here is the first picture of Lucifer Tony ever drew. For some reason he figured his legs should be unusually small (wink!). Tony later decided he should be barefoot all the time, I resisted at first but later I caved in. I think it worked out. We made his wings smaller for the book too, I figured that God made them little and useless when he was cast out of heaven.

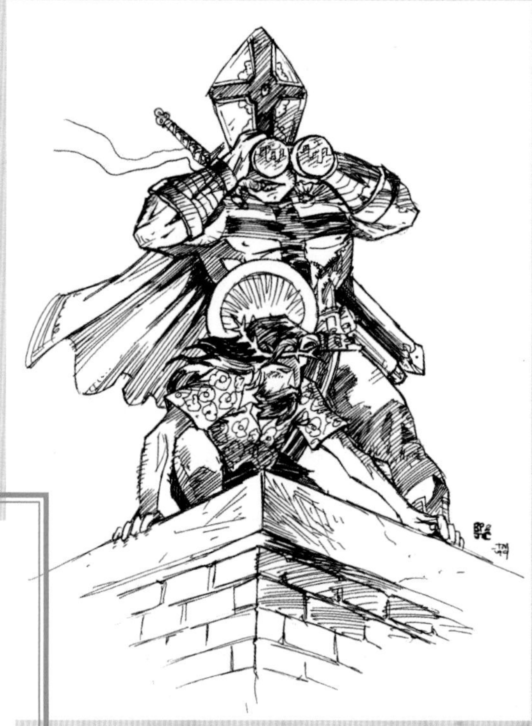

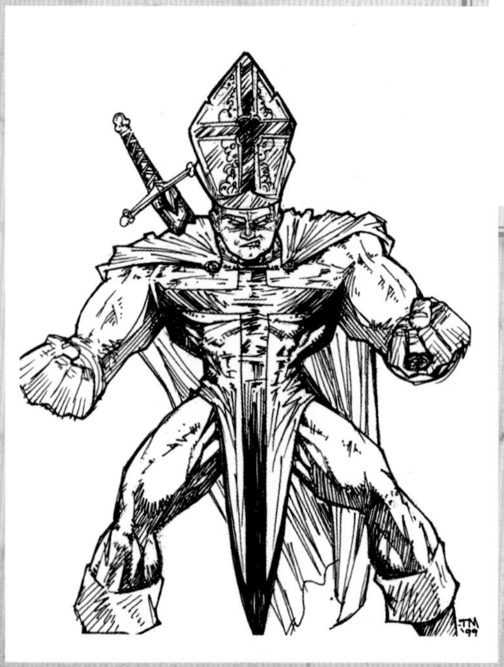

Also we have an illustration Tony did shortly after he decided to do the book. I liked the thing so much I made it the first page of issue two.

And last but not least on this page: This is the first picture of Pope Tony ever drew. Done the night I pitched the concept to him. NO BELT!

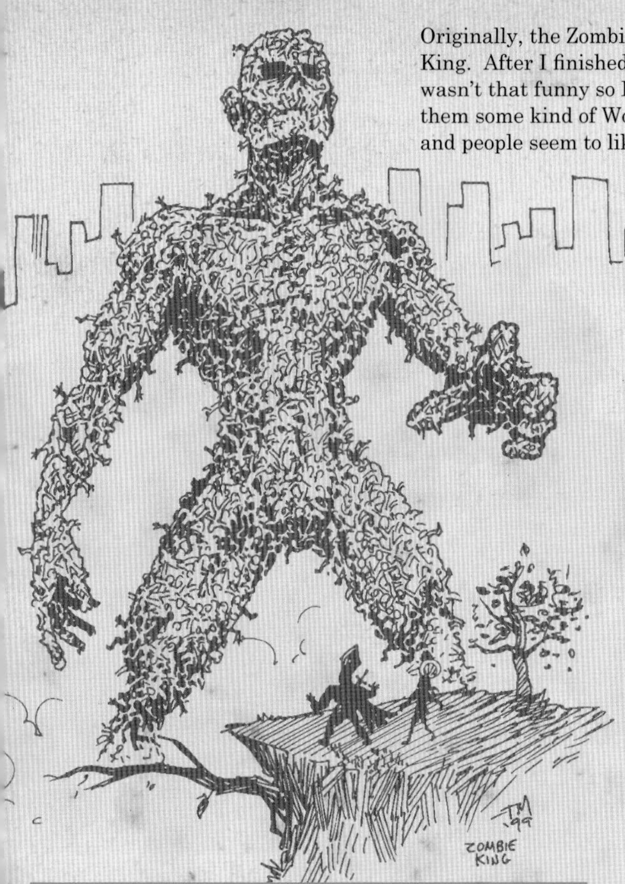
TM '99
ZOMBIE KING

Originally, the Zombie Twins were one character, called the Zombie King. After I finished plotting the second issue, I decided that it wasn't that funny so I split him into two guys. I decided to make them some kind of Wonder Twins spoof. I figured it would be funny and people seem to like the "Zombie Twins, unite!" gag. Tony was originally against the split. He said the name "Zombie King" was too cool to replace. Fast-forward five years and Frank Cho does his damn Zombie King book. Now I guess I can't do crap with the name. Oh, well.

My idea for the Zombie Twins was for them to be made up of motorcycle engines and gears and stuff. With Belaam getting the cybernetic arm and jaw it kinda worked for all of Lucifer's henchmen to be cybernetic in some way. As mentioned before, Tony hated the "Zombie Twins" so much he wanted to change the name to "Zombot Twins" I thought it was too much. He has since warmed up to them; they're pretty popular.

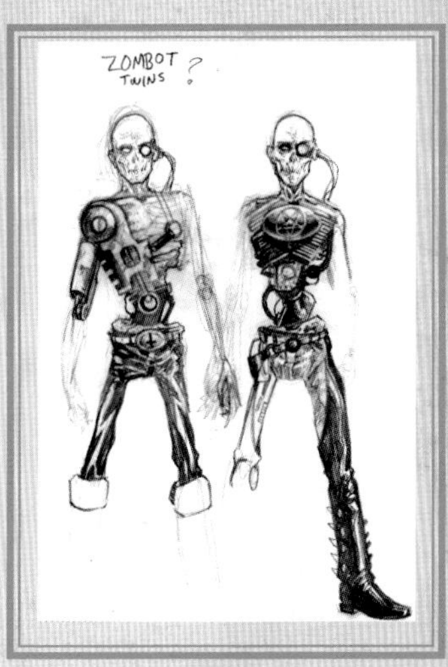
ZOMBOT TWINS ?

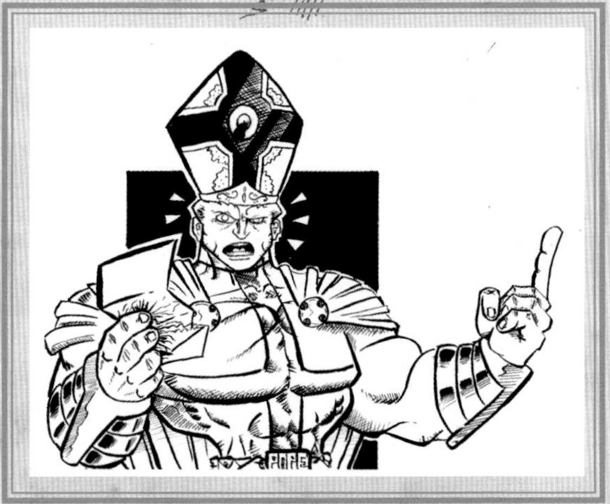

This is a little Pope illustration I did for the letter column of issue one. I used it for issue 2 also, although later I decided it took up too much space and resorted back to the Pope and Jesus heads Tony drew for the website. I used those EVERYWHERE.

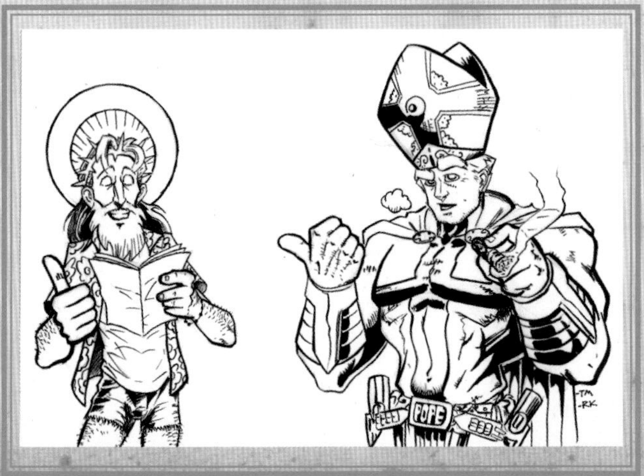
POPE
-TM
-RK

Tony penciled this and I inked it. We used it on the Savage Dragon ads we put in the original mini-series. Everyone who knows me knows that I'm a HUGE Dragon fan so when we started putting Battle Pope together I contacted Erik Larsen about putting the ads in the book for free. He said it was cool, I think they helped make us look a tad more professional somehow. I always have an ulterior motive. (This part was written five years ago. I was sucking up to Erik Larsen WAY before he was the publisher at Image).

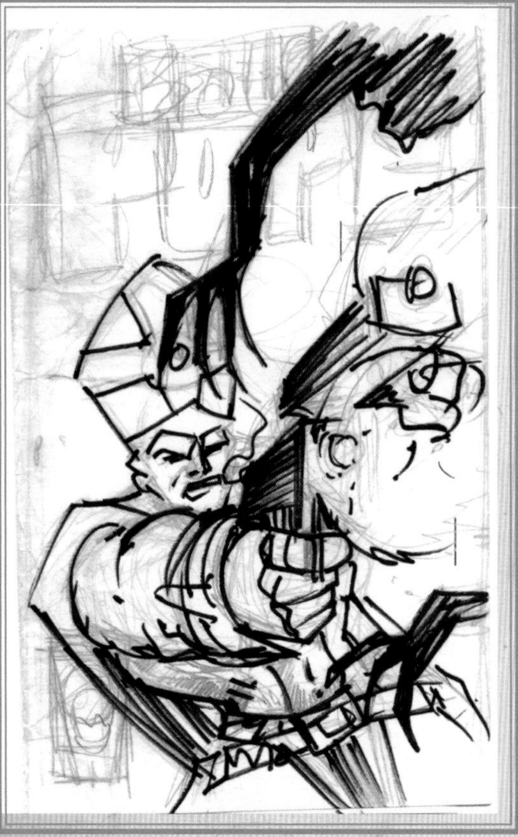

The layouts for the covers to Battle Pope issue 3 by Tony and issue 4 by me.

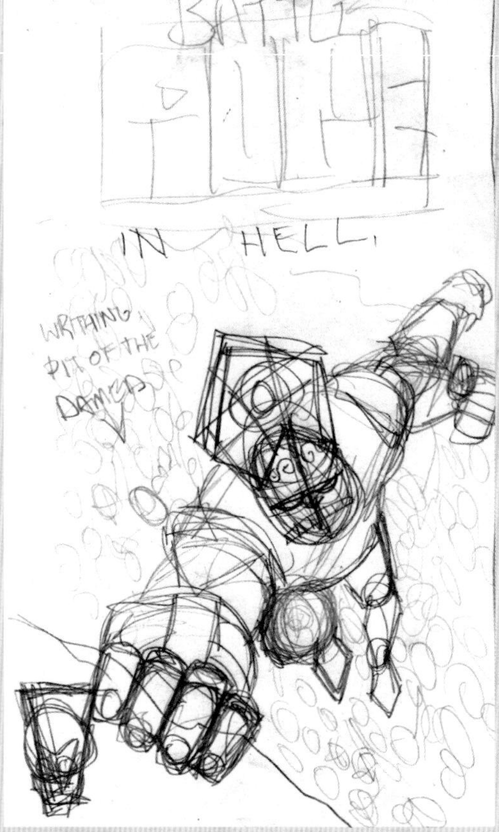
BATTLE
POPE
IN HELL
WRITHING PIT OF THE DAMNED

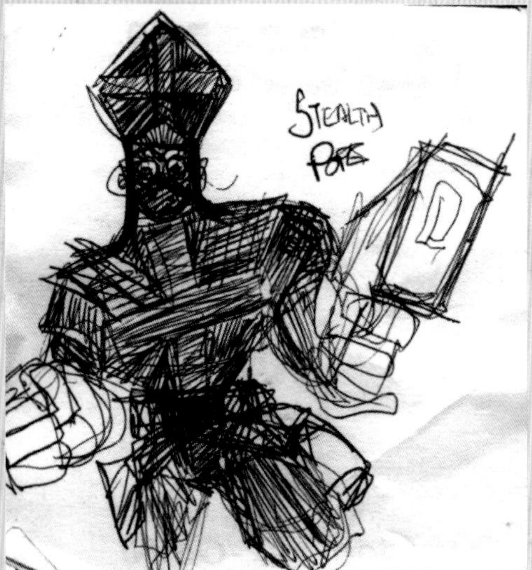
STEALTH POPE

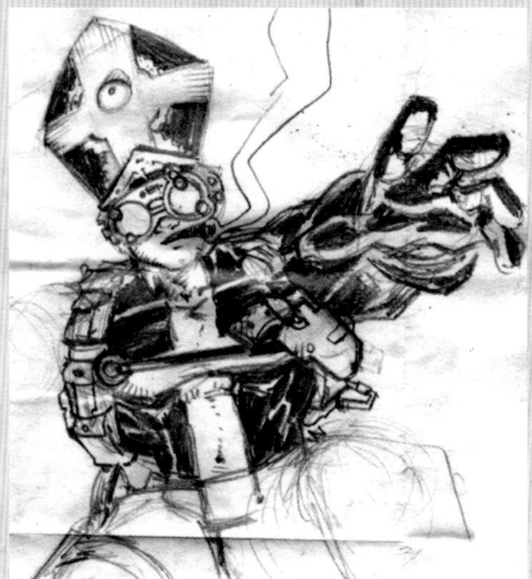

Also on this page, Tony showed up at my house with a sketch of "stealth Pope" he did for fun. I then pulled out my sketch of the same thing! Great minds think alike... or something.

Here is a manga doodle of Pope and Jesus by Tony.

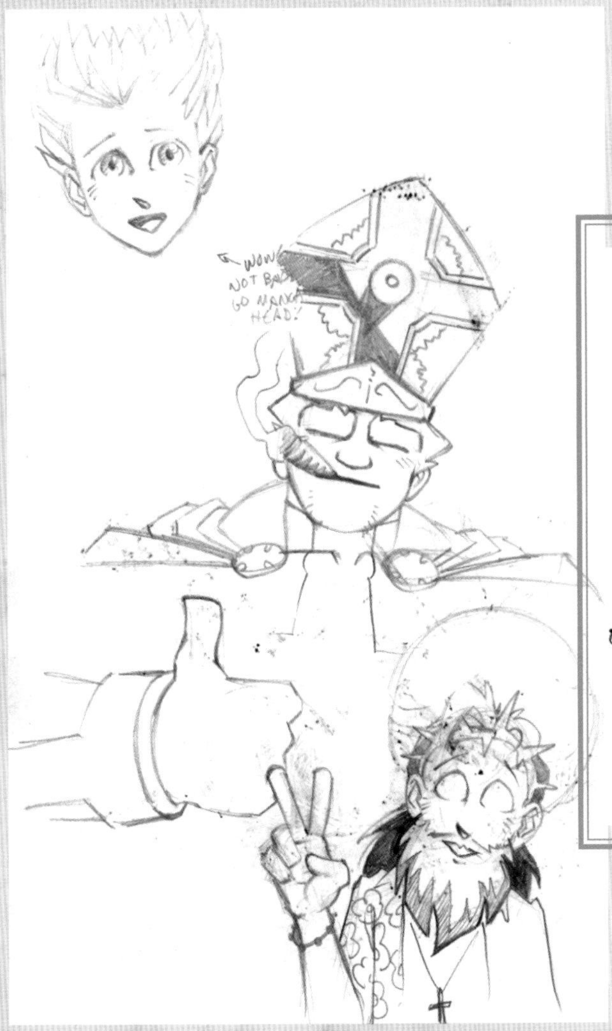
WOW
HEAD!

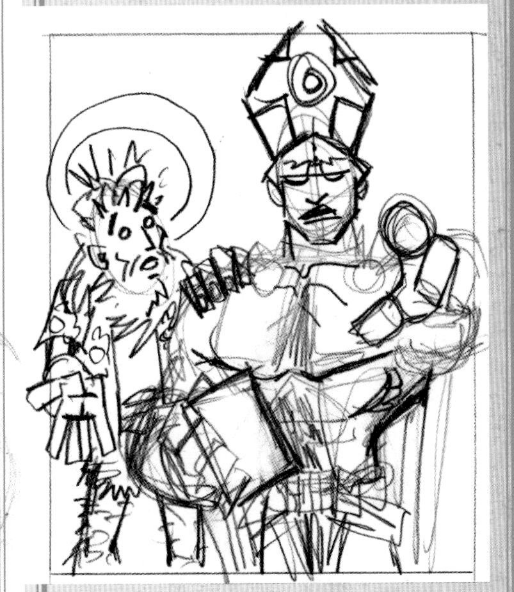

This is the layout I did for the ad for the original volume 1 TPB. Originally Pope was going to be saying "This book is so good it'll make yer pecker hard!" to which Jesus replied, "What's a pecker?" The people at Previews decided it was inappropriate. In a last minute scramble, my pal Eli 5 Stone came up with what we used. The actual ad is seen in a couple of pages.

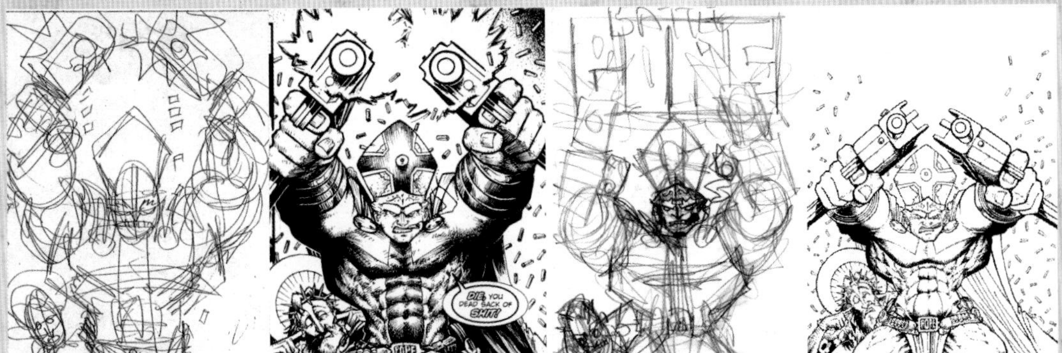
DIE, YOU DEAD SACK OF SHIT!
POPE

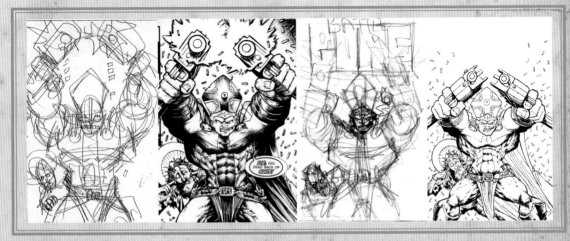

The various stages of this TPB's cover, from my layouts for pages 17 of issue two, to Tony's inks from that page, to my rough layouts for the TPB cover, to the finished inks. This image was used in the ad for issue one, a mini-poster we released for issue one, and a planned poster that never came about.

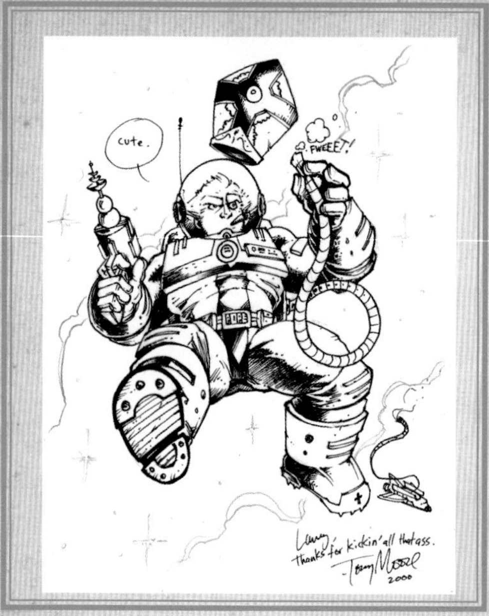
cute.
FWEEE!
POPE
Larry, thanks for kickin' all that ass.
Tony Moore 2000

I had Tony do these illustrations for a couple of REALLY helpful people. The one on the left was for Larry Young, of AIT/PlanetLar fame. He gave me advice and let me ask him questions, which was a huge help back when I was publishing comics. The other one was for Chris Schaff the nicest guy working at Diamond Comic Distributors. Chris is an all around cool guy, too, and even though he was eventually replaced by Filip Sablik when he moved to the toy department at Diamond he still lives on in our hearts and minds as CHRIS, the character who first appears in Battle Pope: Shorts 2/Battle Pope 9. Also, Filip and Chris' names were used to come up with the imaginary creator of Science Dog, Filip Schaff, over in Invincible.

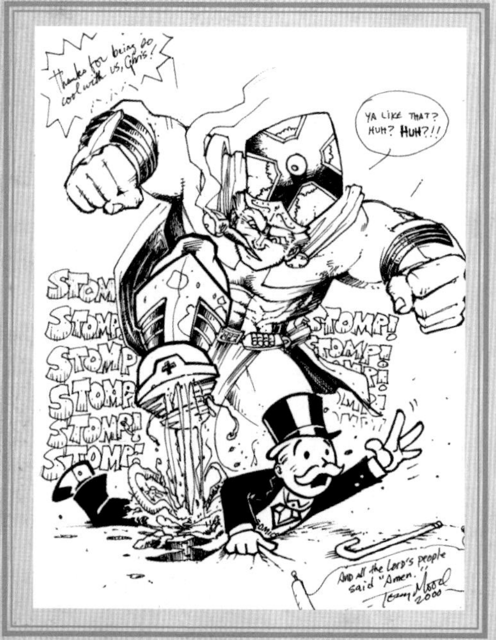
thanks for being so cool with us, Chris!
YA LIKE THAT? HUH? HUH?!!
STOMP!
STOMP!
STOMP!
STOMP!
STOMP!
STOMP!
STOMP!
STOMP!
And all the Lord's people said "Amen."
Tony Moore 2000

Here's a side by side comparison of the line art for the first issue's cover, the original first issue's cover and the Battle Pope Preview cover. If any of you out there actually have a copy of the Preview, feel special, 'cause only 75 copies exist. It's something we printed and bound at a local printer and sent out to Diamond and various other people for advance review. I only have like two copies myself.

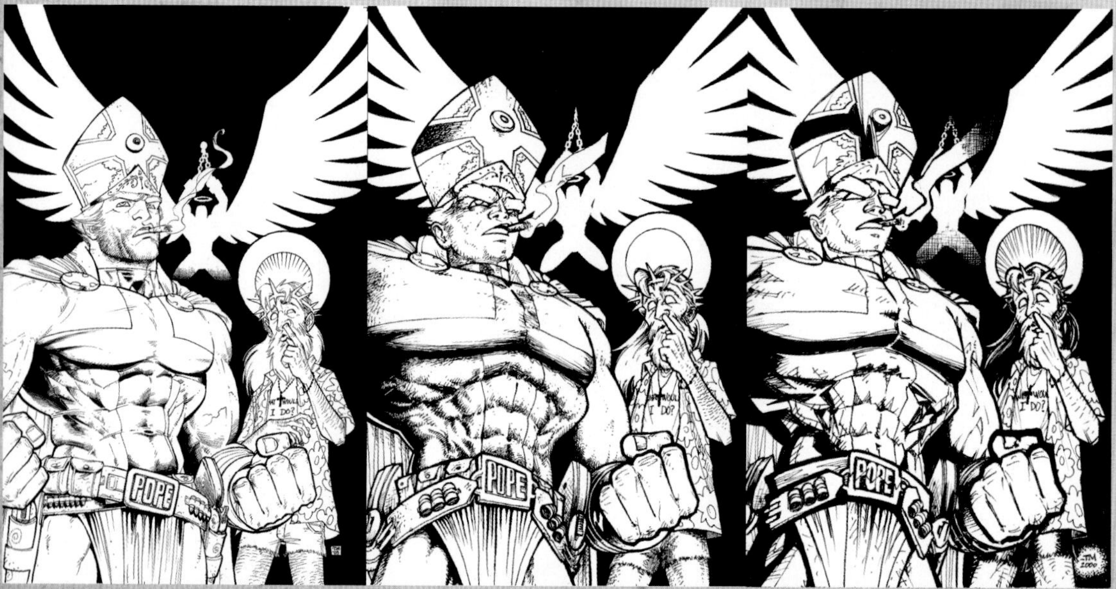
POPE
POPE
POPE

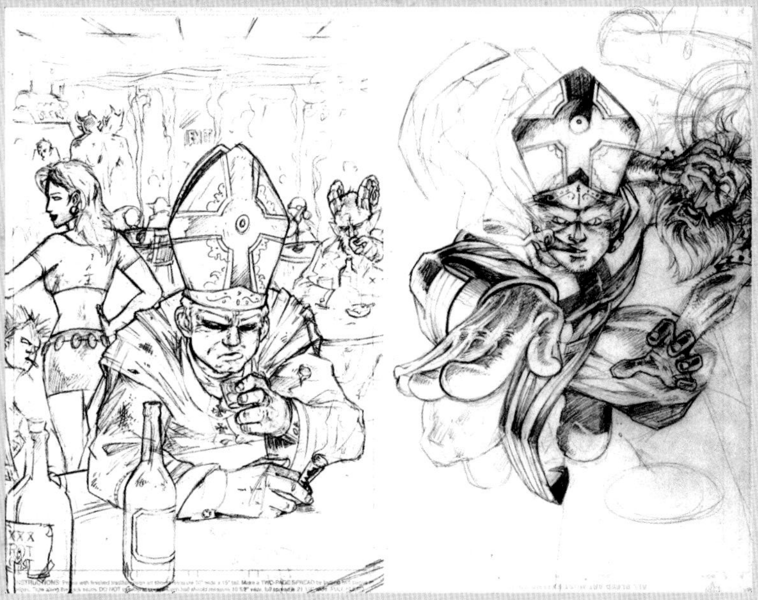

Here's a side by side comparison of the Tony's pencils for the first page of issue one and the last page of issue four. Drawn almost a year to the day apart, you can really see how Tony's skills as a penciler improved over the span of the mini-series.

And here, we have a selection of penciled pages. If you look closely, you'll notice just how much stuff Tony changes from the pencils to the inks. I've also had him change panels back that he changed from my layouts, like the one second from the right on the bottom row.

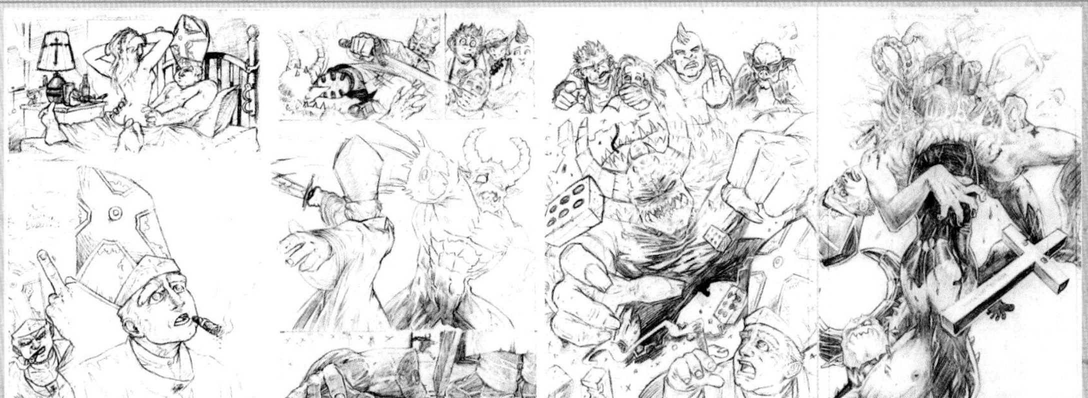

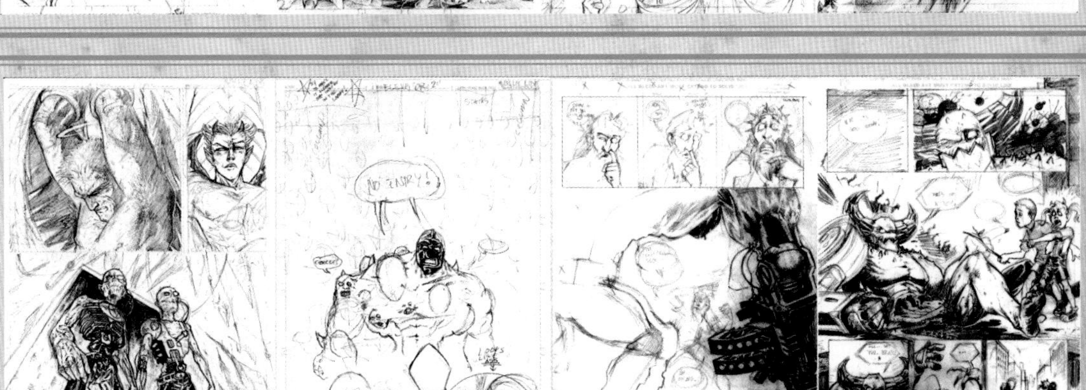

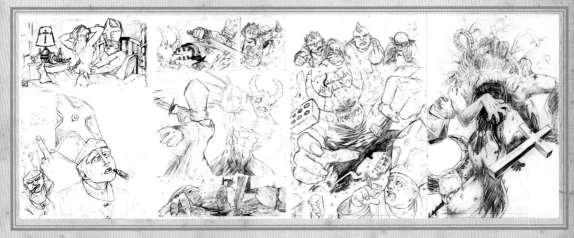

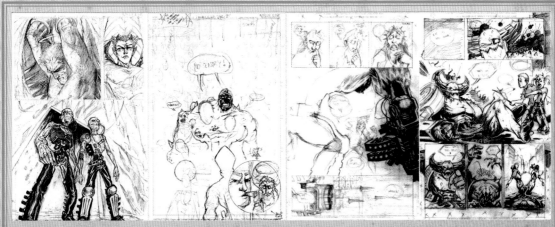

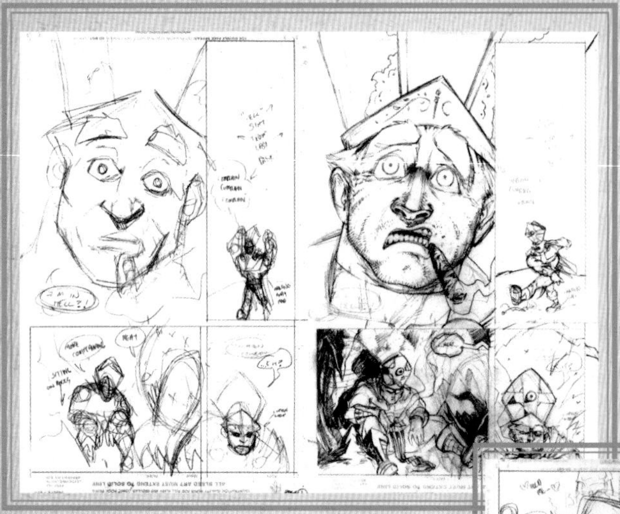

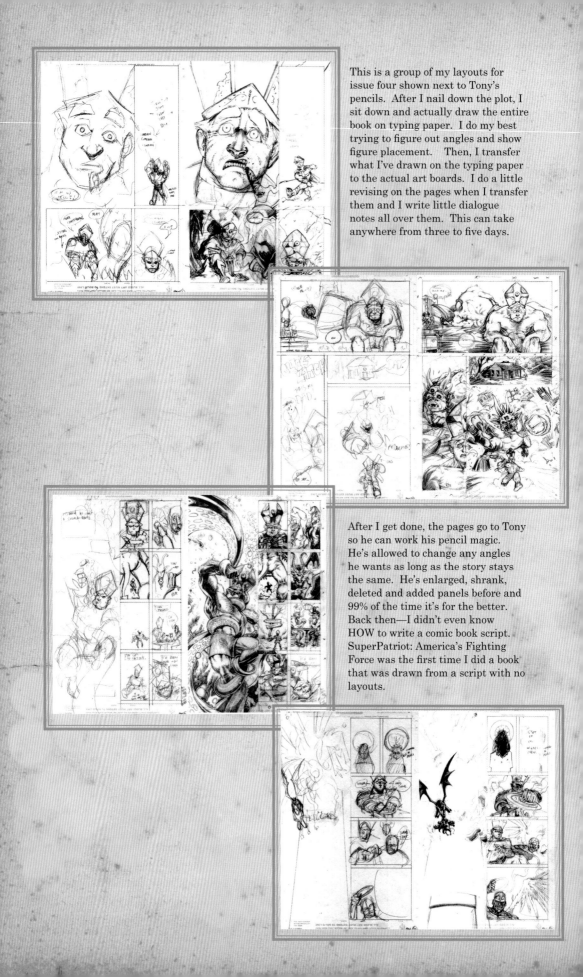

This is a group of my layouts for issue four shown next to Tony's pencils. After I nail down the plot, I sit down and actually draw the entire book on typing paper. I do my best trying to figure out angles and show figure placement. Then, I transfer what I've drawn on the typing paper to the actual art boards. I do a little revising on the pages when I transfer them and I write little dialogue notes all over them. This can take anywhere from three to five days.

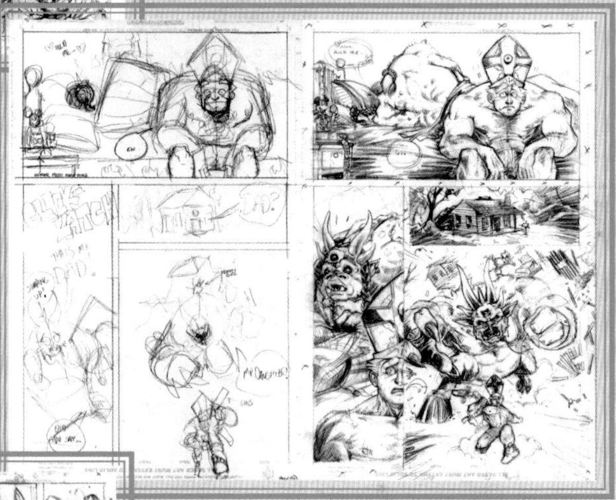

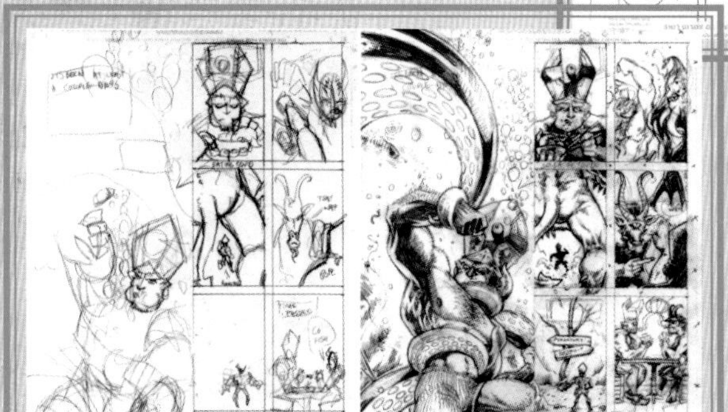

After I get done, the pages go to Tony so he can work his pencil magic. He's allowed to change any angles he wants as long as the story stays the same. He's enlarged, shrank, deleted and added panels before and 99% of the time it's for the better. Back then—I didn't even know HOW to write a comic book script. SuperPatriot: America's Fighting Force was the first time I did a book that was drawn from a script with no layouts.

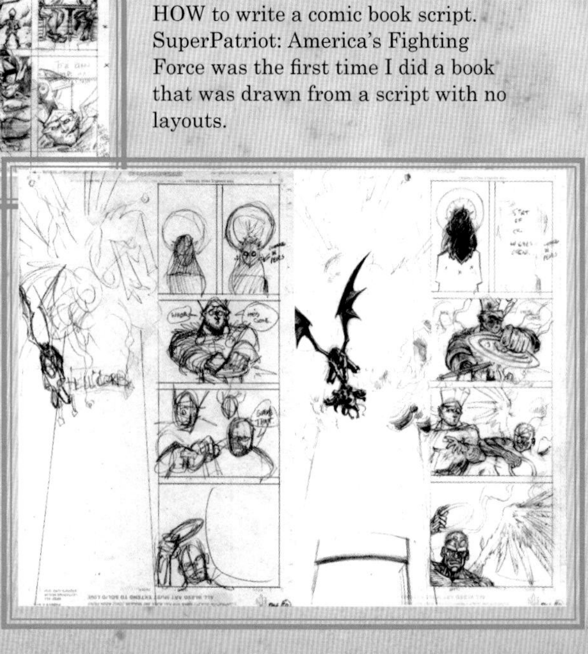

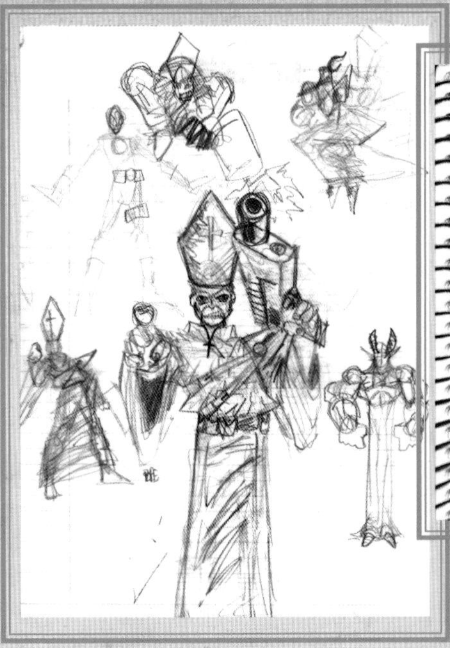

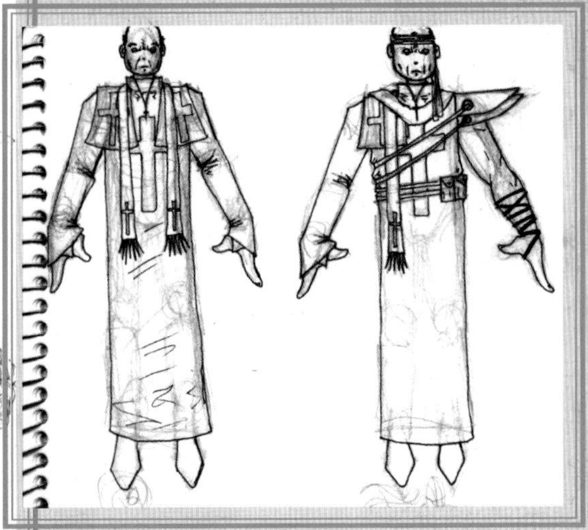

These are the first two drawings I did of Battle Pope, circa 1997. At the time I didn't have a name for him. I forgot all about him until I came up with the title "Battle Pope" in spring of 1999. I then hooked up with Tony and the rest is history. Fun Fact: These were drawn in World Civilizations class during my senior year of high school. In that class I sat next to a girl named Sonia, who later became my wife. She was probably sitting right next to me when I drew these. Weird. And Tony was probably down the hall in English class or something.

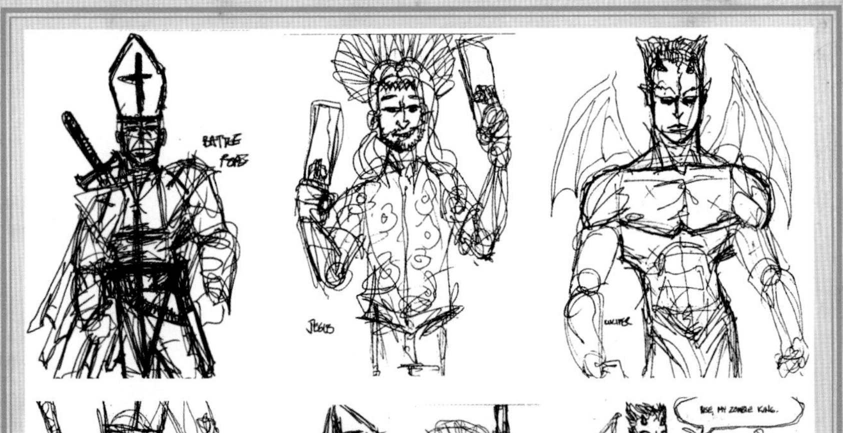
BATTLE POPE
JESUS
LUCIFER
RISE, MY ZOMBIE KING.

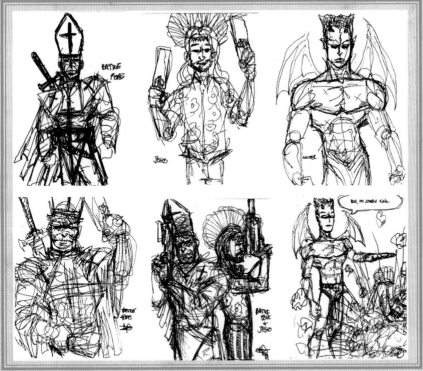

These are a few of the doodles I did after I decided to make a comic based on Battle Pope. The top row features the first ever drawings of Lucifer and Jesus, and the first drawing of Battle Pope since I came up with the title. They ain't too pretty, but I drew them on the can (where I did most of my plotting) so I don't fell so bad. Fun Fact: Half of these were drawn at work, where I would keep a note pad in my pocket and layout pages and doodle characters when I was supposed to be working. I was still at that job when the first version of this book came out— so I was probably too scared to mention that. Wakka wakka.

On the following two pages are the ads for issues one, two, three and the old TPB as they appeared in Diamond Comics "Previews" catalogue back when I was publishing this book through Funk-O-Tron. Enjoy!

-Robert Kirkman

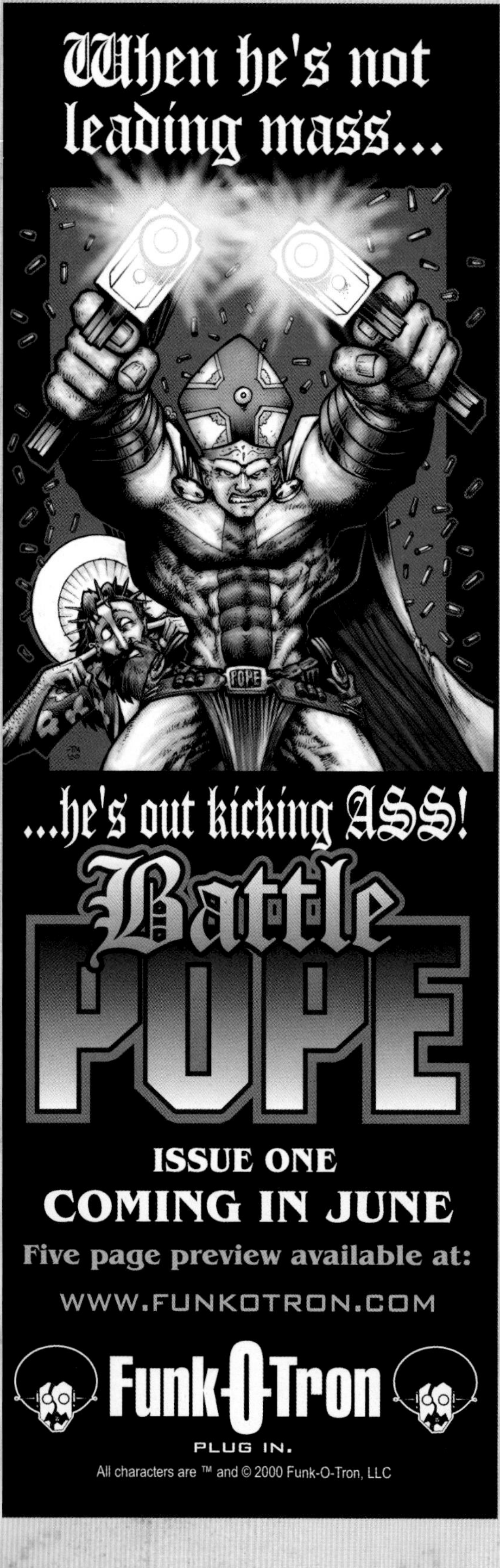
When he's not leading mass...
...he's out kicking ASS!
Battle POPE
ISSUE ONE
COMING IN JUNE
Five page preview available at:
WWW.FUNKOTRON.COM
Funk-O-Tron
PLUG IN.
All characters are ™ and © 2000 Funk-O-Tron, LLC

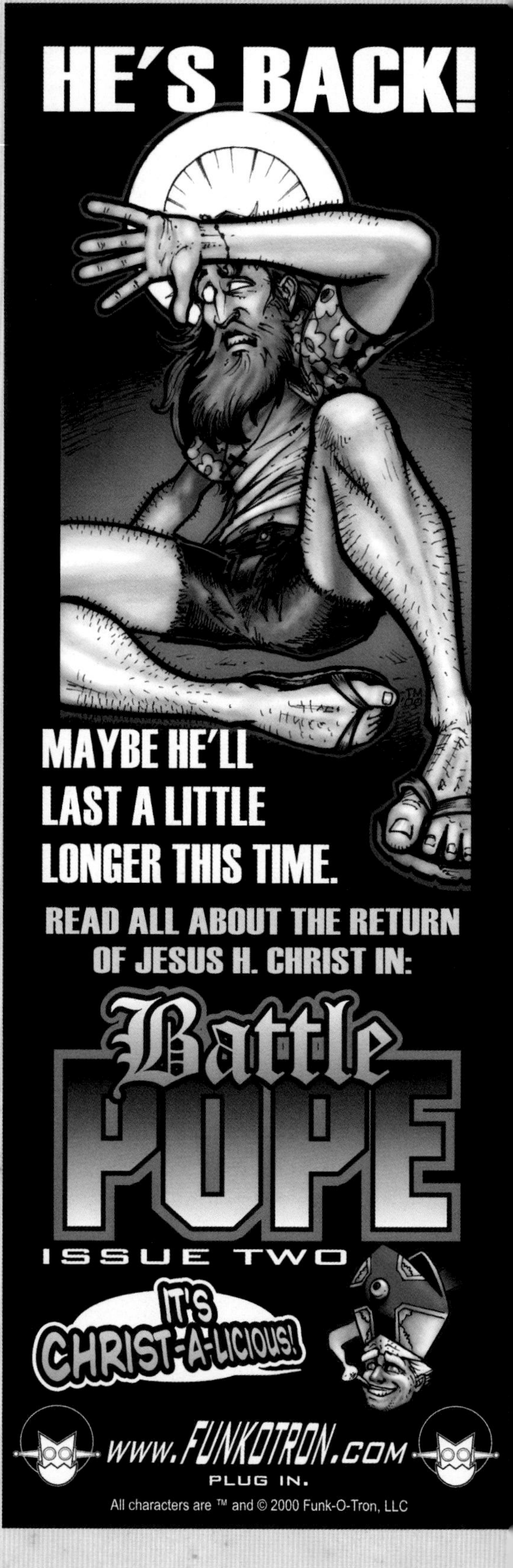
HE'S BACK!
MAYBE HE'LL LAST A LITTLE LONGER THIS TIME.
READ ALL ABOUT THE RETURN OF JESUS H. CHRIST IN:
Battle POPE
ISSUE TWO
IT'S CHRIST-A-LICIOUS!
www.FUNKOTRON.com
PLUG IN.
All characters are ™ and © 2000 Funk-O-Tron, LLC

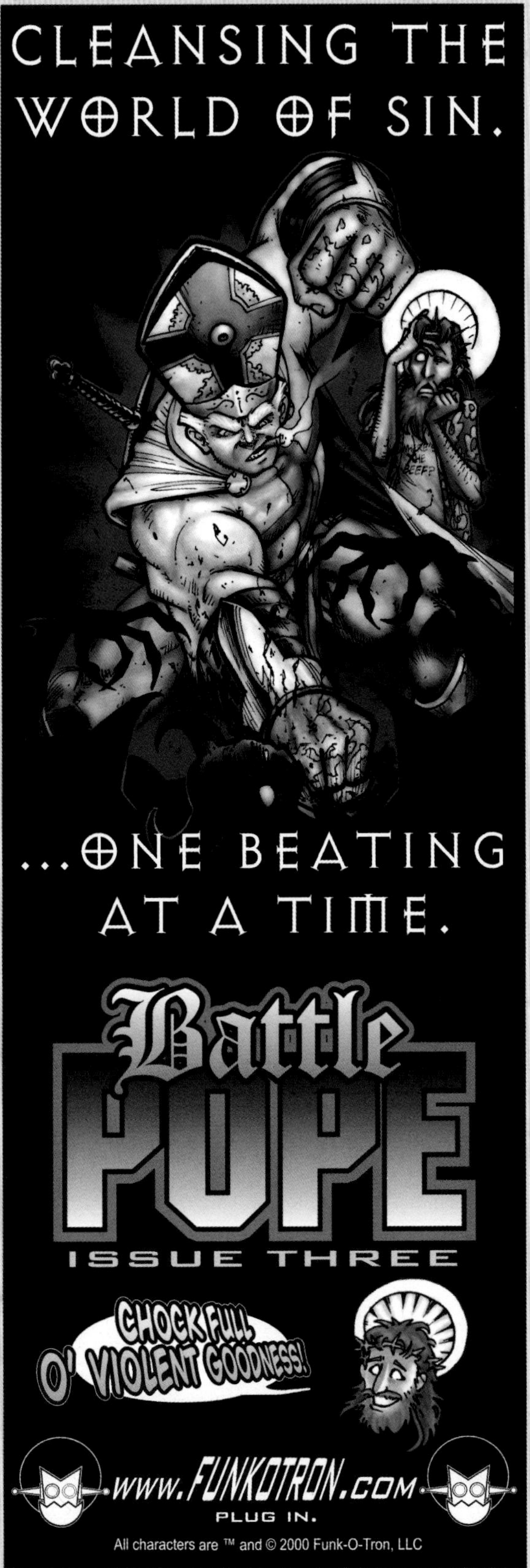

CLEANSING THE WORLD OF SIN.
...ONE BEATING AT A TIME.
Battle POPE
ISSUE THREE
CHOCK FULL O' VIOLENT GOODNESS!
www.FUNKOTRON.COM
PLUG IN.
All characters are ™ and © 2000 Funk-O-Tron, LLC

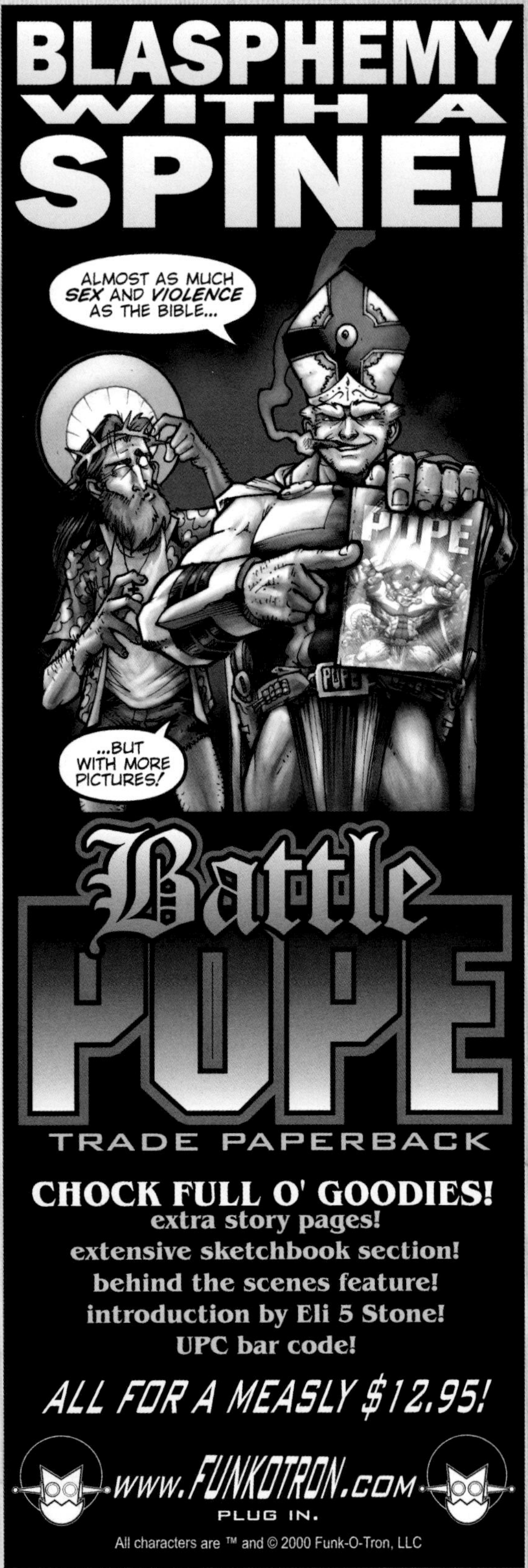

BLASPHEMY WITH A SPINE!
ALMOST AS MUCH SEX AND VIOLENCE AS THE BIBLE...
...BUT WITH MORE PICTURES!
POPE
Battle POPE
TRADE PAPERBACK
CHOCK FULL O' GOODIES!
extra story pages!
extensive sketchbook section!
behind the scenes feature!
introduction by Eli 5 Stone!
UPC bar code!
ALL FOR A MEASLY $12.95!
www.FUNKOTRON.COM
PLUG IN.
All characters are ™ and © 2000 Funk-O-Tron, LLC

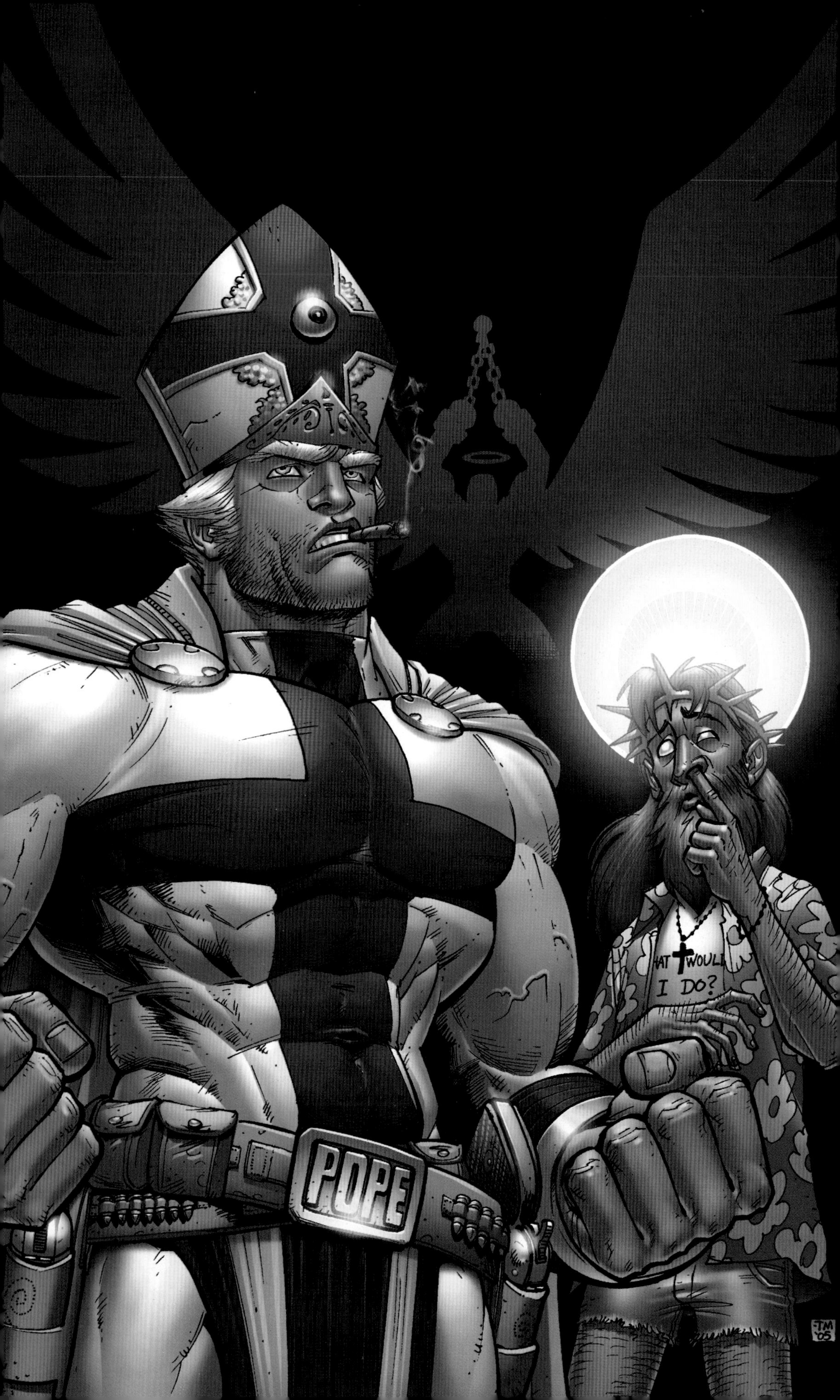
POPE
I DO?
TM '05

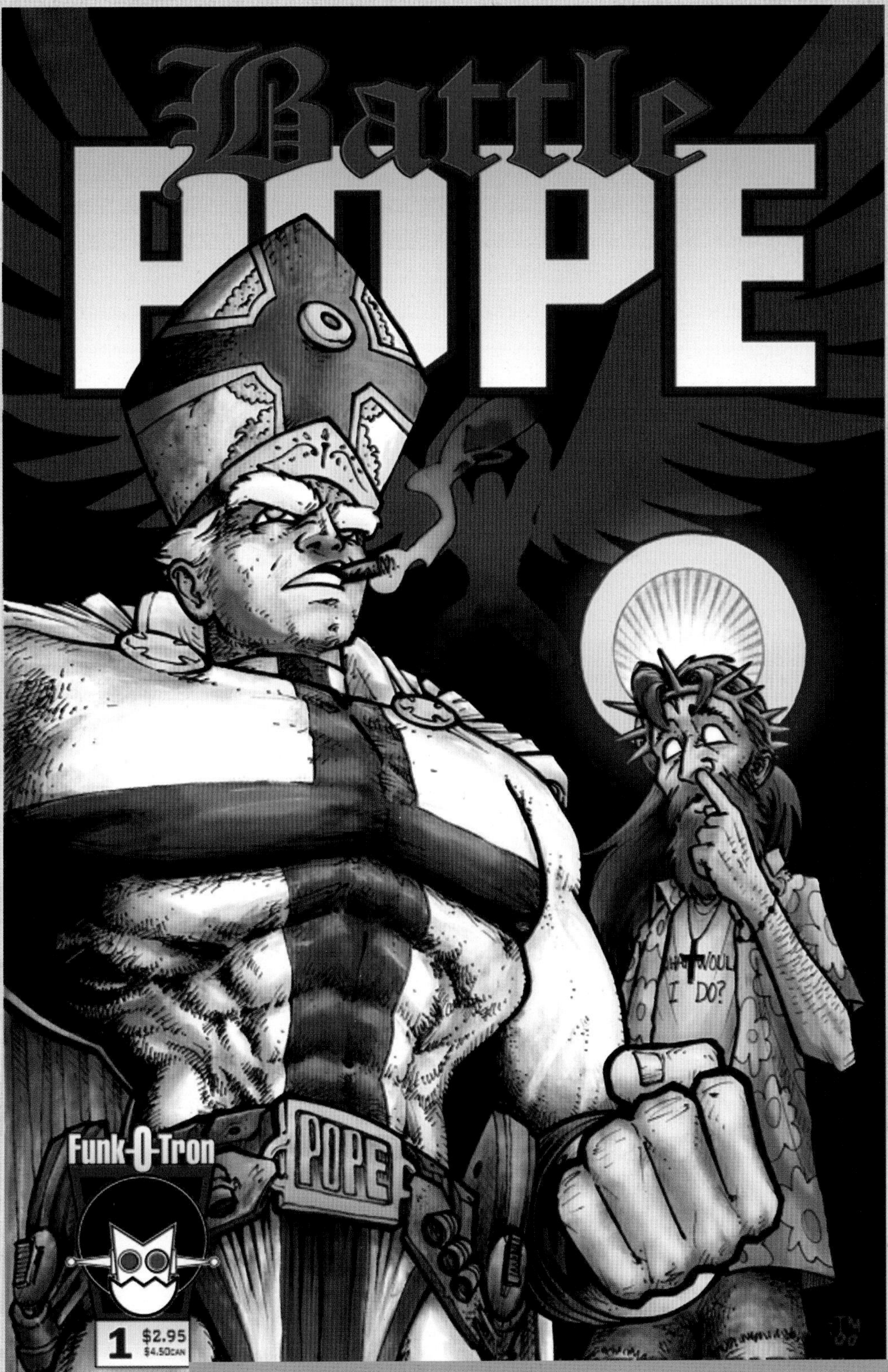
Battle
POPE
Funk-O-Tron
POPE
1 $2.95
$4.50CAN
I DO?

On the left page over there you should see the shiny new cover for Battle Pope #1 by Tony Moore and Val Staples. On this page you should see the old cover from the original black and white series.

I always dug this cover. I really liked Tony's design including Saint Michael in the background. And you know... Jesus picking his nose secured us a cozy spot in hell. The new cover, I think, is an INSANE improvement on the old, as well it should be. Working so closely with Tony for all these years—I never really noticed just how much he improved. And y'know, Val is an amazing colorist so this cover really was stunning.

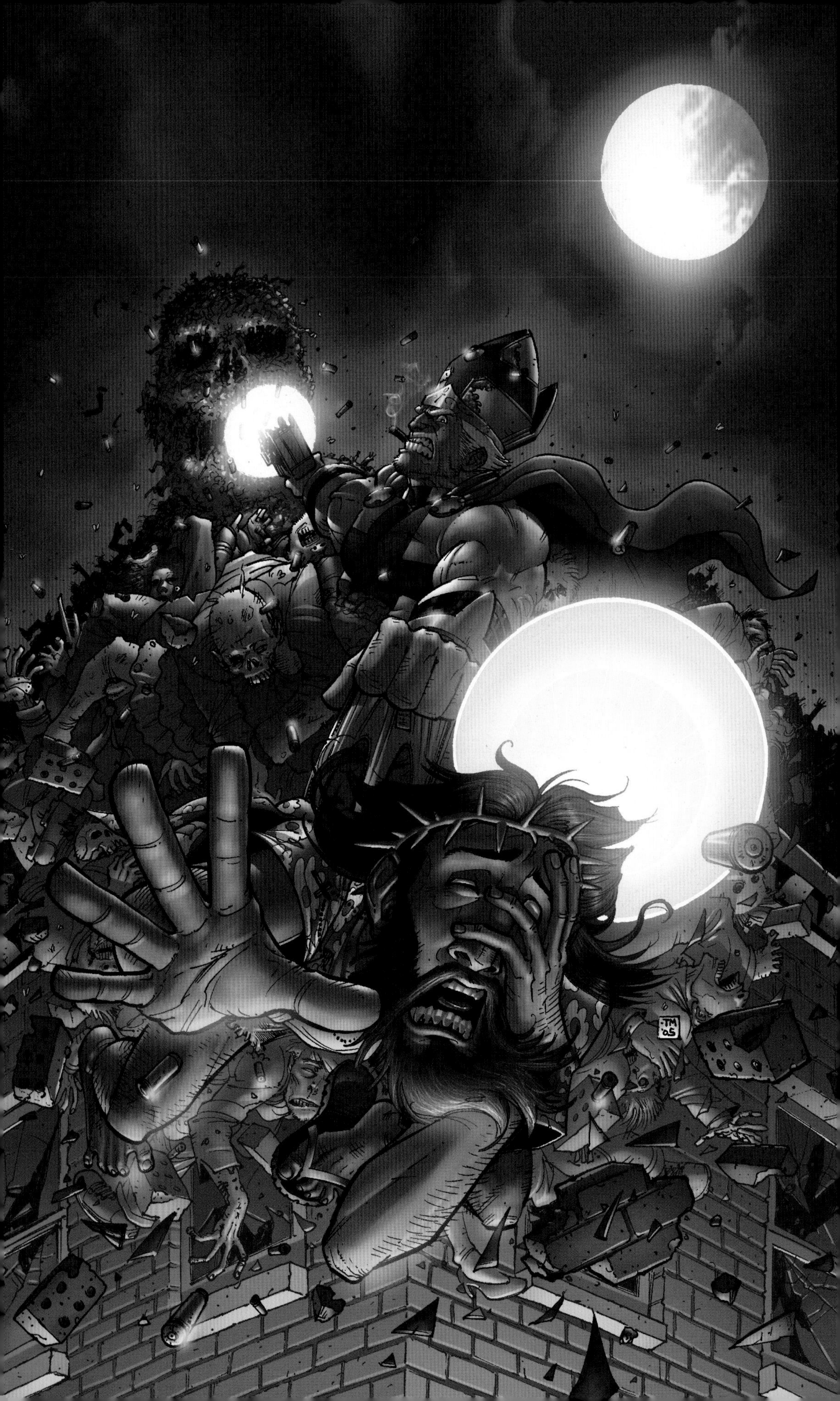
TM
'05

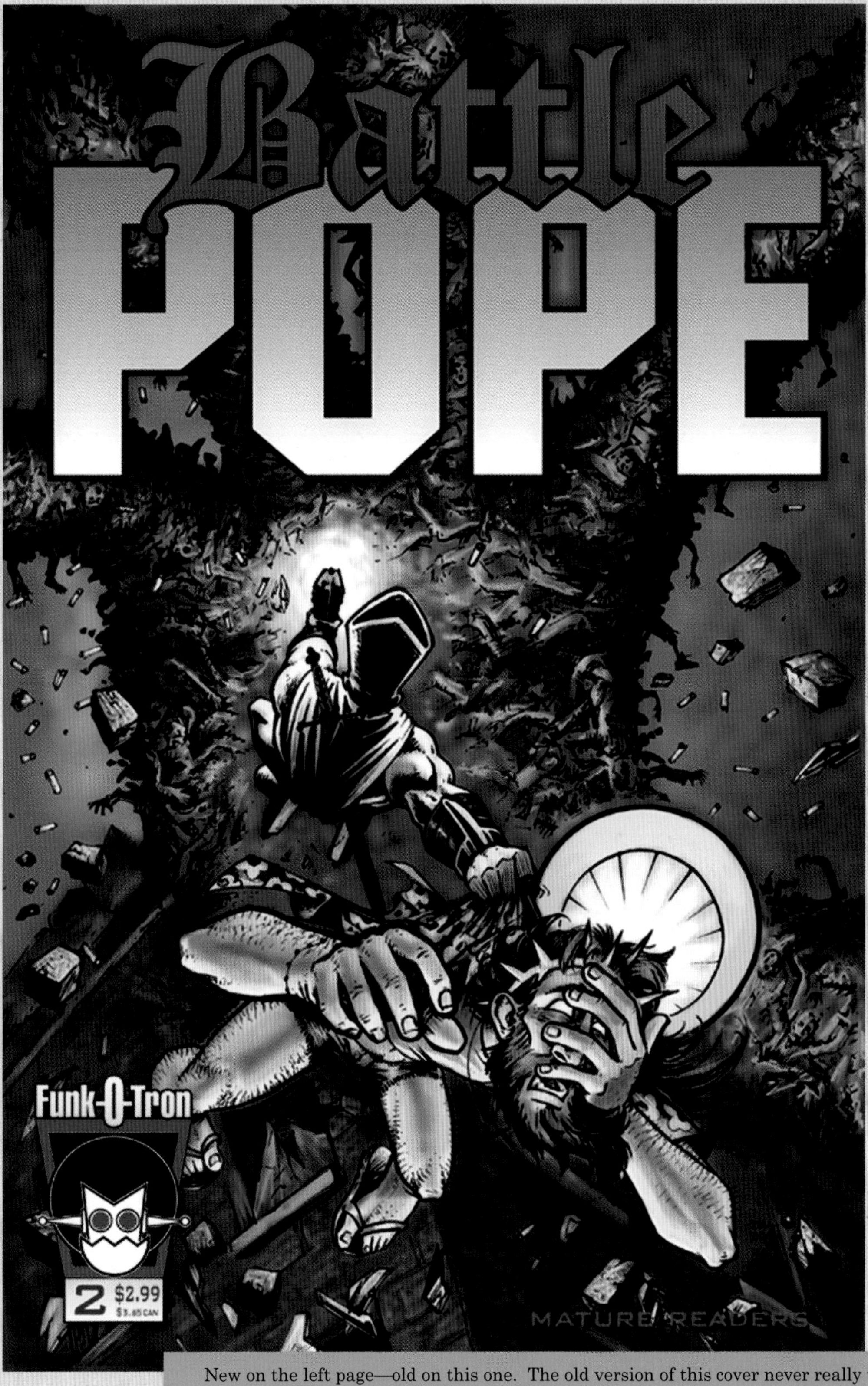
Battle
POPE
Funk-O-Tron
2 $2.99
MATURE READERS

New on the left page—old on this one. The old version of this cover never really worked for me. I wanted more Pope on the cover. I always thought Pope looked like a milkman with his back to us like that. Also, and really, I couldn't make this up, we got a couple comments about the zombie king hand looking like a pot leaf.

The new version gives you a better look at the fully compiled Zombie King and a better look at Pope. It's altogether better. I really dig Val's color choices for this one, too.

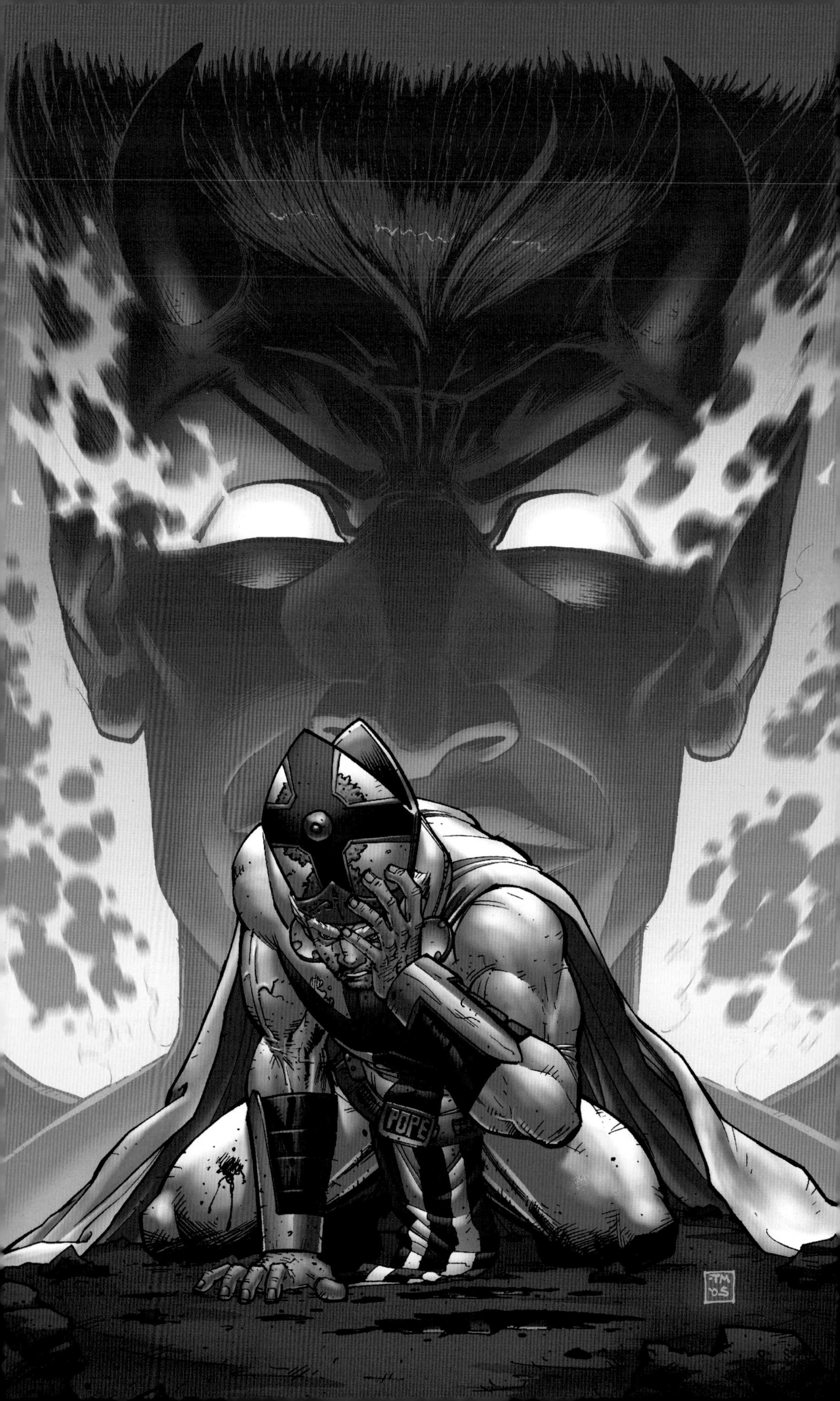
POPE

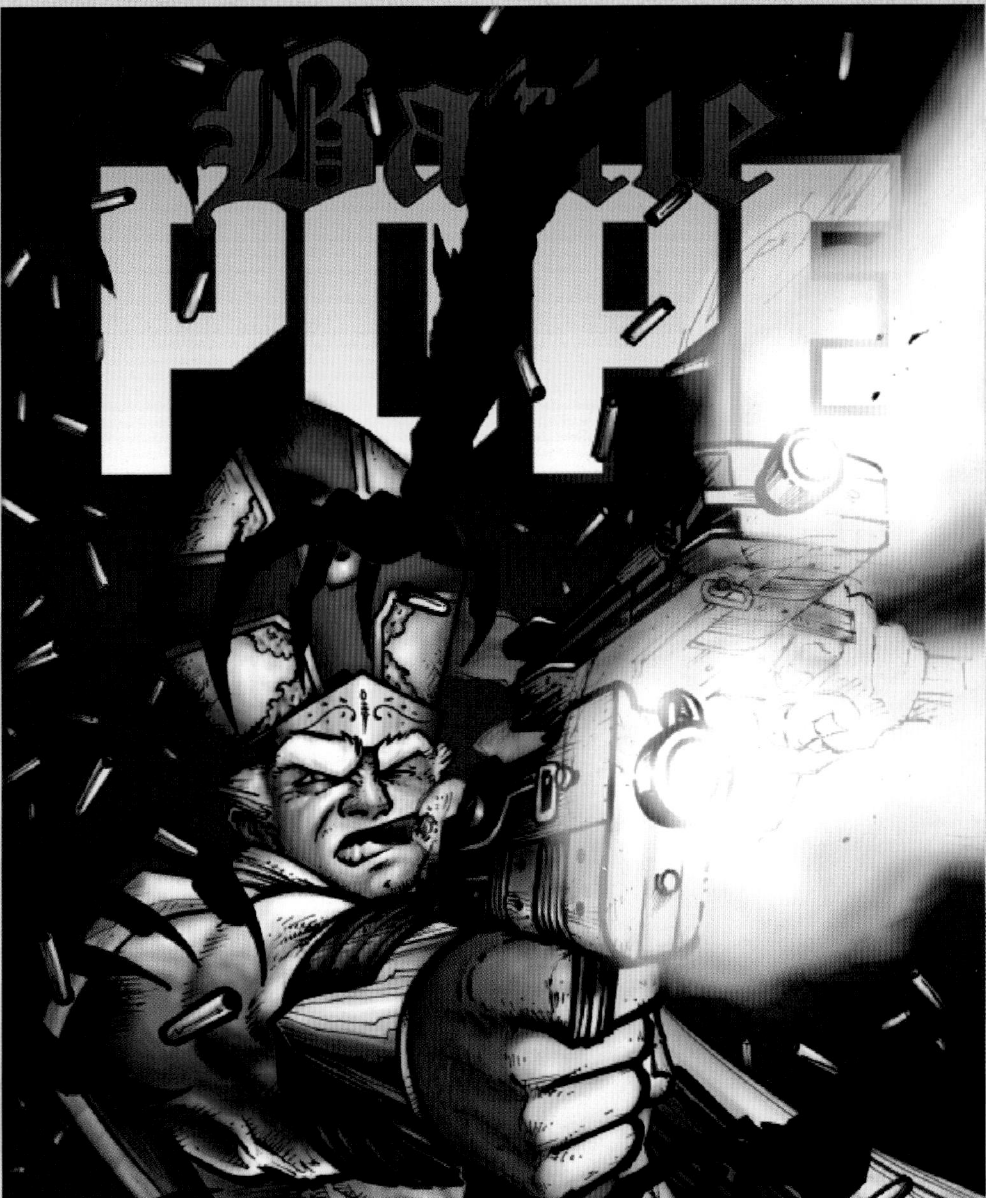
POPE
Funk-O-Tron
3
$2.95
$4.50CAN
POPE

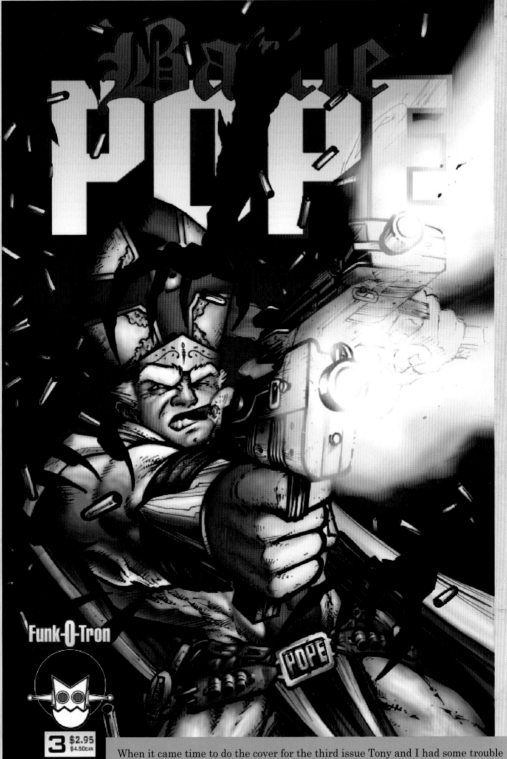

When it came time to do the cover for the third issue Tony and I had some trouble figuring out what to do. Eventually, I suggested Pope fighting Lucifer on the cover—just the two of them trading blows. Tony went into his corner, and came back with Pope shooting his guns at us. I would have preferred Lucifer make it on the cover, for no other reason than we would have gotten to establish his color (since this was a black and white book, the covers were the only place to do that), but this cover turned out so cool looking, I let it slide. I was always impressed by the rendering on Pope's face here that Tony did in the colors.

The new cover—we finally got Lucifer on there—not in his true colors—but he's there. It's a good cover, but it's probably my least favorite of the four new covers done for this series.

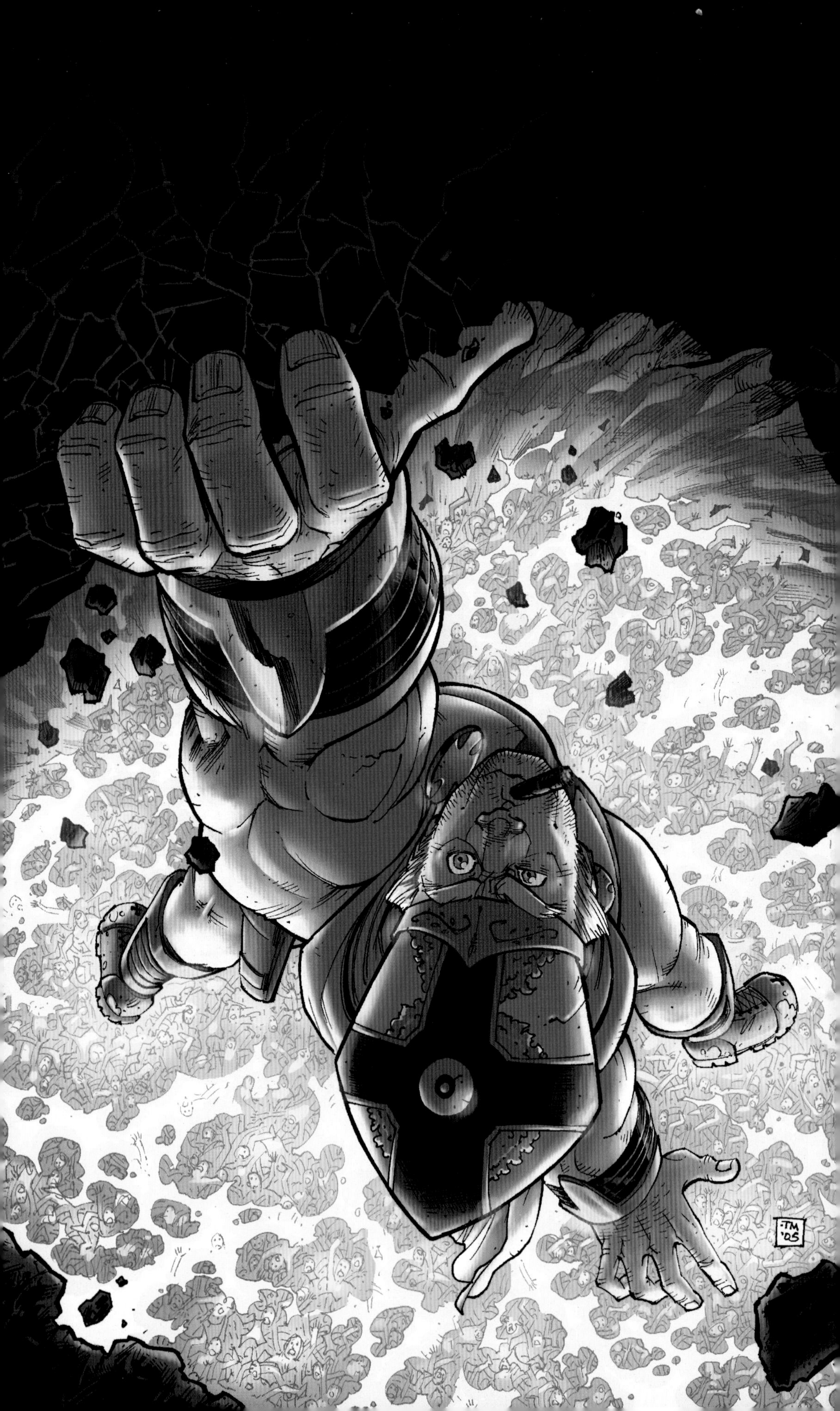
TM
'05